P9-CDC-002

Google Apps
Meets
Common
Core

Google Apps
Meets
Common
Core

Michael J. Graham

CORWIN
A SAGE Company

CORWIN
A SAGE Company

FOR INFORMATION:

Corwin
A SAGE Company
2455 Teller Road
Thousand Oaks, California 91320
(800) 233-9936
www.corwin.com

SAGE Publications Ltd.
1 Oliver's Yard
55 City Road
London EC1Y 1SP
United Kingdom

SAGE Publications India Pvt. Ltd.
B 1/I 1 Mohan Cooperative Industrial Area
Mathura Road, New Delhi 110 044
India

SAGE Publications Asia-Pacific Pte. Ltd.
3 Church Street
#10-04 Samsung Hub
Singapore 049483

Acquisitions Editor: Arnis Burvikovs
Associate Editor: Desirée A. Bartlett
Editorial Assistant: Mayan White
Production Editor: Amy Schroller
Copy Editor: Amy Rosenstein
Typesetter: C&M Digitals (P) Ltd.
Proofreader: Theresa Kay
Indexer: Sheila Bodell
Cover Designer: Scott VanAtta
Permissions Editor: Jennifer Barron

Copyright © 2013 by Corwin

All rights reserved. When forms and sample documents are included, their use is authorized only by educators, local school sites, and/or noncommercial or nonprofit entities that have purchased the book. Except for that usage, no part of this book may be reproduced or utilized in any form or by any means, electronic or mechanical, including photocopying, recording, or by any information storage and retrieval system, without permission in writing from the publisher.

All Google screenshot images contained herein are used with permission of Google Inc.

Common Core State Standards are included with the permission of NGA Center/CCSSO.

Student work depicted in Figure 4.5, "Collective Note-Taking Part II" and Figure 8.11, "How to Open Your Locker" is used with permission.

Lesson Plan 6 "Contrasting Peter Pan" and Lesson Plan 7 "Introduction to the Salem Witch Trials" are used with the permission of the contributors.

Printed in the United States of America.

A catalog record of this book is available from the Library of Congress.

ISBN 9781452257334

This book is printed on acid-free paper.

13 14 15 16 17 10 9 8 7 6 5 4 3 2

Contents

Preface

Forty-five states, three territories, and the District of Columbia have embraced the *Common Core State Standards* in hopes to reform education and make positive change. The United States has been left behind when compared with other countries in mathematics, science, and technology. Most educators are aware that our students entering college must take remedial courses that are not credit bearing, and business leaders complain that students graduating from high school do not have the skills to perform basic job duties. The Common Core State Standards intend to be a solution to these problems. The standards bring into focus the most important student learning expectations to make students ready for the challenges of college and career in the 21st century.

The architects of the Common Core State Standards realize the world is becoming increasingly technology dependent. The standards force educators to incorporate 21st century skills into the classroom so that students will be ready to face problems in our technologically based society. Teachers, administrators, and curriculum specialist must realize the expectations that the Common Core State Standards place on them. It is not a choice, but a mandate that students be ready to enter college or the workplace with the proper skills to perform in the world. Given this problem, some questions for educators today are:

- How will educators incorporate technology into their lesson plans to meet the expectations of the Common Core State Standards?
- What level of skill using technology is needed for teachers and students to be successful?
- What will the Next Generation Assessments look like?
- What technology or software used in classrooms could bring together Common Core and technology and give students the experience needed so that they can perform well on the Next Generation Assessments?

One of the best ways to tackle these questions is to use the free service from Google built exclusively for schools called Google Apps for Education. Google provides a robust and vigorous suite of educational tools for schools that include everything necessary to meet and exceed the technology integration components of the Common Core State Standards.

Because Google offers this package for free to educational institutions, many K–12 and universities are using it to their advantage, saving money and labor. According to Google, more than 16 million students and teachers are currently using Google Apps for Education in the world, with more added every day. If your school uses Gmail as its e-mail, then your school is a Google Apps for Education school. If your school is not a Google Apps institution, it is easy to get started. Direct your technology department to http://www.google.com/apps/intl/en/edu/k12.html to get signed up. Even if your district does not sign up for Google Apps for Education, educators may still use most of these tools to organize, collaborate, and *share* content with students and faculty when they sign up for a free Google Account.

PURPOSE

This book was written to inform educators of ways to incorporate technology into their lessons using Google Apps for Education to maximize learning while adhering to the rigors of the Common Core State Standards. It has step-by-step tutorials that can help even technologically challenged teachers master Google Apps, while challenging the techno-savvy teachers to think of new ways of learning with tech. This book will give lesson plan ideas directly in the commentary about the apps giving educators ideas how to implement technology with a focus on the Common Core State Standards. Ultimately, this book is written as a resource and a guide for educators to use Google Apps to meet Common Core. It is as if Google read the Common Core State Standards, then created free software to meet and exceed them.

TARGET AUDIENCE

Educators from prekindergarten to postsecondary will find this book a valuable source of how to implement technology into the teaching and learning environment. The Common Core State Standards and technology integration is the book's main focus, but the step-by-step tutorials are helpful for educators from any nation, state, or educational institution. College and career readiness is a worldwide goal. It is not restricted to the United States or for PK–12 schooling. Many teachers, curriculum specialists, administrators, and college instructors will find the information in this book worthwhile and meaningful. Professors of education at universities are encouraged to read and recommend this work to their students. Teachers who come directly out of college with the skills and understanding of this book will be ready to lead in the fight to get students college and career ready.

HOW THIS BOOK IS UNIQUE

This book was written because there is nothing like it available to educators. Most books about Google only tell educators about the wide swath of tools that Google provides. This book narrows the focus on the tools in Google Apps for Education and shows how they can be used to exceed the Common Core State Standards. It also provides teachers with a direct relation to which Google App is most appropriate to specific Common Core State Standards, with step-by-step tutorials on how to implement it directly in the classroom to maximize learning. This book seeks to provide educators with the path of least resistance when implementing technology into the curriculum. Education technology tools are quickly entering the market, each with their own quirky and sometimes complicated uses. Learning how to use hundreds of tools would be overwhelming for a busy educator. With Google Apps for Education, the apps are all easily accessed in one place and all follow the same basic principles of use.

This book is unique because it has the ability to demystify some of the Common Core State Standards and reduce the anxiety of teachers that are fearful of technology. I have worked to provide professional development to teachers who are scared of implementing technology because they feel that it is too complicated or out of their skill set. Many veteran educators I have talked to are contemplating retirement because of the changes brought about by Common Core and its mandatory technology integration. If you are one of these educators, please consider this book to help you. Although it may seem difficult to implement technology as an older teacher, give this book a try because your wisdom and experience as a veteran teacher are still needed and play a vital role in the school community. This book can dispel your fears, but also challenge you to break out of your comfort level to give your students what they need to be ready for college and their careers.

ORGANIZATION OF THE BOOK

To make it clear for the reader, I have organized this book around the core components of integrating Google Apps for Education into a Common Core State Standards curriculum. Each chapter is designed to highlight specific Common Core standards. Each standard discussed is followed by an explanation of how Google Apps for Education can be used to meet or exceed it with real classroom examples. Along the way, some authentic student work will be displayed to showcase the power of Google Apps for Education.

Step-by-Step Tutorials

This book will feature step-by-step tutorials with clear instructions through screenshots. The screenshots are pictures of my computer screen that explain in detail exactly when and where to click. These tutorials make it easy for anyone to access the features of Google Apps, no matter what level of experience you have with technology. For an example, see the short tutorial in the next section.

How to Use Google's URL Shortener

Oftentimes, links to Web addresses can be long and complicated. Google has made a way to take long *URLs* or links to Web pages and shorten them to make them more manageable to access. For example, the link to a Google Doc that I want readers to access is https://docs.google.com/document/d/1gYavpNndG8vJtnE-Dr_hWpjSjosh-rGEms1-cgt-I_E/edit. It would be very difficult for the reader to type this exactly as it is into a Web browser. Using Google's URL Shortener, the link can be converted to http://goo.gl/Kaz6M. This link is much shorter and can be easily typed into any Web browser to access the file. These links never expire. All links are *case sensitive*, meaning that capital and lowercase letters must be typed in exactly as shown. Follow the steps below to use Google's URL Shortener.

1. Go to http://goo.gl in a Web browser.

2. Copy any Web address to shorten.

3. Paste the Web address in the box shown in Figure P.1.

Figure P.1

4. Click [Shorten URL] to reveal the shortened link found in Figure P.2.

5. E-mail, Tweet, Facebook, or write the shortened link down to access later or share with friends.

Figure P.1

Every link in this book follows the process above. Readers are asked to pay attention to these links to enhance their experience.

Technology-Infused Teaching Tips

Throughout the book, notice the boxed feature *Technology-Infused Teaching Tip*. This feature offers readers commentary on how to explicitly use Google Apps to meet the rigors of the Common Core State Standards. These boxes often contain lesson plan ideas and short descriptions on how to maximize learning using technology.

Resource Link

The Resource Link is a boxed feature at the end of each chapter that will provide the reader with links to at least three full lesson plans that use various Google Apps at each grade band (elementary, middle, and high school). Lesson plans will not be included for Chapters 1, 2, and 10 because they do not directly tie to classroom instruction, but these chapters certainly support the Common Core State Standards.

Find the entire collection of Web resources that I have gathered or created at http://goo.gl/Envlf.

Lesson plans are located at the end of the book because most of the lesson plans developed use more than one Google App. To help the reader align the various Google Apps, Common Core State Standards, and grade levels of the lesson plans this book contains the *Lesson Plan Correlation Chart* found at the beginning of the Resource section. Using the chart, readers can connect various apps they are learning about with real-world lesson plans found in the Resource section.

Companion Website www.21learning.net

The purpose of this website is to provide the reader with more resources, links, and videos to go beyond what is offered in the book. One great feature of the website is Lesson Cloud. Lesson Cloud is a database of lesson plans that come from readers of this book and the Google Apps for Education community. These plans are submitted directly to the website to provide ongoing resources for educators interested in Google Apps. Educators are an excellent resource, and the expertise in your subject and grade levels should be shared. If you have an excellent lesson plan that uses Google Apps or have an existing lesson plan that could be modified to use Google Apps, please submit it to Lesson Cloud. This is an opportunity to get involved and share some great learning experiences using Google Apps. Directions for submitting lesson plans are located on the homepage of www.21learning.net.

Follow me on Twitter (@mjgraham0) and at my website (www.21learning.net) to access more lesson plans as they are written or submitted. In addition, share your lesson plans on the website to show how you use the power of Google Apps for Education.

THREE REASONS TO BUY THIS BOOK

1. Simplicity. This book is an easy-to-use guide to help you implement Google Apps for Education into your classroom with step-by-step instructions.

2. Innovative. This book will enhance your teaching practice with cutting edge, classroom-tested ideas that implement technology in your classroom.

3. Common Core Connected. This book is directly correlated with the Common Core State Standards, giving teachers practical examples of how Google Apps can help educators exceed the rigors of the Common Core.

FINAL NOTE

Buying this book will enhance your professional practice, giving you the tools to become knowledgeable of how the Common Core State Standards use technology to enhance learning using Google Apps for Education. Use the information in this book to make a commitment to your professional practice and your students to implement the highest level of technology to create, collaborate, and share learning.

Acknowledgments

This book would not have been possible without the support of Harrisburg Middle School's amazing teachers and staff. In particular, I would like to thank Mrs. Karli Saracini, principal of Harrisburg Middle School, for her support of this project and for her exceptional leadership in providing her students with a top-quality, technology-rich education. Find out more about Harrisburg Middle School at www.facebook.com/harrisburgmiddle.

I would also like to thank my wife Jessica Graham, Jay Harper, Michelle Chappell, Denise Doyle, Danny Sample, Heather Eggers, and my editing staff (Deb Stollenwerk, Desirée Bartlett, and Daniel Richcreek) for their continued support and guidance of this project. It would not have been possible without all of you.

See more and sign the guest book at http://goo.gl/5emGM.

PUBLISHER'S ACKNOWLEDGMENTS

Corwin wishes to acknowledge the following peer reviewers for their editorial insight and guidance:

Lisa Graham, Program Supervisor, Special Education
Berkeley Unified School District
Berkeley, CA

Heidi Guadagni, Learning Specialist
French Prairie Middle School
Woodburn, OR

Deborah Howard
Teacher of the Deaf, Teacher ESL, Teacher EFL,
Consultant with several school districts
Pownal, ME

Michelle Kocar, Curriculum Specialist
North Olmsted City Schools
North Olmsted, OH

Betty Rivinus, Special Education Teacher
Canby School District
Canby, OR

Dr. Susan Stewart, Assistant Professor
Ashland University
Ashland, OH

About the Author

 **Michael J. Graham** is the instructional technologist for Harrisburg Middle School in Harrisburg, Arkansas. Michael specializes in providing professional development to teachers on his staff and across the nation to maximize the learning experience for students through the implementation of technology into the classroom. His strength lies in working directly with teachers, motivating them to become 21st century learners so they can pass those skills directly to students. Michael received a B.A. in chemistry and M.S.E. in educational leadership from Arkansas State University. His teaching experience includes five years of eighth-grade mathematics and two years as instructional technologist. Besides his work at Harrisburg Middle School, Michael is involved with the Arkansas Department of Education's Technology Infused Education Cadre, board member on the Arkansas Association Middle Level Education, board member of Hot Springs Technology Institute, board member of Schools Without Walls, and serves as an advisory board member to Arkansas iTunes U Portal sponsored by the Arkansas Department of Education.

Michael is a Google Apps for Education Certified Trainer certified by Google to provide professional development to teachers and others who use Google Apps for Education.

To my wife Jessica, my best friend and true love.

1

Common Core State Standards and Technology

The world is changing. Education should be changing with it. The Common Core State Standards has provided the catalyst for change that schools need in the United States. The Common Core State Standards ask the teachers to slow down and teach fewer standards more deeply by exploring key concepts and concentrating on mastery. They call for students to understand and apply concepts, read closely more nonfiction texts, and support claims with evidence in mathematics, English language arts, and speaking and listening. In addition to these underlying principles of the Common Core State Standards, students will need to have a wealth of 21st century skills to complement their learning. Using Google Apps for Education, students and teachers can prepare for the rigors of the Common Core State Standards and the Next Generation Assessments.

The Common Core State Standards drive teaching and learning to become more in depth and to foster critical thinking skills across the curriculum. When reading the standards, it is apparent that the authors want technology to be a part of the learning process. Standards like *Anchor Standard* 6 for Writing call for students to "produce and publish writing using the Internet." That standard progresses from K–12 with various levels of complexity. Thankfully, the architects of the standards did not separate technology into its own set of standards. Rather, technology integration is too important to single it out as its own discipline. It is a part of everything we do today: how we learn, work, and live. Technology use is embedded in almost every aspect of the standards, and teachers should look for ways to use it, even when it does not specifically say to, as in Anchor 6 for Writing. Teachers must have the courage to learn new ways of thinking about using technology. It is not a toy or a reward; it is an integral tool for learning as mighty as the pen.

Technology is embedded in every facet of our world. It is nearly impossible for a person to work or learn in today's society without interacting with some form of technology. For example, Wendy's, Kroger, and other corporations have abolished paper applications. It is impossible to get a job with these companies without having some basic computer skills, including the use of the Internet. One thing is certain, technology and its use in education will not go away. Moore's Law implies that technology and its capacity will double every 18 months. The kindergartener who starts school in 2012 will graduate in 2026. That means that in the 13 years that the student will attend K–12 schooling, the capacity of our technological society would have doubled 8.6 times. What will work and college look like then? Students must be prepared for college and career. Teachers must implement technology into the classroom if we want our students to succeed in the future. Educators, especially classroom teachers, have a responsibility to integrate technology into their teaching practice to meet and exceed the Common Core State Standards.

NO TEACHER LEFT BEHIND

Take the opportunity of the mandates the Common Core State Standards provide and take back your license to teach. Explore concepts deeply, have the courage to slow down, teach fewer standards, and implement digital citizenship in your lessons. Follow these recommendations, and the transition to Common Core will be a great experience for you and your students.

ASSESSMENT

No Child Left Behind forced states to set in place some form of student learning expectations that guided student learning throughout the year and assess it at the end of the academic period. Each state had separate standards and a separate, one-time assessment. Some states had less rigorous assessments and standards than others, but each state was mandated to perform its own assessment. Using this model, comparing student learning across states was nearly impossible because every state had a different assessment. How could the Apple test from the state of Washington compare with the Orange test in Florida? With the Common Core State Standards, student achievement data can be compared across states because each state will have the same standards with nearly identical assessments, depending on the testing consortia. With the Common Core, poor students in the U.S. Virgin Islands will be held to the same high standard of learning as affluent communities in California. For the first time in American education, a student's ZIP code will not determine the level of academic rigor to which students are exposed.

Next Generation Assessments

Two testing consortia were chosen by the federal government to provide the Next Generation Assessments. They are the Partnership for Assessment of Readiness for College and Career and the Smarter Balanced Assessment Consortium. The majority of the funding comes from a $360 million grant from the federal government and the Bill and Melinda Gates Foundation. These consortia will provide, write, and implement the Next Generation Assessments. The two consortia are very similar. They will both provide tests for Grades 3–11, with the promise of providing Grades K–12 tests in the future. See which consortia your state chose by going to http://www.smarterbalanced.org/ or http://www.parcconline.org/.

The assessment piece of the Common Core State Standards is named the Next Generation Assessment. The name is fitting because both tests contain testing elements that are embedded with 21st century skills. For example, students in sixth grade through 12th grade will perform their test on an electronic device. The test will be a mix of adaptive questioning (Smarter Balanced only), multiple choice, and technology-enhanced research events. Both testing consortia have not confirmed what software and hardware are needed for the Next Generation Assessments, but they have released guidelines for new instructional technology purchases. They recommend that any new hardware purchased have the requirements shown in Figure 1.1.

| **Figure 1.1** | Minimal Guidelines for New Hardware Purchases |

Hardware	Operating System	Networking	Device Type
• 1 GHz or faster processor • 1 GB RAM or greater memory • 9.5 inch (10 inch class) or larger screen size • 1024 × 768 or better screen resolution	• Windows 7 • Mac 10.7 • Linux (Ubuntu 11.10, Fedora 16) • Chrome OS • Apple iOS • Android 4.0	• Wired or wireless Internet connection	• Destops, laptops, netbooks, thin client, and tablets that meet the hardware, operating system, and networking specifications

Used with permission from PARCC. Taken from http://www.parcconline.org/technology on 10/3/12.

Students in Grades K–5 will perform their test on a mix of electronic devices and paper. Pilot assessment programs are underway to research the ability of students in K–5 to perform the assessment on a device. Technology in the classroom is more important than ever. Not only is it the right thing to do to prepare students for college and career, but it is required on the assessments. In some states, students' scores on the Next Generation Assessments will count toward teacher evaluation. The Next Generation Assessments will require students to be technology savvy to perform certain tasks that if left unpracticed in the regular classroom will greatly impair their ability to perform well on the test. The testing medium for the majority of students is an electronic device. For example, students in sixth grade are required to produce and publish writing with a minimum of three pages in a single setting using the Internet and an electronic device. They are expected to collaborate and share their work with the testing company for scoring using the Internet. Student exposure to technology is an imperative. Google Apps for Education in conjunction with their teachers can prepare students for this challenge by providing the platform for them to practice and learn from their mistakes.

On the Next Generation Assessments, students will be asked to produce and publish writing using the Internet. Consider the steps here for writing and compare them with what the Common Core State Standards envision for students to master for the modern world.

Poor Practice

- Take out a pencil.
- On paper, prepare the writing, including graphic organizers.
- Complete a rough draft.
- Go to the computer lab.
- Type the handwritten document in Microsoft Word.
- Print the document for teacher to review.

In this formula, the writing is created by handwriting, which is an important skill but looks nothing like what students are reading in books. Using technology to create writing lets the document live on to be edited or shared. Using older techniques, the writing dies as soon as it is handed into the teacher for grading. Its best chance for review by peers, parents, and professionals is the off chance that the work is posted in the classroom or hallway. That model is not the intent of the Common Core State Standards. The steps below *are* the way professionals and college students write:

Modern Common Core Style Writing Procedures

- Take ideas from brain to keyboard on an Internet-enabled word processor *(Google Docs)*.
- Compose the document using the Internet.
- Share and collaborate with others.
- Share or e-mail the document to the teacher for scoring or to coworkers for review.

Think of the last time you performed a formal writing piece that was produced in the Poor Practice example. With the Next Generation Assessments, our students must be able to do the Modern Common Core Style to be successful in college, career, and the Next Generation Assessments. Chapter 4 will connect specific Common Core State Standards to the Modern Procedures.

Types of Devices

One reason why Google Apps for Education is the best solution for implementing technology for the Common Core State Standards is because the service is *device neutral*. Device neutrality means that no matter what device the student is using, he or she will have access to Google Apps for Education. In contrast, Apple's word-processing software Pages can only be accessed on an Apple device. Using the programs available through Google Apps for Education requires only access to the Internet and a Web browser. The Next Generation Assessment is very similar to Google Apps because it may operate virtually on any device. With Google Apps, students can access and produce their documents, files, and other work from any device (PC, Mac, Android Tablet, or iPad). The Next Generation Assessment may be given on any device that matches the requirements in Figure 1.1. That is a possibility of eight different operating systems and many different types of computers, including tablets, desktops, and laptops. That is a large combination of devices to prepare students to work with. Google Apps for Education helps students become ready for an ever-changing device market just like the Next Generation Assessments. At the moment, Apple's iPad is the king of student devices, but that will inevitably change as new devices arrive in the marketplace.

Google provides the experience for students to be ready for any device they encounter on the Next Generation Assessments, in college, or in a career.

TECHNOLOGY-INFUSED TEACHING TIP

Teachers are sometimes deprived of quality technology professional development provided by their districts. It is very difficult to target and deploy training when everyone in the building is on a different skill level. Accept the challenge that implementing technology will be difficult but necessary. Start small—learning technology that can impact students the most with the least amount of learning. Over time, things will get easier. Follow these tips for successful technology integration.

1. If you don't know, ask someone (this person is most likely a student).

2. Research on your own.

3. Read online message boards for how-tos.

4. Follow tech gurus on Twitter, Google Plus, Facebook, and Pinterest (social media—the secret weapon when learning new teaching strategies with or without technology).

GOOGLE?

The Common Core State Standards set high expectations for both students and educators. One of the most challenging for educators is finding the right way to integrate technology into the learning process. Google Apps for Education provides nearly all of the tools to get educators on the path of using technology while implementing the Common Core State Standards. Google's apps are free, easy to use, and are trusted by more than 16 million students and teachers worldwide. The services Google offers follow the company's motto of "do no harm." They are providing the most sophisticated, easy-to-use software experience for free, because it is the right thing to do for teachers and students.

This book is filled with exciting new ideas and processes for the educator to get started with Google Apps for Education and how it can be used to meet and exceed the Common Core State Standards. Hopefully, it can excite the veteran teacher to implement new strategies while calming fears and help the novice teacher get familiar with Common Core State Standards and their technology component. Step-by-step tutorials with screenshots will be provided to explain in detail how to get your students learning and working with these amazing 21st century tools as well as full lesson plans in the Resource Link section. Get ready to learn how Google Apps for Education meets Common Core!

RESOURCE LINK

Find additional content on the Web, including videos, websites, links to the Common Core State Standards, and testimonials, at this link:

- http://goo.gl/n1MkN

2

Google Apps
for Education

It is imperative that students are exposed to working and learning with technology to prepare them for life after high school. Computer skills such as writing documents, creating presentations, writing e-mail, and collecting data on spreadsheets must be commonplace in the classroom because they are commonplace in college and in a career. Many K–12 and higher education institutions across the country are using Google Apps for Education in their schools to help provide this vital experience.

Google Apps for Education is a suite of applications that is offered at no cost and advertisement-free to educational institutions. These applications provide educators with the tools to successfully integrate technology into their teaching, and they prepare students to be college and career ready with relevant 21st century skills. The Common Core State Standards require teachers and students to be fluent in digital technologies. The architects of the standards address the need for students to be able to work and learn in a technologically based society. That is why the standards demand that students be able to work in an atmosphere of collaboration, with special emphasis on creating and sharing learning. Google Apps for Education will make these goals a reality in the classroom by providing teachers and students with the ability to create, collaborate, and share ideas.

THE APPS

Google offers Gmail, Google Calendar, Google Docs, Google Video, and Google Sites in a package that students and faculty can access from anywhere. This virtually unlimited access of Google Apps allows students and teachers to extend learning and work beyond the school walls. This gives users vital real-world experience with digital tools to manage their work and life.

Gmail

Gmail is a Web-based e-mail service that provides students and school employees with a school-managed e-mail account. This is done under a school's unique *domain* that users can access from any Internet-enabled device. For example, a student or faculty member at a Google Apps for Education school will have a Gmail address with this format: username@yourschool.org. This is different from personal Gmail accounts that have the format username@gmail.com. Features located within Gmail for schools keep Gmail safe, secure, and controlled by the school's *domain administrator.* Gmail can be accessed from home, school, a smartphone, or any Internet-enabled device. Gmail is packed with features like search, filters, labels, chat, and labs that extend the user experience. For example, when enabled, the labs *Send SMS* and *Call Phone* allow users to send SMS text messages to cell phones and to call any phone number directly from their Gmail account. This is great for teachers, giving them a phone in their classrooms that provides a way for easy parent contact. With the ability to text or call directly from their Gmail account, teachers can stay in touch with parents regardless of the parents' communication hurdles.

Gmail also includes other features (see Figure 2.1). Notice chat, video chat, and call phone features are available for use directly in Gmail without having to open other applications. The green video camera icon next to "Michael Graham" signals that he can receive video calls to and from his Gmail. When video chat is not available, a green dot will appear signaling that only text chat is available.

Figure 2.1	Gmail Features

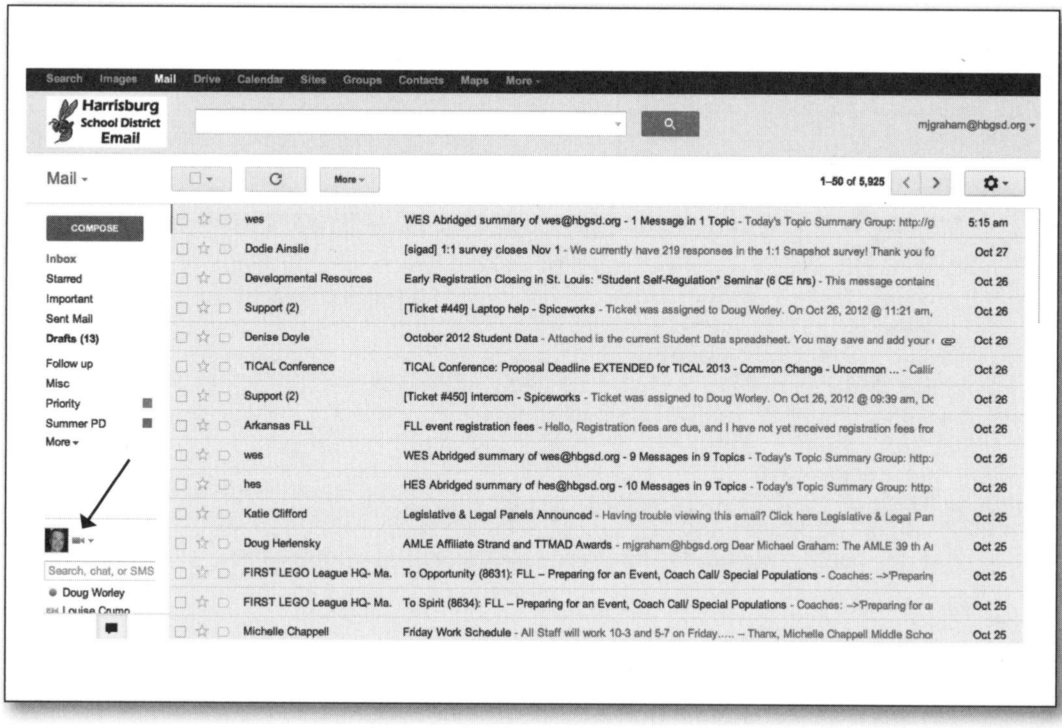

Google Calendar

Google Calendar is a Web-based calendar that lets users make appointments, schedule meetings, set due dates, and share that information with others in a live online calendar. Teachers can create class calendars and share them with specific students or with groups of contacts organized by class period, making it easy to share material with large numbers of students. Teachers and students can also create multiple calendars that manage their busy lives. For example, the student council secretary could create a calendar of the meetings and events for the organization. He could then share that calendar with the members of student council. That calendar will appear along with that student's basketball game schedule, freshman English assignment calendar, and the student's personal calendar. All of the calendars are color-coded accordingly, making them easy to distinguish from one another. Calendar makes it possible to see events of multiple friends, classmates, or teachers' schedules in one online calendar. Figure 2.2 shows how different calendars are represented by different colors. Each event that belongs to a particular calendar has the same color.

Google Docs

Google Docs is a Web-based software package that includes Document, Presentation, Spreadsheet, Form, and Drawing applications that can fully replace expensive office software. In Google Docs, students have the ability to share a document with teachers or peers, allowing for a collaborative writing experience. Students can write on the same document at the same time, but be on different devices. In addition, students can share the document with the teacher allowing immediate feedback on writing assignments.

Figure 2.2   Calendar

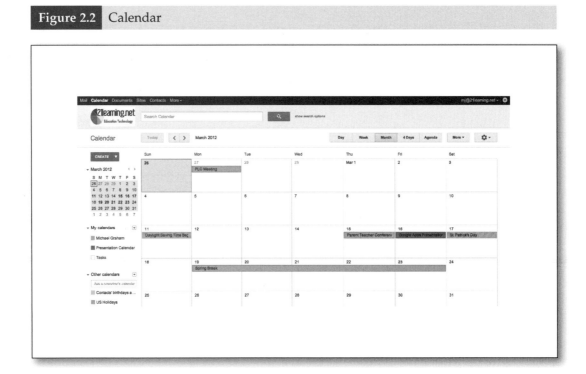

Google Docs is where the work gets done using Google Apps for Education. Built into Google Docs is the ability to share. Sharing provides a collective environment where student work that is created in any of the Google Docs programs can be collaboratively viewed, edited, or published to the Web. Google Docs saves the user's work every few seconds to the cloud-based storage service called Google Drive. Google Docs and Google's cloud-storage service eliminate the need for physical student data-storage devices such as USB flash drives, reducing clutter and decreasing the chances that the dog will eat their homework.

Figure 2.3 displays the Google Drive homepage. Clicking on the Drive tab at the top left of the screen while signed into any of the Google Apps will take the user here. Clicking on the Create tab will enable the user to choose what type of Doc to create. The Google Drive homepage includes links to Document, Presentation, Spreadsheet, Form, and Drawing programs. Next to Create in Figure 2.3 is the Upload button. Use this to upload any file type to the users' Google Drive. See size limits in Table 2.1.

Google Video

Google Video provides a place where videos can be uploaded for student viewing. This is different from YouTube, where inappropriate comments and advertisements are unpredictable. The videos available through a school Google Apps for Education account are videos that are uploaded by the domain administrator or their designee. Students are unable to search for videos that are not specifically chosen by an educational professional. School officials who are allowed to upload videos can tag those videos, allowing the videos to be given keywords making searching

| Figure 2.3 | Google Drive |

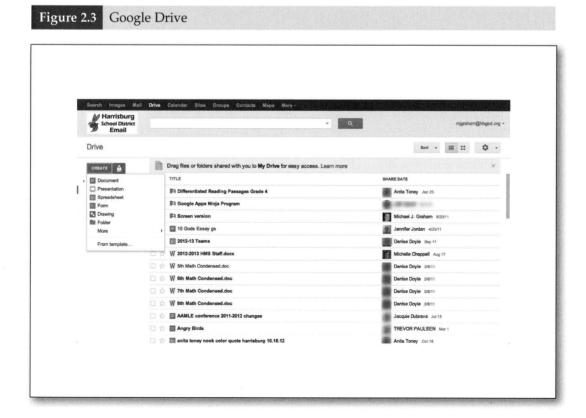

Table 2.1	Google Apps for Education Storage Limits	
Apps	*Storage*	*Practical Sizes*
Gmail	25 *gigabytes*	This amount of space stores Gmail messages that contain pictures, video, and text; 25 gigabytes is the equivalent to 36 blank CDs or five blank DVDs.
Google Docs format created in the online Google Apps account	• Each document can have 1.024 million characters of text regardless of number of pages or font size. • Each spreadsheet may contain 400,000 cells, with a maximum of 256 columns. • Each presentation can be up to 10 *megabytes*. • Drawing files are unlimited. The number of Google Docs that can be created is unlimited. Each Doc must adhere to these requirements.	• That is equivalent to about 500 double-spaced pages of a Microsoft Word file without pictures or clip art. • Spreadsheets with 400,000 cells contain a massive amount of data. For example, a spreadsheet that has 1,250 rows and five columns totals 7,500 cells. • Presentations that are 10 megabytes contain approximately 200 slides without image files or video. • Google reports on its website that it has never had a person produce a drawing that was too big. Google politely ask Google Apps for Education customers not to try.
Uploaded files **not** created in Google Docs	1,024 megabytes	1,024 copies of Chapter 4 of this book. It contains 8,500 words and 24 pictures. In other words, Google Apps for Education offers a tremendous amount of space to store student and teacher work.

by students and teachers easy. For example, an uploaded video could contain the tags *science, 8th grade,* and *topography.*

Students and teachers are able to search for videos uploaded to their school domain using the Google Video page (see Figure 2.4). Uploading videos is not allowed unless the domain administrator has turned it on for the specified user. Only 100 users under the entire domain may upload videos. This restriction is meant to limit the possibility of inappropriate or irrelevant content being posted to the school's domain.

Google Sites

Google Sites is a free website creator that allows teachers and students to make websites that are fully compatible with Google Calendar and Google Docs. These are kept under the school domain, and students may share websites with the outside world if approved by the domain administrator. Google Sites does not require the use of complicated Web design language such as HTML.

Figure 2.5 displays the Google Sites main menu. Sites that are created under the school's Google Apps domain are listed here. If sites are enabled for students and

Figure 2.4 Google Video

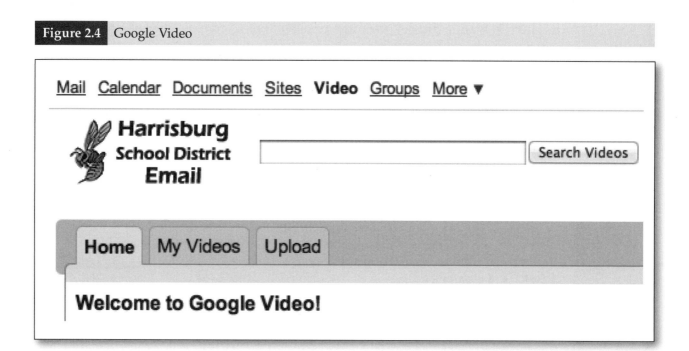

Figure 2.5 Google Sites

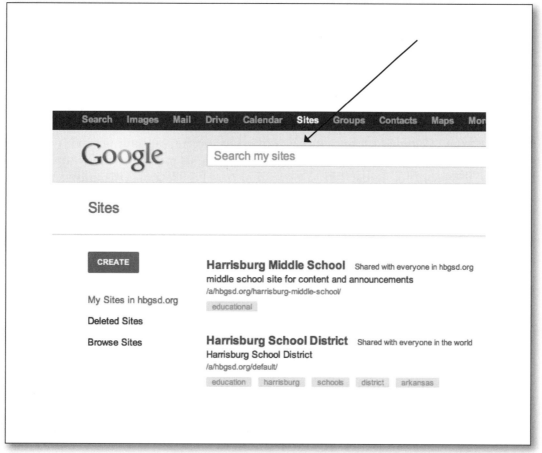

teachers in a large district, then it is possible that a large number of sites would be listed here. Using the *search bar* to narrow down sites is the most efficient way to find the site the user is looking for.

Google Video and Google Sites in This Book

Google Video and Google Sites will not be addressed in detail in this book. Google Video and Google Sites are important and should be considered as part of a school's solution for delivering high-quality technology-related instruction. The purpose of this book is to directly relate Google Apps for Education with the Common Core State Standards and to offer teachers lesson plan ideas and insight to make that possible. Additionally, Google Sites' user controls are complex and would require more space than is appropriate for this work.

THE CLOUD

Google Apps for Education are cloud based, meaning they can be accessed anywhere from any device that has an Internet connection. Cloud computing makes it possible for users to store, create, and share content without saving it to a physical hard drive. For example, a student writing an essay in Google Documents on a laptop in English class can save the file to her Google Drive and later access that file from her home computer. With Google Drive, it doesn't matter if the computer gets a virus and is completely destroyed. The student's essay can be accessed anywhere there is an Internet connection through the user's Google Apps for Education account. This ability allows students and teachers to create, collaborate, and share their work across any device using any platform. It does not matter if students are working on a Mac, PC, or smartphone. Students may even upload other formats of student work such as Microsoft Word, Excel, PowerPoint, Apple's Pages, .PDF, or .CSV data files and share them with anyone.

If the student or teacher uploads a format other than Google Docs to his or her Google Drive, the user may not edit the document in the Google Docs program. It is just for storage. Alternatively, the user could convert the file to Google Docs format, creating a new Google Doc that may be edited in the corresponding Docs program. During the upload process, Google Docs will ask the user if he or she wants to convert the document to its matching Doc format (see Figure 2.6). This allows the user to edit the document with the corresponding Google Docs program.

Figure 2.6 Upload Settings

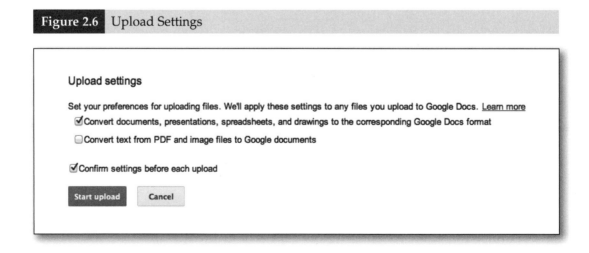

SHARE

Sharing is one of the unique features of Google Docs that gives it the upper hand by offering collaboration to users. Traditional office software packages that reside on the hard drives of computers do not offer the ability of collaboration and sharing. Sharing in Google Docs allows users to be able to work collaboratively in any of the programs. The user can give others the rights to edit, view, or comment on any document that they own in real time by setting visibility options and share settings. The default share setting is private, but users can share with anyone through a URL or use share settings to send the person an e-mail notification alerting them that a document is being shared. Options in sharing allow the user to make the Google Doc searchable on the Web, public for users in your domain only, or public for anyone with the Web link.

Students' motivation for doing high-quality work will increase because they are doing the work not only for the teacher to read, but also they are producing work that can be shared with parents, peers, and other adults, giving them a sense of pride and responsibility to produce excellent work. Vannessa Rivera, a sixth-grade student at Harrisburg Middle School, was quoted saying, "Using Google Docs is way easier than writing our essays on paper, it also gives me a way to show off my writing . . . I can really share it with anyone . . . plus we're not killing all of the trees we used to." Vannessa now has another purpose for her writing. Her writing has the possibility of being read by parents, peers, and professionals around the world, giving her pride, motivation, and validation. Sharing work with others outside the student-teacher relationship is a possibility, not a requirement. Students, teachers, and parents may have conversations on what is appropriate for sharing with parents, peers, or the world.

With Google Apps for Education, users can share Google Docs within their domain or, if their domain administrator has approved out of domain sharing, students and teachers may share with anyone. This includes neighboring school districts, professionals in the field, or colleges and universities. One of the hallmarks of the Common Core State Standards is learning through collaboration. Through sharing and collaborating, students gain a sense of community and responsibility for the group's work. Google Apps for Education gives students the tools to create, collaborate, and share their understanding of the world and to find their place in technologically rich college and career settings.

THE DOMAIN ADMINISTRATOR: BEHIND THE SCENES

Google Apps for Education is hosted by Google, which means all of the content created by students and teachers is safely stored on Google's servers. However, the data that students and teachers create with their Google account is the property of the school and the user. Google Apps for Education customers benefit from two features that will help district technology personnel allocate human and financial resources more appropriately. There is no software to install and no hardware to purchase: Google provides the entire apps package and services for free. The ability of the school domain administrator to manage the Google Apps for Education service adds the special security measures that are appropriate for the school setting.

Figure 2.7   School Logo in Google Apps

Domain administrators are able to use their school's custom logo instead of the default Google Apps logo (see Figure 2.7). This is good because students and teachers can easily tell if they are logged into their Google Apps for Education account. Plus, the logo adds to school spirit and looks professional.

The domain administrator can control many features of Google Apps for Education. For example, the domain administrator can select certain features to become available to groups of users. He or she may allow teachers and support staff to access Gmail Labs, but they may be turned off for students. Your school community would benefit from a committee that is designated to review what features of Google Apps for Education are available for use by students and teachers so that they may reflect the values of the community. The domain administrator may add features or take them away at any time for individual users or groups of users. For example, if a middle school student sends an e-mail to a fellow student that contains bullying language, then the domain administrator may disable Gmail for the offending student but leave on Google Calendar and Docs so that the student may complete assignments. After the student has been held accountable and counseled on the proper way to communicate online and has earned the trust back, the domain administrator can restore the privilege of Gmail to the student. All e-mails sent to the student during that time will be saved and may be accessed when the students' Gmail is reactivated. Groups of users from an elementary setting may benefit from more restricted access to sharing and Gmail outside the domain while middle and high school students may need to contact peers, parents, or professionals outside the domain.

Although dangers exist, proper classroom management and student online safety education will create a student who is ready for college and a career. Blocking outside forms of communication may leave the student unprepared to handle the digital world. Relaxing the content filters and share settings can educate students about dangers such as bullying and access to inappropriate content. When a student abuses the trust, the student can be counseled on the appropriate way to use digital tools. If left uneducated, students may not know how to behave properly online once out of the more secure Google Apps for Education setting.

RESOURCE LINK

For more information about Google Apps for Education, including:

- domain setup for tech administrators videos,

- overviews and Google training materials,

- the author's favorite websites, and

- testimonials and interviews of schools currently using Google Apps, access this link: http://goo.gl/843B1.

3

Gmail

KEY FEATURES

❖ E-mail assignments to students
❖ More involved parent, teacher, and student communication
❖ Gmail Labs
❖ Video and text chat
❖ Call phone
❖ Text message

Connectivity through digital communication is one of the best aspects of the Internet age. Collaborating and communicating using Gmail empowers students and teachers to connect with each other to facilitate learning. The Common Core State Standards support digital communication and want students to become responsible and ready to work and learn with it.

In this chapter, we will look at how Gmail can serve as the command center of communication with Google Apps for Education. We will also discover how students and teachers can use Gmail as an e-mail application and learn how Gmail goes beyond simple e-mail. Follow the screenshots and step-by-step procedures to see how Gmail can exceed the expectations of the Common Core State Standards.

GMAIL

• 25 gigabytes of e-mail storage for Google Apps for Education schools (enough space to store 6,000 copies of the King James Bible)
• Easy access to Drive, Calendar, Sites, and Video

(Continued)

- Gmail is more than just e-mail
  - Filters
  - Labels
  - Labs
  - Call phone
  - Text, video, and voice chat
  - Calendar and document sharing notifications

STUDENT MAIL ACCOUNTS

Gmail has evolved into much more than sending and receiving e-mail. The other features embedded into Gmail will open possibilities for teachers and students to exceed the ideas in the Common Core State Standards. One of the fundamental principles of the Common Core State Standards is for educators to focus on deep learning using the most up-to-date technology that will prepare them for college and a career. The standards suggest that technology and its use in everyday life is so important that it does not require a separate set of standards. Instead, they are woven into every standard because that is how technology is woven into our lives. Living and thriving in a technologically based society requires mastery of skills such as e-mail and digital citizenship.

Digital citizenship is an important part of becoming a responsible member of a technologically based society, but there is more to it than behaving properly online. It is about learning how to organize the massive amounts of digital information that students and teachers are bombarded with daily. The digital age has brought us easy access to information, but it also has burdened us with the task of sorting, indexing, and recalling that information with clear purpose. Gmail can help students gain skills on how to manage this influx of information while learning the essential skills of e-mail and proper use of electronic communication. The introduction to the Common Core State Standards says of students that meet the standards: "They habitually perform the critical reading necessary to pick carefully through the staggering amount of information available today in print and digitally." Using Gmail to its full potential as a command center of Google Apps for Education can help students and teachers wade through the massive quantity of information they encounter, reinforcing college and career readiness skills that are paramount in today's world.

Student Versus Adult Accounts

Student Gmail accounts can differ from teacher or administrator accounts. The domain administrator has the ability to turn on or off certain features. For example, the chat feature in Gmail could be turned off for students but may be open for faculty. Additionally, Labs may be turned on or off depending on the domain administrator. Labs are new services that Google and its partners are working on to make Gmail better.

COMMAND CENTER

Gmail is the cornerstone of Google Apps for Education. It allows for constant communication between all Google Apps. Most users sign in to Gmail first because this is where notifications are displayed to alert the user of Google Docs that are being shared and upcoming calendar events. It is best for students and teachers to use Gmail as the starting point for working in Google Apps for Education. For example, if the Algebra teacher placed an event on her shared Algebra Google Calendar reminding students of an upcoming assignment, Google Calendar will automatically notify the students of time, location, and description of the event through Gmail. The students do not have to remember to check their calendar. Instruct students to sync their Gmail to their smartphone so they can be in constant contact with their academic responsibilities. In addition to classroom purposes, students who are college and career ready will have an e-mail address and use it effectively to communicate.

Learning appropriate e-mail etiquette will help students make checking e-mail part of their daily routine, just as people in the workplace. This is an important routine to follow because most notifications from work or school come through e-mail. Students at Harrisburg Middle School are allowed to check their e-mail during their lunch break and other appropriate times. Mrs. Anita Toney, the school's library media specialist, has scheduled computer access during lunch so the students can have time to check their e-mail. She says, "When students have time to explore Google Apps on their own outside the classroom setting, they gain more experience with using the tools and it makes it easier when they apply those skills in the classroom." Allowing time for students to check for notifications, e-mails from friends, and e-mails from teachers is good practice. The idea is for students in the early grades to become familiar with e-mail and its ubiquity in college and career. Students as early as fifth grade became fluent sending and receiving e-mail with purpose within the first semester they had access.

SIGN IN

Sign in by visiting http://www.gmail.com in a Web browser. This will open the standard Gmail sign-in box as shown in Figure 3.1.

This is different from the official Google Apps for Education sign-in screen managed by a Google Apps for Education school, but it will take the user to the school-managed domain by typing the full e-mail address into the username box, for example, user.name@yourschool.org.

The school-managed sign-in looks different from the personal sign-in and has the school's logo as shown in Figure 3.2. To access the school sign-in page, the domain administrator may have a link on the school's website or access the default link at mail.google .com/a/yourschool.org

Every school that uses Google Apps for Education has its own domain. For example, the 21 Learning Academy's domain is www.21learning.net. Every e-mail address assigned by the domain administrator in

Figure 3.1 Standard Gmail Sign-In

this domain will end in @21learning.net. To access the school's official Google Apps for Education sign-in page, type google.com/a/yourschool.org. For example, the sign-in for my school district is google.com/a/hbgsd.org. At this Web address, the user will find the official school logo and sign-in as shown in Figure 3.2. The google .com part directs the user to Google, then the "a" part represents "account" followed by the school's domain registered through Google. These are unique for every Google Apps for Education account.

Look at the arrow to the school's domain address listed under the username box in Figure 3.2. With this sign-in option, the user will not type the entire e-mail address to sign in, just the username. All Google Apps for Education sign-in boxes are colored, as opposed to the personal Gmail sign-in boxes, which are gray.

Sign-In Procedures

1. In the *address bar* of a Web browser, type www.gmail.com or www.google .com/a/yourschool.org.

   a. If the user chooses www.gmail.com, then he must place the entire e-mail address into the username box like in Figure 3.1.

   b. If the user chooses www.google.com/a/yourschool.org, then he only places his username in the username box as shown in Figure 3.2.

2. Enter the password.

3. Press **Enter** or click the ⌈Sign in⌋ button.

Figure 3.2   Google Apps Sign-In

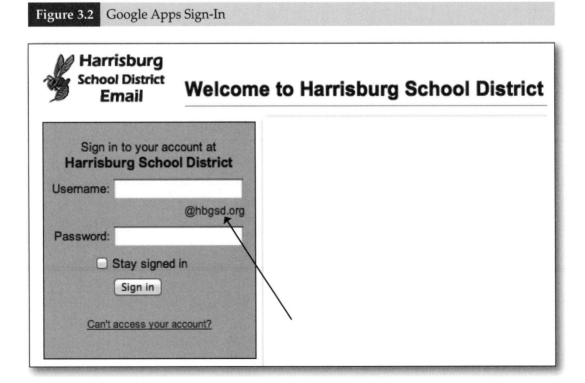

Figure 3.3	After Sign-In

Figure 3.3 displays the command center of Google Apps for Education. To access Mail, Calendar, Documents, or Sites, click on their respective links above the school logo. From here, users can manage their apps.

Elementary Students and Sign-In

It is possible for elementary students to master the sign-in process. Working with elementary students and explaining Internet terms will be challenging, but they should be familiar with the basic aspects of e-mail, Internet, and collaboration. The Common Core State Standards demand it. Students in kindergarten will be asked to use Internet tools to "produce and publish writing, including collaborating with peers." E-mail is the foundation for the Common Core State Standard quoted above. To make the transition easier to a technology-based curriculum, technology managers could create easy sign-on options for younger students. For example, the students could have an icon on their desktop that takes them directly to the school-managed sign-in page. Teaching elementary students the basics of Web browsing and e-mail will be a challenge even to the tech-savvy teacher, but it is necessary to fulfill the Common Core State Standards. The key is to persevere. High expectations of students will lead them to become college and career ready.

SEARCH

Google is the king of search. Its search engine is the most used in the world. *Time* magazine reports that as of 2011, there were more than 34,700 Google searches per second worldwide (the next closest is Yahoo, with 3,200 per second). Google offers the best search experience, according to its popularity, and it has applied its massive search power into Gmail. Using Gmail search will let the user find anything in their Gmail account. Google Gmail provides 25 gigabytes of storage to Google Apps for Education customers; with the number of e-mails that amount of space can hold, the ability to search for a particular message becomes important. For example, a student needing notes that a fellow student has e-mailed him or her at the beginning of the semester can find them by searching for keywords found in the notes.

When searching in Gmail, place any keyword into the search bar to gain results concerning the query. For a more specific search, look at Table 3.1; it shows how to do advanced searches within Gmail. Figure 3.4 is a screenshot of the Google Search box found in Gmail.

> ### TECHNOLOGY-INFUSED TEACHING TIP
>
> Enable the Lab *Apps Search* to allow Gmail to search the user's Google Documents. This will display relevant documents related to the query that are in the users Google Drive below the results found in Gmail.

| Figure 3.4 | Gmail Search Bar |

To activate advanced search in Gmail, use the list of operators found in Table 3.1. Operators are words that search for only specific results found in Gmail. To use operators, follow these steps:

1. Type the operator into the search bar followed by a colon.

2. Type the keyword to be used with the operator after the colon (no spaces after colon).

3. Press **Enter** or click the blue box with the magnifying glass to search.

The results will appear on the next page. See Table 3.1 for an explanation of the operators and their functions.

| Table 3.1 | Advanced Search |

Operator	What it does	Example
To:	Finds messages the user sent to a specific person or e-mail address	To:Brett Finds all e-mail that was sent to Brett
From:	Finds messages from a specific person or e-mail address	From:bently@21learning.net Finds all e-mail that was sent to the user by bently@21learning.net
Subject:	Finds messages that have particular words in the subject line	Subject:science lesson plan Displays messages that contain the words "science lesson plan" in the subject line
After: Before:	Search for messages after or before a certain date	After:10/26/2012 Will find messages that were sent after this date
Quotes " "	Searching something with quotes finds exactly the words in quotes in the same word order	"faculty meeting" Searches Gmail for messages containing the exact phrase "faculty meeting"

TECHNOLOGY-INFUSED TEACHING TIP

Use quotes in the regular Google Search bar, found at www.google.com, to specifically search websites that have the exact phrase in quotes. If quotes are not placed around a phrase, then Google will find websites that have those words anywhere in the website in no particular order.

LABS

Gmail Labs are experimental features that third-party developers and Google's software engineers are working on to improve the Gmail experience. Google thrives on innovation by its employees to make its products better. Every Google employee spends 20 percent of his or her work time on a project of his or her choice. Many of the amazing features Google offers in its Gmail service come from this "20 percent innovation time." Labs are invented and maintained by Google and their partners, but the domain administrator controls the Labs that are available in Google Apps for Education. The domain administrator may turn off Labs for specific users or groups of users. One disadvantage of Labs is that they are experimental and could crash at any time so users beware, but this is highly unlikely. If a Lab you are working with crashes, refresh Gmail and the problem will be taken care of. Once Labs are proven to be effective and stable, they will be considered to become a permanent feature in Gmail.

TECHNOLOGY-INFUSED TEACHING TIP

The Common Core State Standards want students to be able to think critically about problems that affect them. The standards also give students the tools necessary to speak with conviction and to back that up with data and evidence. It's about overcoming the obstacles they face in college and career and teaching them that, with determination, their goals can be reachable. To accomplish this, it would be great if teachers took a few lessons from Google and allowed their students guided but independent work time to study things that they are interested in. Most of the innovations that make Google special come from their "20 percent innovation time." Students are more inclined to produce high-quality work when they are emotionally invested. Teachers who have the courage to slow down and help students explore their world will have more success implementing the standards. The Common Core State Standards give us back the license to be innovative.

Some administrators and teachers may feel uncomfortable allowing students to text message, text chat, video chat, or call phones from Gmail while in school. However, Labs and other features like this should be allowed for everyone under the domain. Students need the ability to communicate and collaborate with peers. The Common Core State Standards explicitly say in Writing Anchor Standard 6 to "use technology, including the Internet, to produce and publish writing and to interact and collaborate with others." Limiting students' ability to communicate and collaborate

Figure 3.5   Accessing Labs

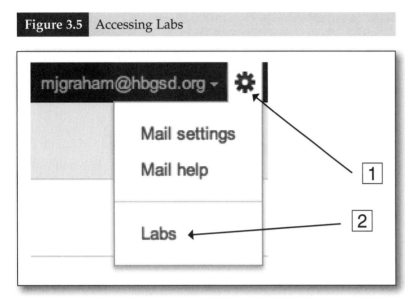

with others goes against the ideas outlined in the Common Core State Standards. The standards focus on the next generation of 21st century college and career skills. People in this cohort need these skills of communication. Where better to teach them responsible ways to use digital tools than at school, where it is safe? Some students will abuse it, allowing for a teachable moment on how to properly behave in the digital world. Some students may write inappropriate notes with paper and pencil, but I do not foresee administrators taking these tools for learning away.

To access **Labs** (see Figure 3.5)

1. Click on the gear next to the username in the upper right-hand corner of Gmail.

2. Then, click **Labs** to reveal Figure 3.6.

Figure 3.6   Labs Selection Page

General   Labels   Accounts   Filters   Forwarding and POP/IMAP   Chat   Web Clips   **Labs**   Inbox   Offline

Harrisburg School District Mail Labs: Some crazy experimental stuff.

Harrisburg School District Mail Labs is a testing ground for experimental features that aren't quite ready for primetime. They may **change, break** or **disappear** at any time.

If (when) a Labs feature breaks, and you're having trouble loading your inbox, there's an escape hatch. Use https://mail.google.com/mail/ca/u/2/?labs=0.

Search for a lab: [   ]   e.g. search, gadget, preview   1

[Save Changes]   [Cancel]

Enabled Labs

Old Snakey
by Dave C
⊙ Enable
○ Disable

Kick it old school with Old Snakey! Enable keyboard shortcuts and hit '&' from the main page to play a game of snake.
Send feedback   3

gmark
506 132 2314 ▾
me: I enjoyed dinner last ni(
thanks for inviting us

SMS (text messaging) in Chat
by The SMS Team
⊙ Enable
○ Disable

Allows you to send and receive text messages (SMS) in Chat.
Send feedback

– Send SMS

SMS in Chat gadget
by The SMS Team
⊙ Enable
○ Disable

Figure 3.6 shows the Labs available for this domain. The user may search for a Lab by keyword.

To search for a specific Lab or a property you may enjoy as a Lab, follow these steps:

1. Enter the search term into the box **Search for a lab.**

2. Press **Enter** to reveal a list of Labs that meet your criteria.

3. Click on the bubble to enable the Lab.

Labs require the user to sign out and then sign back in to Gmail activate.

Labs for Productivity

Google Calendar gadget: This Lab lets users see their Google Calendar directly from Gmail. For example, students who are collaborating on a project for a mathematics class can confirm due dates for each of the group's assignments without having to open their Google Calendar. It makes it easy to communicate the user's schedule when in Gmail. This Lab also lets the user see the details of the calendar event such as upcoming events, locations, and event details on the left side of Gmail.

Google Docs preview in mail: This Lab lets the user preview documents, spreadsheets, and presentations directly from Gmail. When users share a link to a Google Doc by e-mail, this Lab will let the user view it without opening it in Docs. For example, an elementary teacher could require third-grade students to type their journal entries in a Google Document. The students would then share the link to the journal entry by e-mail with the teacher. This Lab allows the teacher to preview the work, confirming its length requirement and completion. Later, the teacher could open Google Docs and read the entire entry for grading.

Inserting images: Enabling this Lab will place the picture insert icon ![icon] into the Gmail toolbar, allowing images to be inserted into the body of an e-mail. See the Gmail toolbar below in Figure 3.7. When making a point by e-mail, adding images can be useful. For example, instead of creating a formal Google Document that contains images, teachers can pose questions directly from Gmail to their students that contain diagrams or pictures. Informal assessments like this could be valuable as bell ringers or as the ticket-out questions that teachers often use as a quick assessment of the day's learning. Students in science class could be asked to identify the parts of a flower from a picture sent directly in the body of the e-mail. This saves the teacher and students the time of attaching and opening the image. Students can quickly answer the question based on the image and send their responses back for grading. This icon will not be present if this Lab is not enabled.

Figure 3.7 Gmail Text Edit Toolbar

Undo send: Gmail and most e-mail applications send immediately when the user presses the send button. The Gmail Lab *Undo send* can help the user avoid mistakes by delaying the e-mail being sent by a short amount of time. For example, a student who is assigned to reply to an e-mailed quiz could undo send a few seconds after he or she clicks the send button. The default time for a message to be undone with this Lab is 10 seconds. But the user can change the amount of time it is delayed up to 30 seconds. Follow the steps below to change the default undo time.

1. Enable the Lab *Undo send* outlined in the steps under Figure 3.6.

2. Click the ⚙▾ gear icon next to the username in the upper right-hand corner of Gmail as shown in Figure 3.5.

3. Click on **Settings**, then **General**.

4. Look for *Undo send* under the General tab like in Figure 3.8.

5. Click the drop-down arrow to select the time Gmail waits to allow for an undo send.

Figure 3.8	Undo Send Settings

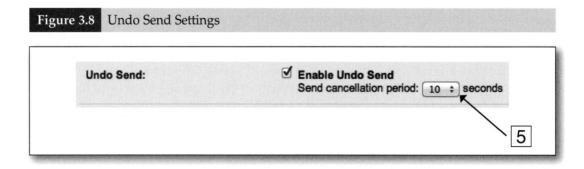

After the Lab is enabled, each time an e-mail is sent the user has the option to click on the Undo button at the top of the Gmail Inbox page like in Figure 3.9; however, the user has only seconds to act.

Figure 3.9	Undo Send Button

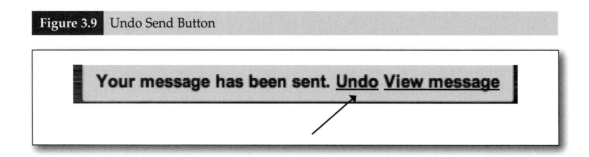

LABELS

Gmail automatically places messages with the same subject line into one conversation. Each time a message is replied to, it is nested under the original message, creating an easy to follow discussion. This is a good organizational tool that can help students and teachers keep up with the information being passed back and forth through e-mail. One extension of this is labels. Labels are a powerful tool that will allow the user to group messages according to any attribute the user chooses. Labels are like folders but better. Folders only allow the user to place a message in one particular file. Labels allow the user to place multiple labels on the same message. For example, a second-grade teacher who teaches all subjects is working on a lesson plan with the special education teacher by e-mail. The lesson contains both mathematics and social studies standards. The teacher can place mathematics, social studies, and special education labels on the same message, allowing for easy recall of the contents by searching for any of these keywords.

To make a label, follow these steps:

1. Click on the gear ⚙ in the upper right-hand corner of Gmail next to the username like in Figure 3.10.

2. Click **Mail settings.**

3. Choose the **Labels** tab next to **General.**

Figure 3.10	Creating a New Label

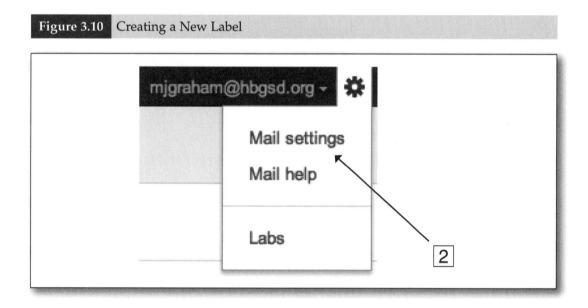

4. Click on the **Create new label** option [Labels / Create new label] to reveal Figure 3.11.

5. Enter a label name in the box in Figure 3.11.

*Create a **nest label,** similar to a subfolder, by checking the box shown in Figure 3.11.*

Labels appear under the default labels Inbox, Sent Mail, Important, and Drafts that are located on the left side of Gmail. The label icon 🏷 appears when a box is checked like in Figure 3.12. To place a label on an existing conversation, follow these steps:

1. Check the box or boxes next to a conversation to label as shown in Figure 3.12.

2. Select the **Label as** icon 🏷▾ .

3. Check the box to give it a label (Figure 3.11).

Figure 3.11 New Label

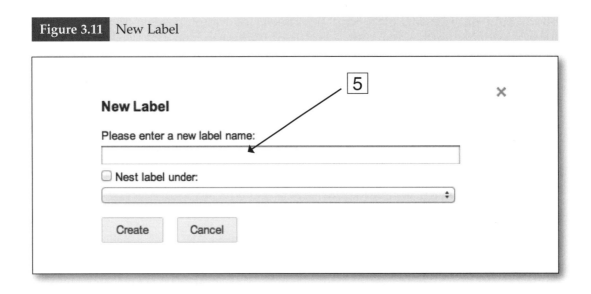

Figure 3.12 Label Existing Conversation

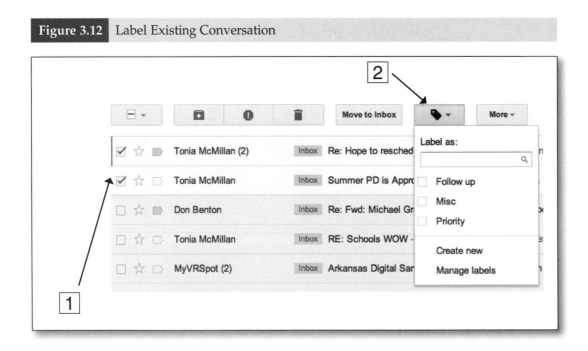

In Figure 3.12, notice the "2" in parenthesis next to Tonia's message. That indicates that there are two messages in this conversation with the same subject. Both messages in this conversation will have the same label. In Figure 3.13, after the label "Summer PD" has been placed on a message, it will appear next to the default label, "Inbox." This conversation could be found under the Inbox label or Summer PD label list on the left side of Gmail.

| Figure 3.13 | Managing Labels |

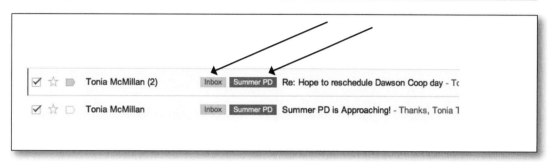

Default Labels

- Inbox
- Starred
- Sent
- Drafts
- Trash

FILTERS

Filters allow the user to manage incoming messages. Sometimes users have messages that they want to automatically apply a label to, skip the inbox, or forward. Creating a filter will redirect incoming messages and apply a preset command for the type of message. For example, a teacher who assigns an e-mail quiz will have responses from many different students from different class periods. These messages can overtake the teacher's inbox, creating confusion and disorganization. To overcome this, the teacher may create a filter to redirect the messages and apply a label automatically before they come to the inbox. For a classroom example, follow these steps:

LESSON IN FOCUS

The teacher will . . .

1. E-mail a quiz to students in third-period English class with the subject line "Third-Period Quiz."

2. Instruct the students to reply to the message containing answers to the quiz.

   When the quiz is replied to, the subject line "RE: Third-Period Quiz" is automatically generated.

3. Create a filter to collect messages with the words "Third-Period Quiz" in the subject line to skip the Inbox label and go directly to the label **Third-Period Assignments** as shown in Figure 3.14.

When the teacher gets ready to grade the work, all of the third-period quizzes will have skipped the regular Inbox label and will be labeled Third-Period Assignments. This allows the teacher's e-mail inbox to not be cluttered with third period's assignments. The teacher can access the assignments to grade from any Internet-enabled device, just as easy as checking e-mail.

Figure 3.14   Creating a Filter

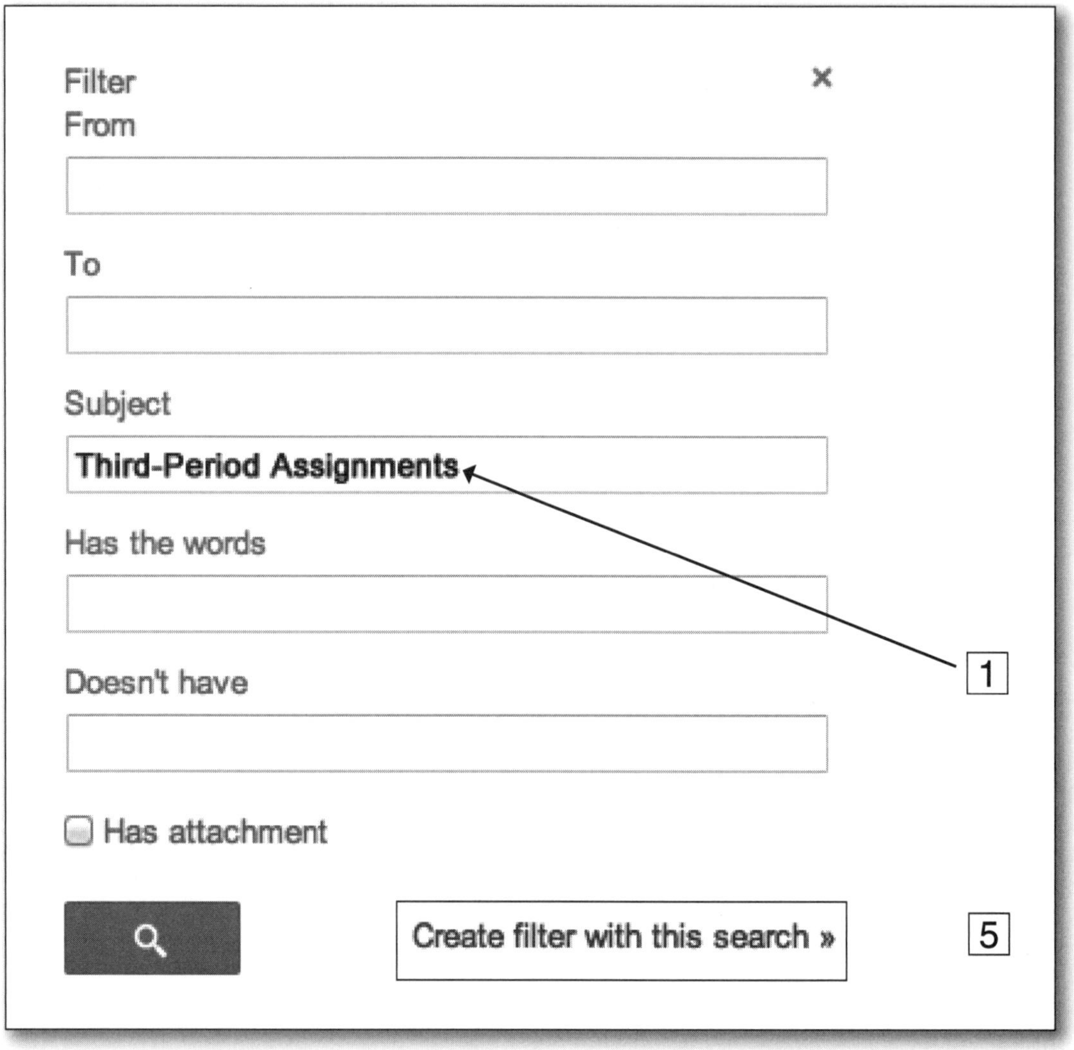

Create a New Filter

1. Click on the gear icon ⚙▾ in the upper right-hand corner of Gmail.

2. Select **Mail Settings.**

3. Click **Create New Filter.**

4. Type "Third-Period Assignments" in the Subject field.

    a. If the user wants to filter for other keywords, fill in the appropriate box.

5. Click Create Filter With This Search to set the filter.

Figure 3.15   Filtering Options

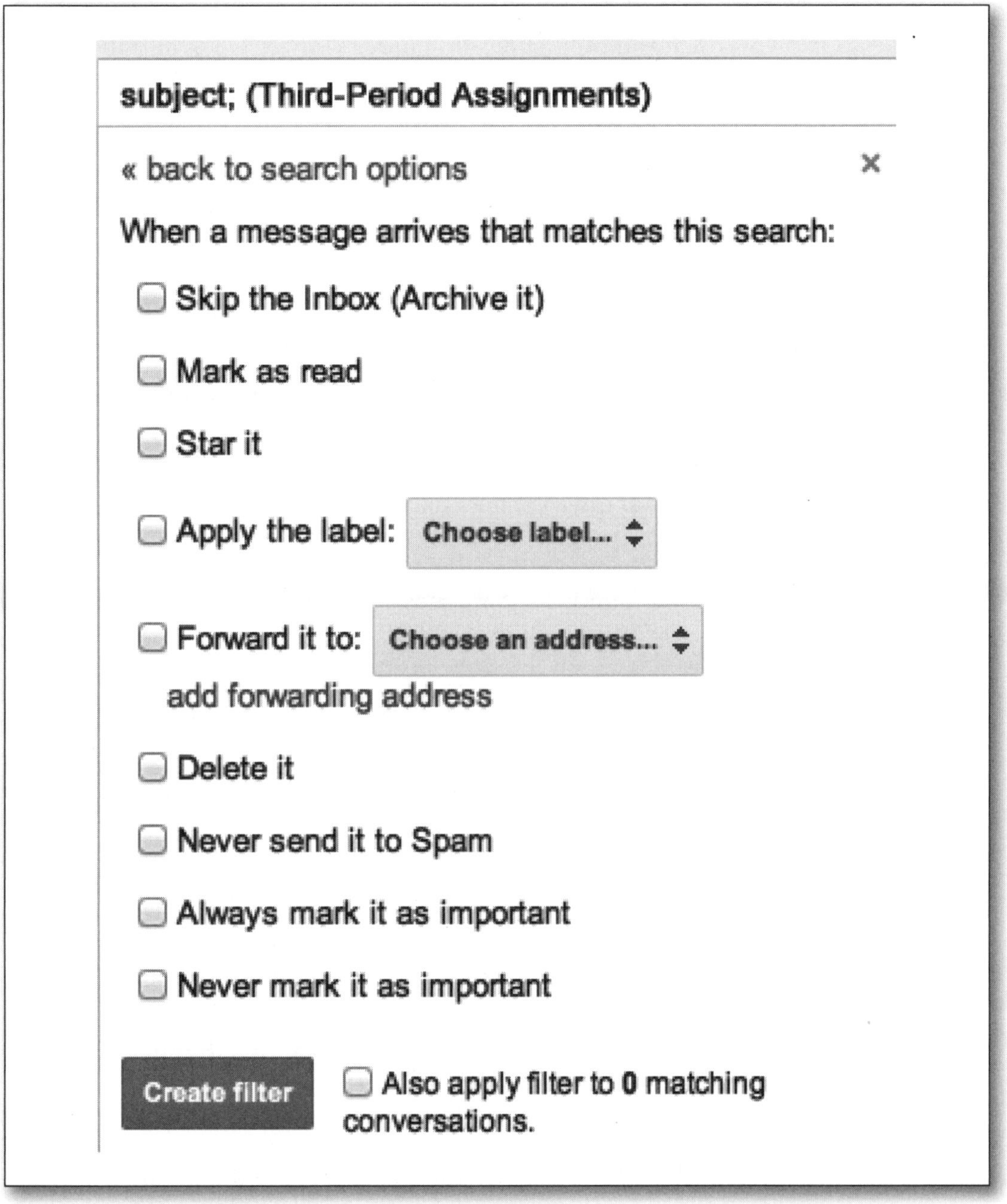

subject; (Third-Period Assignments)

« back to search options   ✕

When a message arrives that matches this search:

☐ Skip the Inbox (Archive it)

☐ Mark as read

☐ Star it

☐ Apply the label: **Choose label...** ⬍

☐ Forward it to: **Choose an address...** ⬍
   add forwarding address

☐ Delete it

☐ Never send it to Spam

☐ Always mark it as important

☐ Never mark it as important

Create filter   ☐ Also apply filter to **0** matching
                     conversations.

• **Skip the Inbox (Archive it)** means that the message will not appear in the user's regular mailbox (also called the Inbox label). This will prevent a large number of student e-mails from cluttering the teacher's Inbox label. Ms. Maghen Nelms, a seventh-grade English language arts teacher, uses labels and filters to sort student work from various class periods. She says, "Labels and filters have saved my life, organizing essays into manageable groups by class period." At our school, the literacy department practices Common Core State Standards–inspired writing events where the students study a piece of informational text. Over the next few class periods, the students are given time to research and understand the piece. Later, the students produce and publish writing using Google Docs, and they share that writing with their teacher, where student and teacher can collaboratively edit the document. Sharing creates an e-mail notification sent to the teacher. Ms. Nelms creates labels and filters to redirect student document notifications, skipping the inbox. Ms. Nelms said, "Before I learned about filters and labels, I would miss important communication from the administration and staff because it would get lost in the sea of unread messages from students." Writing events such as the one described here help students and teachers be immersed in technology that is thought provoking and that meets the requirements of the Common Core State Standards.

- **Mark as read** allows the user to mark the message as read.

- **Star it** is a default label in Gmail along with Inbox, Important, and Sent Mail. These labels are found on the left side of Gmail. Starring is used to quickly notify this message as significant. For example, teachers may want to star messages that come from the principal or administration. These messages most likely contain certain information that will need to be reviewed later. Starring a message places an automatic label so it can be easily found. To star a message, follow these steps:

1. Click on the star next to the e-mail message as shown in Figure 3.16.

2. Access starred messages by clicking on the starred label located on the left side of Gmail.

3. Star e-mail in Gmail and star any Google Doc for easy access in Google Drive.

| Figure 3.16 | Star an E-mail |

- **Apply the label** allows the user to place the message automatically into a preexisting label or a new one. In the example "Third-Period Assignments," teachers will select this label to automatically label student assignments from third period. Use this in conjunction with **Skip the inbox** for student assignments to be placed automatically in an easy-to-find label for later grading.

TECHNOLOGY-INFUSED TEACHING TIP

Avoid printing. Gmail has done the work by filtering and labeling student assignments like in the example about Ms. Nelms. The student work is nicely marked with labels in the teacher's Gmail, where the teacher can grade them anywhere there is an Internet connection. Printing the papers for the purpose of grading will take away from the benefits of cloud computing. Google offers all the tools necessary to grade the papers online. Common Core State Standards not only want students to be college and career ready, but also they push teachers to become proficient in 21st century skills.

CHAT

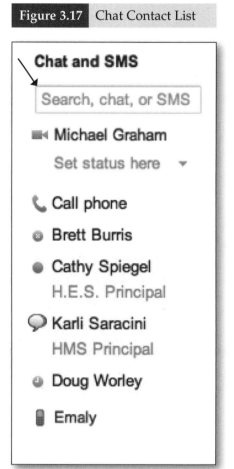

Figure 3.17 Chat Contact List

Chat is another powerful feature tucked into Gmail. Gmail includes text chat, video chat, voice chat, call phone, and if Labs are enabled, the user can text-message phones directly from her school Gmail account. Chat is located on the left side of the Gmail page. Look at Figure 3.17 and the bullet points here to see some of the features and their explanations.

- The box labeled **Search, chat, or SMS** allows the user to either search for a contact or type in the name of the person to chat with. This makes it easy to find people in a long list of contacts. For example, if a teacher needed to ask the technology coordinator about a troubleshooting issue, chatting by text can provide quick answers in a classroom technology crisis.

- A **green camera** next to a name in the chat list signals that the person has the necessary hardware for video chat. To video chat, there must be a video camera and microphone attached to the computer.

- A **green circle** denotes that the user is online and available for text or voice chat. Voice chat is only available if both parties have a microphone attached to their computers.

- A **quote bubble** next to a name signals that a conversation is in progress.

- An **orange clock** next to a name indicates that the user is away or has set his or her status to busy.

- A **cell phone** beside the name only appears when you have sent the user a SMS text in the past. Clicking on Emaly's name, for example, would bring up a text box for SMS.

- A **gray circle with an "X"** denotes that the person is offline and cannot be reached by chat. This does not mean that the person is unreachable. If the user knows the cell phone number of the person who is offline, he or she can use the Lab SMS text or call phone feature.

- **Call phone**—see the "Call Phone" section for a full description.

To chat with a person in the contact list, follow these steps:

1. Click on the name of the person, and the chat box in Figure 3.18 will appear.

2. Enter text into the box and press **Enter** to send.

3. Click the icon to video chat.

4. Click the icon to voice chat.

    a. This is different from call phone. Voice chat calls someone's Gmail account while they are online, NOT their phone.

5. Click on the icon to add participants to the text or voice chat.

Figure 3.18   Chat Box

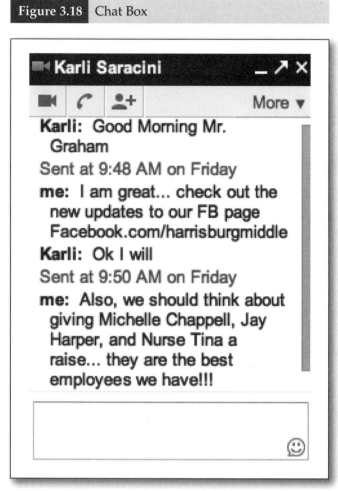

Call Phone

Gmail has a feature built into chat that will allow users to call phones within the United States for free. This item is accessed directly in chat and can connect the user to any phone number. Many schools enable this feature for parent contact. Parent contact is an important part of a successful teacher's duties. Informing parents and guardians about successes and shortcomings can have a valuable impact on students. The call phone feature allows teachers to have a private phone number connected to their Gmail account. Many teachers are wary about their personal phone number being displayed on the parent's caller ID. Teachers can take advantage of the call phone feature so that they can make and receive calls from their Gmail with a free additional phone number that is strictly for school business. Connecting to the call phone service requires the teacher to install the Google Voice software and register using his or her school Google account. Download the plugin and get started at http://voice.google.com. When Google Voice is activated, the teacher can be assigned an active telephone number from Google that when called, will ring just like a telephone. If the user is not logged into Gmail, then Gmail will take a voice message and e-mail the audio file as well as a text transcript of the message. Download the Android or iPad Google Voice app to receive and make calls from the teacher's mobile device.

Figure 3.19   Call Phone

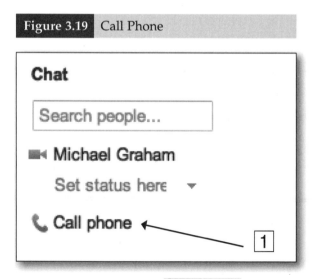

Parent Contact

Teachers can call immediately from Gmail and access a detailed call log for their parent contact records. Teachers are able to enter each student's parent information into their Gmail contacts. If this is done, the teacher never has to ask the office for parent numbers. The call phone feature in Gmail works like any other feature in Google Apps for Education; the only requirement is Internet access. Teachers can use call phone from home, work, or while sitting in a café. These services are not limited to the school network.

To access the phone dialer in the chat window, follow these steps:

1. Click Call phone located in the chat window on the left side of Gmail as shown in Figure 3.19 to open the phone dialer.

2. Dial the phone number you wish to call, area code first, as shown in Figure 3.20.

   a. In Figure 3.20, notice the words **search or dial.** If you have previously placed people's phone numbers in your Gmail contacts, then type their name and the phone number will appear.

3. Click **Call** to connect.

4. Click on the **Clock** ⊙ to show call history with timestamps.

See the Common Core State Standard in Table 3.2 to see an example of how students may use the call phone feature.

The standard in Table 3.2 refers to the student's ability to speak clearly with appropriate usage and mechanics. Practicing speaking on the telephone with eloquent speakers could help students learn to listen and speak with clarity. For example, teachers may meet this standard by interweaving it into a research project in science. In this project, students will research a profession that uses science. As part of their research, students must call a professional in the field using their student Gmail and discuss the science involved in the professional's work.

Figure 3.20 Phone Dialer

TECHNOLOGY-INFUSED TEACHING TIP

Teachers may copy and paste their call history into a Google Spreadsheet. They can add extra columns to record whom and what was discussed for an electronic parent call log. This log will be stored in the user's Google Drive for access anywhere. Don't stop with recording calls—add notes from parent-teacher conference, letters home, or e-mail communication. Documentation of student behavior and parent contact has never been easier. Access a premade parent call log by going to http://goo.gl/a8V0C in a Web browser.

Table 3.2 Common Core Standard Link

Language Grades 6–8 Standard 3 Knowledge of Language
Use knowledge of language and its conventions when writing, speaking, reading, or listening.

Students will call and interview these professionals, listening for vocabulary and speaking with them, "adapting speech to a variety of contexts and communicative tasks, demonstrating command of formal English when indicated or appropriate," skills that are detailed in Common Core Anchor Standard for Speaking and Listening number 6. This activity will help students gain perspectives of listening and speaking. Noticing the professional's tone of voice and word choice will help students grow in their verbal communication. With Gmail's call phone feature, every student computer can turn into a free telephone.

Video Chat

Video chat is another way to assess and practice communication skills of speaking and listening. The Speaking and Listening Anchor Standards mostly evoke live communication that would be found in a classroom discussion or a one-on-one discussion. But, the standards leave room for the use of technology. Consider this note from the Common Core State Standards concerning speaking and listening.

New technologies have broadened and expanded the role that speaking and listening play in acquiring and sharing knowledge and have tightened their link to other forms of communication. The Internet has accelerated the speed at which connections between speaking, listening, reading, and writing can be made, requiring that students be ready to use these modalities nearly simultaneously. Technology itself is changing quickly, creating a new urgency for students to be adaptable in response to change.

This idea of using technology for students to listen and speak can be used with video chat. For example, a student who is chronically ill or who is otherwise prevented from coming to class can call his or her teacher during class time to video chat. If second-period English class starts at 9 a.m., the student can sign in to his or her Google account from home at the appropriate time and select to video chat with the teacher's computer. The student can see and hear the class discussions and participate. Adding the ability for collaborative note-taking with Google Documents the student could participate fully in class, even turning in assignments while being miles away. By allowing the student to participate in class, the teacher has not only provided instruction and collaboration meeting writing standards, but he or she has also let the student experience electronic speaking and listening that will be valuable for his or her college distance learning classes and career meetings that take place through video conference.

SMS Text Message

Gmail allows the user to SMS text message through the SMS text message Lab. If Labs are turned on, the user may enable this feature. It does not come standard. To SMS text message a phone, follow these steps:

1. Enable the Lab *Send SMS* by following the steps outlined under Figure 3.6.

2. Type the phone number, including the area code, into the box like in Figure 3.17, to reveal Figure 3.21.

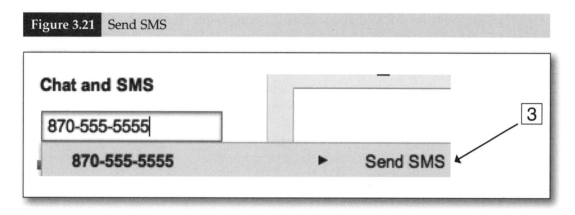

Figure 3.21 Send SMS

3. Click **Send SMS.**

4. Enter the text into the box in Figure 3.22.

5. Press **Enter** to send the text.

Any user who has this Lab enabled may text-message with limits. Every message that is sent will take your daily limit down by one message. If the message is replied to, Gmail will credit your daily limit by five texts up to a max of 50 messages (see Figure 3.22). If the user sends 50 unanswered text messages and depletes their stock, 50 more texts will be credited after 24 hours. The reason for the limit is that Google wants to make sure that the texts are real and not generated by a computer program. Read the information located in Figure 3.22 for more clarity.

Figure 3.22 Send SMS

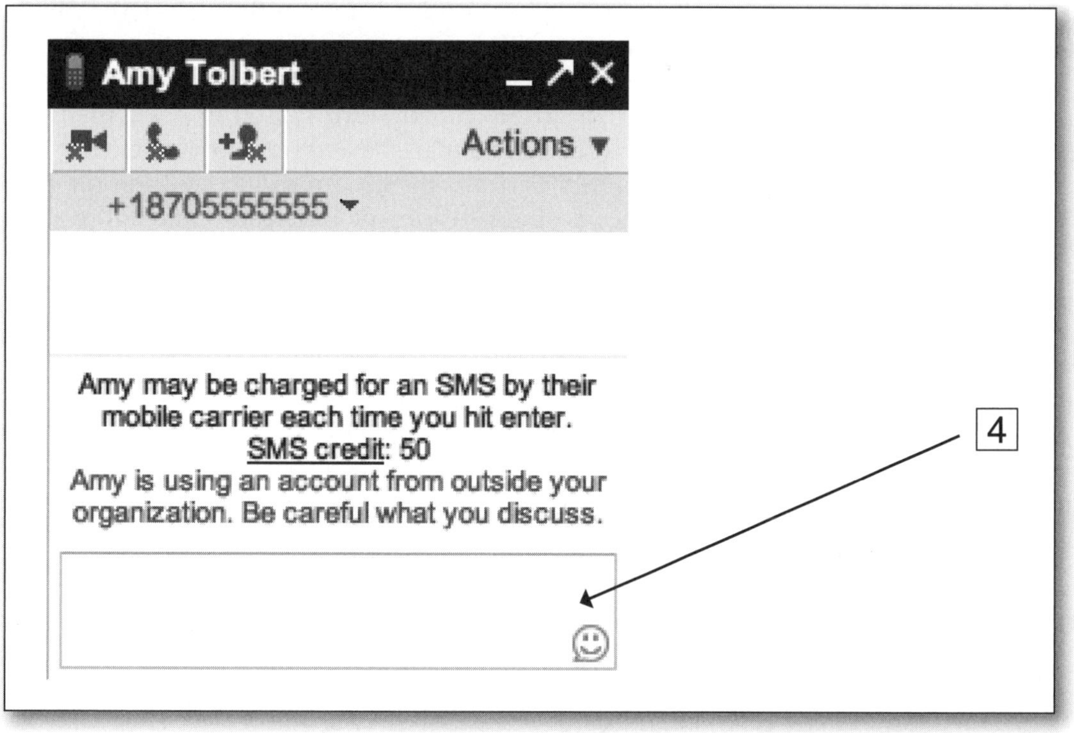

An example of school use is parent communication. Much like the call phone feature, SMS text messaging allows the user to text a phone of a parent without the parent obtaining the teacher's personal cell phone number. For example, a teacher can send home a letter to parents asking them for permission to text them about their child (this is good practice because some cell phone plans charge extra for text messaging, as noted in Figure 3.22). Texts by their nature are great ways to communicate quickly. For example, use this feature to alert parents of things like good behavior or missing school supplies. This feature is great for parents who do not have access to e-mail. Many rural or poor communities that do not have access to the Internet can use SMS text to stay in touch.

A note on chat. Students are connected more than ever to each other and their world using the Internet. Video and text chat, text messages, and calling phones from a school-issued mail account are good ways to introduce students to the educational value of these tools. Some students may not recognize the power of the mobile device that they use every day during out-of-school time. Common Core State Standards issue a paradigm shift in education. Break down the barriers of fear and use the Internet and its power to help students educate themselves wherever they are, even on a phone in your classroom.

Mass E-mail and Managing Contacts

Oftentimes, teachers and students need to share information with a particular group of people. Creating Gmail groups is a great way to organize contacts. For example, a freshman English teacher is going to e-mail part of Dr. Martin Luther King Jr.'s "Letter from Birmingham Jail" to students in her third-period English class. The students will analyze the text with the teacher's help. Over the next class periods, the students will complete a writing assignment. In order to e-mail selected groups, the teacher must first create the group called Third-Period English, then add students into the group. When she is ready to e-mail the assignment, the teacher will select from her groups. Teachers should perform the task of group creation for each class they teach as soon as they receive their rosters for the year. Names of people who have e-mailed the user will automatically appear as the user types her name in the search box, making it easy to add people to groups. As a welcome-back activity, have students e-mail their teachers telling them about their summer. Once they have done this, they can be easily added to their appropriate group. To add groups, follow these steps:

Figure 3.23 Mail, Contacts, and Task

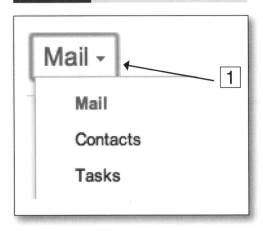

1. Click on the **Mail** drop-down menu as shown in Figure 3.23 and choose **Contacts** to reveal Figure 3.24.

2. Click on **New Group** in Figure 3.24, and name the group accordingly.

3. Click the 👤+ icon to add members to the new group. If they have previously e-mailed the user before, then their names will automatically appear in the search box as the name is typed, as shown in Figure 3.25.

| Figure 3.24 | Contacts | Figure 3.25 | Auto Fill Contacts |

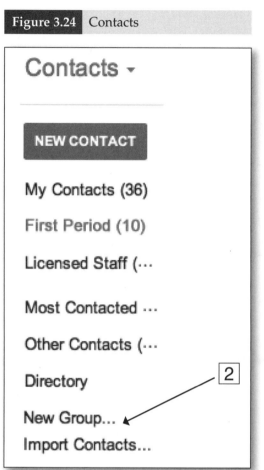

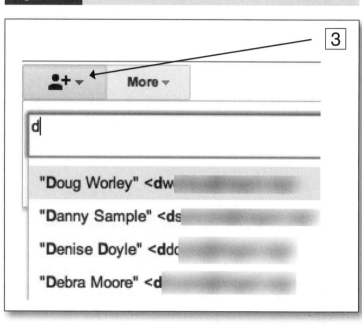

Create a Group by Class

Creating groups by class period not only lets the user e-mail en masse, it also allows the user to share with the group in Google Docs. For example, after the students and teacher have analyzed Dr. King's "Letter from Birmingham Jail," the students will react to a writing prompt about the text. Beforehand, the teacher will create a Google Document, including directions and the prompt. The teacher will then share the document with the group of students. After the students receive the document in their Google Apps account, they will make a copy of the prompt by selecting **File,** then **Make a copy.** Teachers that share community documents need to make sure they share the View Only option. If the teacher created a Google Doc and set share settings so that people it is shared with can edit it, then if anyone typed on the document without first making a copy, it would show up live on everyone's screen. To avoid these mistakes, set the permissions to view only. This forces the students to make a copy of the document before they can edit.

To e-mail a group, follow these steps:

1. Select the **Compose** button on the left side of Gmail as shown in Figure 3.26.

2. Click on the word **To** in Figure 3.26 underneath the **From** section to select the group to e-mail.

3. Select the group and click **All** to e-mail the entire group like in Figure 3.27, or select individuals from the group to notify by e-mail.

Figure 3.26   E-mail Groups

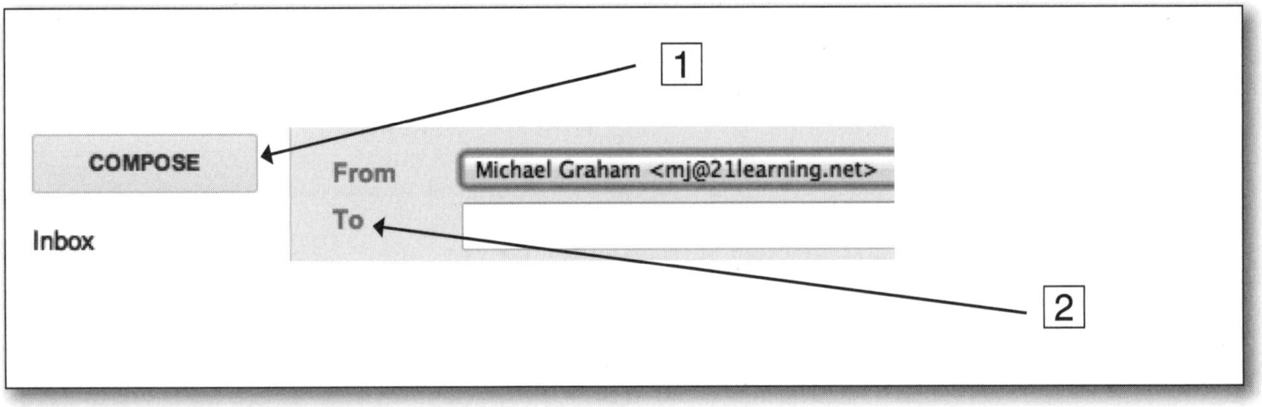

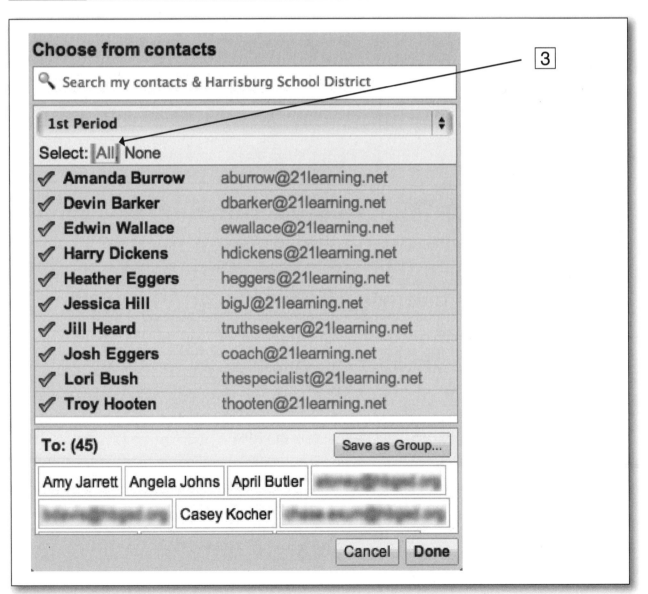

Figure 3.27   Contact Groups

SUMMARY

Gmail gives students and teachers the means to collaborate and communicate. Services like e-mail, voice chat, video chat, text chat, call phone, and SMS text message give Gmail users access to others to share information. Features like labels, filters, and Labs give students and teachers the means to manage large amounts of digital information to prepare them for college and a career. The Common Core State Standards push educators to prepare students for beyond high school. Gmail provides one of the first steps on the road to infusing technology into education.

The next chapter explores Google Documents, the first program in the app Google Docs. Google Documents is a full-service word processor infused with Google's sharing and collaborating capabilities. The Common Core State Standards are rife with collaboration and digital literacy. Google Documents provides an avenue to meet these challenges head on. Gmail is the command center connecting the apps, but Google Docs is where the real work is done in Google Apps for Education.

RESOURCE LINK

Lesson Plans

Grade Level	Lesson Plan Title	Digital copy found at the link. Lesson plans with numbers are in order in the resource section.	
Elementary School	E-mail the Author	http://goo.gl/EOhG7	#1
Middle School	Call the Expert	http://goo.gl/D9WnT	#2
High School	E-mail the Journalist	http://goo.gl/VRTp7	#3

For additional resources including lesson plans, videos, and video tutorials, access this link:

- http://goo.gl/K6lfa

4

Documents

KEY FEATURES

❖ Create original documents

❖ Share documents with peers, parents, and teachers

❖ Store all documents in one cloud space

❖ Work collaboratively among peers, parents, and teachers

❖ Publish work to Web and social networking sites

❖ Meet and exceed Common Core State Standards

Google Documents is the word-processing software offered by Google as part of the Google Apps for Education suite. Google Docs is free and can replace conventional word-processing programs such as Microsoft Word or Apple Pages. An advantage of Google Docs over Word, Pages, or other word-processing programs is the convenience of storing student and teacher work in the cloud. Google's cloud storage space is called Google Drive. Storing in Google Drive helps users avoid being tethered to multiple hard drives that students and teachers may encounter during the school day. Cloud computing means that users may store their work on Google's servers and have access to that content anywhere an Internet connection exists. Google offers virtually unlimited storage for Google Docs and up to 5 gigabytes of storage for other formats, including Word, Pages, PDF, or video files. Some limitations may apply to documents created within Google Docs. A single Google Document can have more than 1 million characters, or roughly 500 pages of text. There are no limits on the number of documents a user can create. Students can take advantage of this storage capacity to start to create electronic portfolios that can showcase their academic progress throughout their school career. With the ability to store work in the cloud, students become mobile learners. For example, students are able to start a writing project in the school's computer lab on an iMac, then later add content during English class on an iPad or Android tablet, and finally revise the paper at home on the family's PC.

With Google Documents, students can work on a document from home, school, or any place where they have an Internet connection. Up to 50 people can work on the same document at the same time from anywhere in the world or in the same room. Google Documents differs from traditional word-processing programs because it goes where the user goes. Students and teachers never have to worry about what programs are installed on which computers. Anywhere there is a Web browser, your personal Google Documents are always available. In addition, sharing and collaboration become a reality with a click of the mouse. This ability to be anywhere and work collaboratively on a document without saving multiple versions of the same document on multiple devices is great for students and teachers. This is important because it can provide a method for organization to keep up with the ever-increasing digital content that is created.

Google Apps for Education is gaining popularity in a time of deep changes in our educational system. Common Core State Standards have arrived in most states, creating a paradigm shift in education. The shift will drastically cut the number of standards, deepen the focus on the standards, and push for the increased integration of technology to prepare students to become college and career ready. This chapter will connect Google Apps for Education directly to Common Core State Standards that will help the teacher meet the needs of students to prepare them for college and beyond.

Table 4.1 highlights three Common Core Anchor Standards for Writing that are particularly important when using Google Documents. Anchor Standards provide a broad understanding of writing that spans all grade levels in the Common Core State Standards. In Anchor Standard 5, revision, editing, and rewriting are key features. Google Documents has a feature that will allow students and teachers to see a revision history of their work giving the students the ability to return to a previous version. Google Documents saves the work every two seconds automatically. This creates a trail of revisions that can be accessed by the teacher and the student. For example, if a student is struggling about a particular paragraph in their writing, a student could delete or edit the paragraph without worrying it will be deleted forever. The student then can make a copy of the work and return to the previous version. This is helpful during the editing process. The teacher now can give feedback to the student, guiding him in the right direction.

Using Google Documents to meet and exceed Anchor Standard 6 is important for student growth. This Anchor Standard aligns fully with the use of Google Documents in the classroom. Students are able to produce writing using the Internet and publish writing to collaborate with peers, parents, and teachers. For example, students working on a piece of writing may create a Google Document and then share the document with the teacher. When sharing is complete, the teacher will be able to comment on the writing and see its progress. Immediate feedback may be given, steering the student in the right direction by leaving comments. After adjusting the share settings learned in Chapter 2, students can publish their content to anywhere on the Web or select specific people with a click of a button.

In Anchor Standard 10, Google Documents could be used to collect research from the Web. For example, when starting a new research project, the student may create a document titled "Research." The student will perform the research and use the copy-and-paste features to gather links, text, or pictures explaining the topic from the Internet. This material is easily saved in Google Documents for review or shared with other members of the research group. It is important to realize that research takes time. Google Documents is a nice way to write over extended time periods because it allows the user to save the work and access it from anywhere. Students are no longer tied to the computer in which they started their work.

Let the Common Core State Standards in Table 4.1 guide you through the chapter. Google Apps for Education, in particular Google Documents, will be used to focus on these standards and more Common Core State Standards in teaching. These provide a road map so you can refer to key standards and see how Google Apps for Education can make a connection to the Common Core in your teaching.

Table 4.1 Selected Anchor Standards for Writing
Selected Common Core State Standards: Anchor Standards for Writing 5, 6, and 10
5. Develop and strengthen writing as needed by planning, revising, editing, rewriting, or trying a new approach.
6. Use technology, including the Internet, to produce and publish writing and to interact and collaborate with others.
10. Write routinely over extended time frames (time for research, reflection, and revision) and shorter time frames (a single sitting or a day or two) for a range of tasks, purposes, and audiences.

GOOGLE DOCUMENTS BASICS AND COMMON CORE

States that have adopted Common Core State Standards will employ either Smarter Balanced or the PARCC (Partnership for Assessment of Readiness for College and Careers) next-generation assessments that are tied to the Common Core State Standards. These assessments will be used to measure student achievement in English language arts and mathematics. Access one of the sample assessment pieces offered by Smarter Balanced by following the link http://goo.gl/GXuZv. This item provides a piece of informational text and asks the students to read the passage, research a particular part of the passage on the Internet, answer questions regarding the passage, and create a brochure describing the passage and research. After the brochure is complete, the students are asked to upload the document to the testing center's website for scoring.

Figure 4.1 QR Code for Smarter Balanced Question

To read the Smarter Balanced sample question, go to http://goo.gl/GXuZv in a Web browser or use a QR reader to access the file linked in the quick-response (QR) code in Figure 4.1.

The example accessed in Figure 4.1 (QR code) and the link provided are for high school students. To perform successfully on this type of question, however, students in the lower grades must also be familiar with the general use of word-processing programs over a wide platform, and they must practice those skills frequently, because beginning in the sixth grade, students will be taking the state mandated writing exam on an electronic device. That means they must know the conventions of writing a formal paper on an electronic device. They must be able to navigate simple toolbars like the ones in Google Documents to shape the piece they are writing—for example, center justified, margins, bullets, numbering, and so on, as shown in Figure 4.2.

| Figure 4.2 | Google Document's Toolbar |

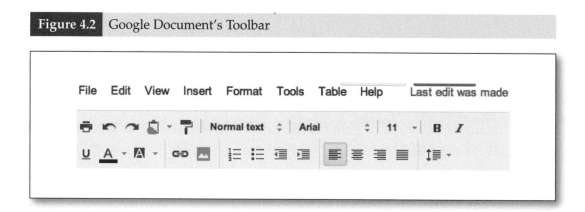

Spell Check

Google Documents offers an automatic spell checker that works the same in all of the Google Docs programs. It does not have a specific button like Microsoft Word that checks the spelling of the document at once. Instead, Google places the familiar red line underneath words that are spelled incorrectly. To correct the spelling of a red underlined word, follow the steps in Figure 4.3 to reveal suggestions the software has matched as possible alternatives.

This type of spelling check has its advantages when addressing the Common Core State Standards. Anchor Standards for Production and Distribution of Writing indicate that students must produce writing using digital tools starting with kindergarten and continuing throughout the grade levels. Correcting mistakes during the writing process makes for more efficient writing and lets the students practice producing writing on the device. The procedures for writing are evolving with the integration of technology into the classroom. In the past, students wrote the content using a pencil and then transferred the

| Figure 4.3 | Correcting Misspelled Words |

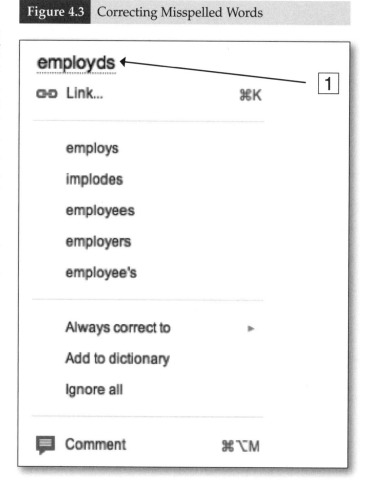

writing to a word-processing program. With Common Core State Standards, students must produce writing on the electronic device, then use the device to edit and revise the work. Google Documents makes this task a reality in the classroom, practicing for the next generation assessments.

1. Right-click on the red underlined misspelled word as shown in Figure 4.3 (Mac users Command+Click).

2. Click on the appropriate word to replace the misspelled word.

   o **Always correct to** automatically corrects chronically misspelled words. This feature is nice because whatever device is used to type a document, Google Docs remembers the user's list of trouble words if she is signed in to her Google account.

   o **Add to dictionary** lets the user add words to his own personal spell check dictionary to avoid placing the red underline. Popular items to place in the dictionary include proper nouns such as people's names or places. Students will automatically recognize their own names being underlined if their name has an uncommon spelling. Instruct them to add their name to their personal spell-check dictionary.

Keyboarding and Technology in the Early Grades

Beginning in kindergarten, the Common Core State Standards will mandate the use of technology in an effort to help our students have a wealth of 21st century skills for college and career. The use of technology rapidly increases throughout the years in Anchor Standard 6, Production and Distribution of Writing. Kindergarten standards indicate that students will *explore* various technologically enhanced tools to create writing. The wording only differs slightly for students in the first and second grades; the standard says *use* digital tools, suggesting that students actually get their hands on devices to input their content. Table 4.2 provides information about technology and writing, especially the use of the keyboard in Grades 3–5.

Since Google Documents can be accessed through any Internet-enabled device, it does not require a traditional keyboard like other word-processing software. Students in the early grades could benefit greatly by writing on devices such as the iPod Touch, iPad, Android tablet, or another similar device without a physical keyboard. Using other devices to build skills of typing could be an important part of the solution of introducing keyboarding skills in kindergarten. In the fourth grade, students will be expected to have a sufficient grasp of keyboarding skills so they are able to type one page in a single writing event as well as collaborate with peers and adults using technology. One page per grade year is added through the sixth grade.

Table 4.2 provides grade-level standards for Common Core Anchor Standards 3, 6, and 8. This table offers guidance about how Google Documents can drive student learning within these Anchor Standards. It is important for the reader to realize that Google Documents is an Internet-based word-processing program much like what students will be exposed to during the next-generation assessments. The more experience students get using technology to publish, produce, interact, and collaborate while using the Internet, the better students will do on the high-stakes tests.

Anchor Standard 6 of the Common Core State Standards refers to using the Internet to produce, publish, and collaborate on writing throughout every grade level. Google Documents makes this standard a reality. Anchor Standard 6 can be

Table 4.2 Writing Standards and Breakdown

Grade	Common Core State Standard	Breakdown
Grade 3		
W.3.6	With guidance and support from adults, use technology to produce and publish writing (using keyboarding skills) as well as to interact and collaborate with others.	Students will be expected to create original work and use the keyboard for input. Google Documents provides the best place for learning these skills, because of easy sharing, collaborating, and publication of writing. For example, teachers can prepare a Google Document ahead of time with pictures of objects students are currently studying. With the help of adults, students may use the mouse to navigate to a text box under the picture and describe the scene using the keyboard. The students will use key vocabulary discussed about previously to add meaning to the picture. Publish this student work to the Web using share settings. After you have the unique link post to the class's Facebook Fan Page or share with parents' e-mail through share settings. See Chapter 2 for details on sharing.
Grade 4		
W.4.6 W.4.3	With some guidance and support from adults, use technology, including the Internet, to produce and publish writing as well as to interact and collaborate with others; demonstrate sufficient command of keyboarding skills to type a minimum of one page in a single sitting. Write narratives to develop real or imagined experiences or events using effective technique, descriptive details, and clear event sequences.	Students in the fourth grade must have a grasp of collaboration and keyboarding skills to create and edit a one-page document. Students will need constant practice using the keyboard to attain the stamina to type one whole page in a single setting. One example to prepare students for this task is to create a recipe book. Students can use Google Documents to type family recipes from home with an added narrative about their experience with the food. Incorporate standard W.4.3 to create a narrative of their experience, giving supporting details in their writing. Students share the documents with the teacher for grading and feedback. After revisions are made, share with parents, peers, and other adults. Collect all pages into a single document. Share the cookbook through share settings, making it easy to post to relevant Facebook Fan Pages or Twitter accounts for community involvement.
Grade 5		
W.5.6 W.5.8	With some guidance and support from adults, use technology, including the Internet, to produce and publish writing as well as to interact and collaborate with others; demonstrate sufficient command of keyboarding skills to type a minimum of two pages in a single sitting. Recall relevant information from experiences or gather relevant information from print and digital sources; summarize or paraphrase information in notes and finished work, and provide a list of sources.	Two pages are required for fifth grade, further reiterating that keyboarding should be practiced as an important skill used for college and career preparation. Fifth-grade students may use Google documents in writing to produce content specific writing that also meets other writing standards. Teachers meeting standard W.5.8 could use Google Documents to create a list of content-specific search terms and websites that describe their topic for the lesson. The teacher will share the document with the class, giving them directions to only choose from these websites listed in the teacher document to research their topic using these specific search terms. The students can click the links that the teacher has embedded (instead of typing in a long URL into the address bar) to navigate to the site. Students research and summarize on a separate document, providing a list of sources. Copy and paste specific links within the website the student chose. Teach students how to hyperlink in Google Documents to create an easy-to-read piece without cumbersome URLs.

linked to most of the other writing standards. For example, Standard W.12.1 wants students to write arguments and support claims in reference to complex text. To produce this type of writing, the student must use skills taken from Anchor Standard 6, Production and Distribution of Writing. To compete globally in a 21st century economy, students must have relevant skills to produce and distribute quality writing using high-tech tools such as Google Documents. Most of the Common Core State Standards for Writing involve production and distribution of writing; therefore, most standards of writing could be exceeded with the use of Google Documents.

Collaborative Note-Taking Example

Table 4.3 highlights an eighth-grade mathematics standard from the Common Core State Standards. This standard is represented in Figure 4.4 and Figure 4.5, where students are taking collaborative notes while writing on the same document at the same time. The students are instructed to type only in their assigned box; if they did not follow these instructions, students would be trying to type on the same line from different computers creating confusion. As the class discussion proceeds, the students are typing what they believe is important about the subject. Later the teacher will help the students revise their notes concentrating on the key parts of the lesson. When they are finished, this document is automatically saved into every student's Google Drive for later review from any location with Internet access.

Table 4.3	Expressions and Equations Common Core Mathematics Eighth Grade

(8.EE.5) Graph proportional relationships, interpreting the unit rate as the slope of the graph. Compare two different proportional relationships represented in different ways. For example, compare a distance-time graph to a distance-time equation to determine which of two moving objects has greater speed.

Figure 4.4	Collective Note-Taking Part I

1. Noah	2.	3.	4. Joey Hi	5.Allie. I learned to get the velocity
6.Connor	7.Dalton	8.	9.john i a i il	10.Ashton Hello
11.	12. gavin Ms.	13.	14.	15.GABBIE
16.	17.	18.	19.Hayden :3	20.Rebecka
21.	22.Savannah :)	23.	24.	25.
26.	27.	28.	29.	30.

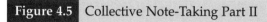

Figure 4.5   Collective Note-Taking Part II

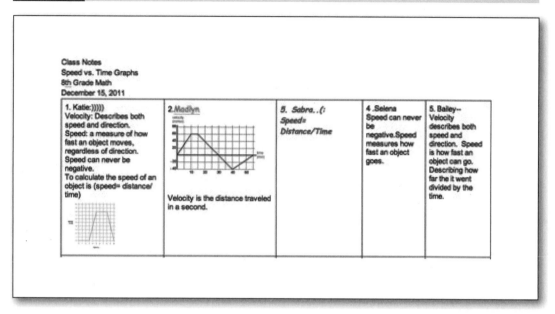

In Figure 4.4, students are in the act of typing on the same document. Notice as they type their username appears highlighted in a color to help differentiate who is typing where. If Connor is typing in Gavin's box, the whole class will know, decreasing the chance for disruption from a discipline problem.

TECHNOLOGY-INFUSED TEACHING TIP

Students are children. They have a unique desire to test limits and break boundaries. Let them know the rules for new technologies early on in the process. Breaking a rule with technology is no different than a student breaking a rule with pencil and paper. Be consistent, and technology integration will be smooth for your students.

Figure 4.5 displays the final product. The teacher has facilitated discussion and with the help of other students and the teacher, each student has refined his or her notes. The teacher, Mrs. Strawn, reported a pleasant surprise during the activity. Katie and Madlyn spontaneously performed a Google Image Search to find examples of distance-versus-time graphs and inserted them into their explanation. This happened live on everyone's screen, and the discussion quickly became more in-depth because the *student* was explaining why it was important not only to have notes about distance versus time, but also to see a picture.

Opening Google Documents

To access Google Documents, follow these steps:

1. Sign in to your Google account as described in Chapter 3 in Figures 3.2 and 3.3.

2. Click on **Drive** located at the top of the screen as shown in Figure 4.6.

Figure 4.6 Opening Google Documents

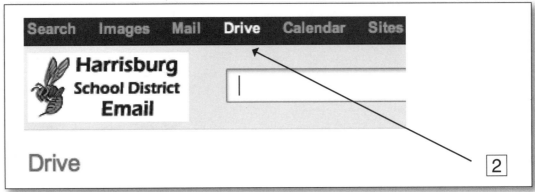

3. Click the  CREATE button to reveal a drop-down menu shown in Figure 4.7.

4. Click **Document** as shown in Figure 4.7 to create a new document.

Figure 4.7 Accessing the Documents Program

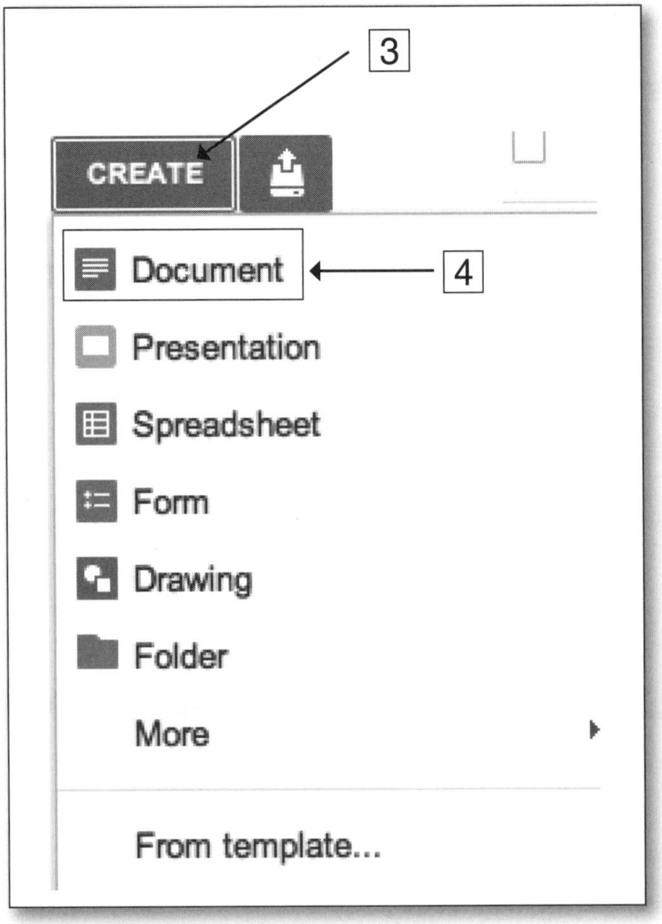

CREATE

3

Document 4

Presentation

Spreadsheet

Form

Drawing

Folder

More ▶

From template...

Upload

Uploading files and folders to be stored in the user's Google Drive makes mobile learning a reality. Google allows the uploading of any file type to its servers for access anywhere there is an Internet connection. For example, if a student uses Microsoft Word to produce writing on a home computer, then the student can upload that work to her Google cloud from home. During the upload process, Google asks if the document should be converted to Google Documents version or uploaded in Microsoft Word format. If the user choses Microsoft Word format, then the document can be downloaded to any device and opened if Microsoft Word is installed. To upload files to Google Drive, follow the steps outlined in Chapter 10: Drive.

Graphical User Interface

The administrator of your school's Google Apps for Education account has options regarding how the page will look. Technology professionals call this the graphical user interface, or GUI (pronounced "gooey"). From time to time,

Google will update its user interface to improve the user's experience. Google will delay the mandated rollout of such a change if it suspects that the user may feel uncomfortable with the difference. Usually, a link exists for users to click to test out the new feel of the page before they decide to make the change permanent. Some Google Apps for Education administrators may allow the user to keep the old version for a period while others may change versions without warning.

FILE MENU

After the user completes the steps associated with Figures 4.6 and 4.7, the Google Documents Program will open. The following describes the contents of the **File** command located in Google Document's toolbar section. These commands are similar to other word-processing programs, but they contain cutting-edge features that take them a step above for classroom use.

Share

Sharing allows the user to give access to a Google Doc to as many or as few people as they prefer. Users may share the document in the following ways.

- E-mail attachment
- Anyone with the link
- Public—on the Web
- Private—allowing only specific people to access the document

Sharing is one of the hallmark features in Google Docs. It is used in every part of Google Docs to work collaboratively and publish content. To share documents from Google Documents, follow these steps. Sharing is discussed at length in Chapter 2.

1. Select **Share** from the **File** menu in the toolbar in Google Docs or click on the blue 🔒 Share button in the upper right-hand corner of any Google Doc program to reveal the share settings as shown in Figure 4.8.

2. Copy and paste the link in box #1 in Figure 4.8 to share the document.
    a. Paste it into:
        i. E-mail
        ii. Social media (Facebook, Twitter, Google Plus)
        iii. Another Web browser's address bar

3. Click **Change** in box #2 to change the visibility options for this document as shown in Figure 4.9.

    a. Click the appropriate circle to select the access level.

4. Type in the names, e-mail, or groups of people that you would like to directly share the Google Doc with in the bar in box #3.

5. Click Done to save your changes.

Figure 4.8   Share Settings

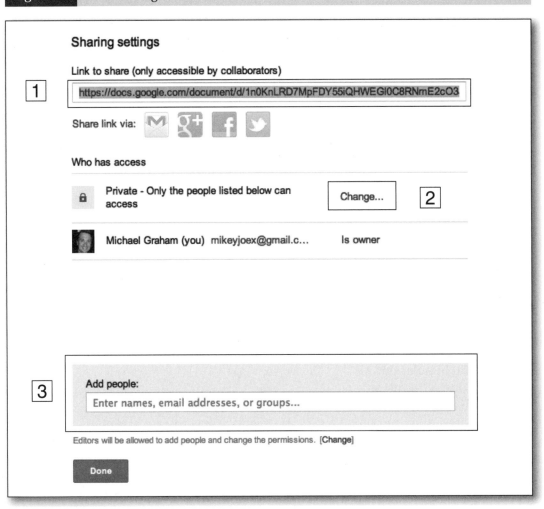

Figure 4.9   Who Has Access

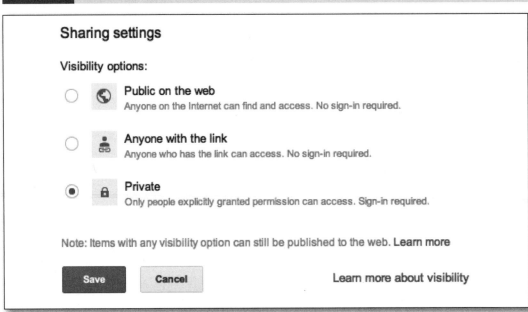

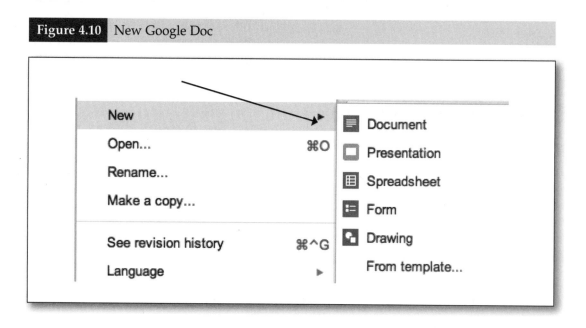

Figure 4.10   New Google Doc

New

Click **New** in the **File** menu to open a new Google Doc as shown in Figure 4.10. This option opens the new Google Doc in another tab or browser window.

Open

Click **Open** in the **File** menu to return to the documents view, also called Google Drive. This is the equivalent of a My Documents folder on a PC. This is where folders are created and files are managed, allowing for management of your cloud storage.

Make a Copy

This option lets the user make a copy of the work. This will be helpful when sharing documents with students. For example, the teacher could share a quiz document with a class and assign the students to answer questions on the page; the students make a copy of the work, answer the questions, and re-share the document by e-mail or share settings to be graded. If the students did not make a copy, all of the students would be typing on the same document at the same time unless the document is made view-only by the teacher.

Revision History

Revision history will allow the user to go back to any point in time to see how the work is progressing or to correct errors in writing. Anchor Standard 5, Production and Distribution of Writing, wants students to "develop and strengthen writing as needed by planning, revising, editing, rewriting, or trying a new approach." This standard is clearly met with the use of this feature in Google Docs. For example, students learning to write informative pieces that examine complex concepts may need to revisit a previous idea. Seeing a revision history will allow the student to look back in time at the writing examining how the progression was made. This allows students to return to a previous version down to a specific keystroke. If two

Figure 4.11 Revision History

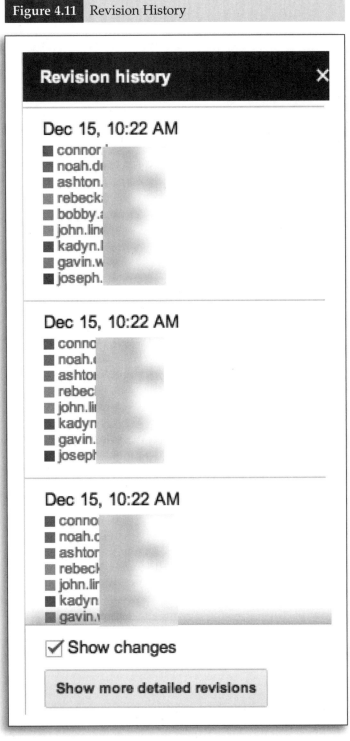

or more people are working on the document collaboratively, then each person could see their revisions and who made the changes. To see the revision history of a document, follow these steps:

1. Select **See Revision History** from the **File** menu in the Document's Toolbar.

2. Click on a revision timestamp in Figure 4.11 to roll back the changes to that particular time.

3. Click Show less detailed revisions to see wider time intervals.

Language

The use of the **Language** feature allows the user to change the language of the dictionary Google Docs uses to spell-check words. For example, if a student is writing a translation of several words in a foreign language, the student may choose to use spell check in that language. It is also useful when students need special characters when writing. For example, the word "niña" in Spanish has the tilde over the second *n*, denoting a different sound associated with that letter when spoken in Spanish. If the student chose the Spanish dictionary to spell-check the document, he or she could right-click (command-click for Mac users) the word to reveal suggested spellings and choose appropriately from words that appear in the Spanish dictionary.

Download As

Choose this option to save the work to your computer's hard drive in various formats. Google doesn't discriminate. It even lets the work be saved in Microsoft Word format for sharing with others who do not use Google Docs. Plus, Google offers a variety of formats, including PDF, TXT, and HTML.

Publish to the Web

Publish to the web is a sharing option that is similar to the *Anyone with the link* option shown in Figure 4.9. It gives instant access to publish work directly to the

Figure 4.12	Publish to the Web

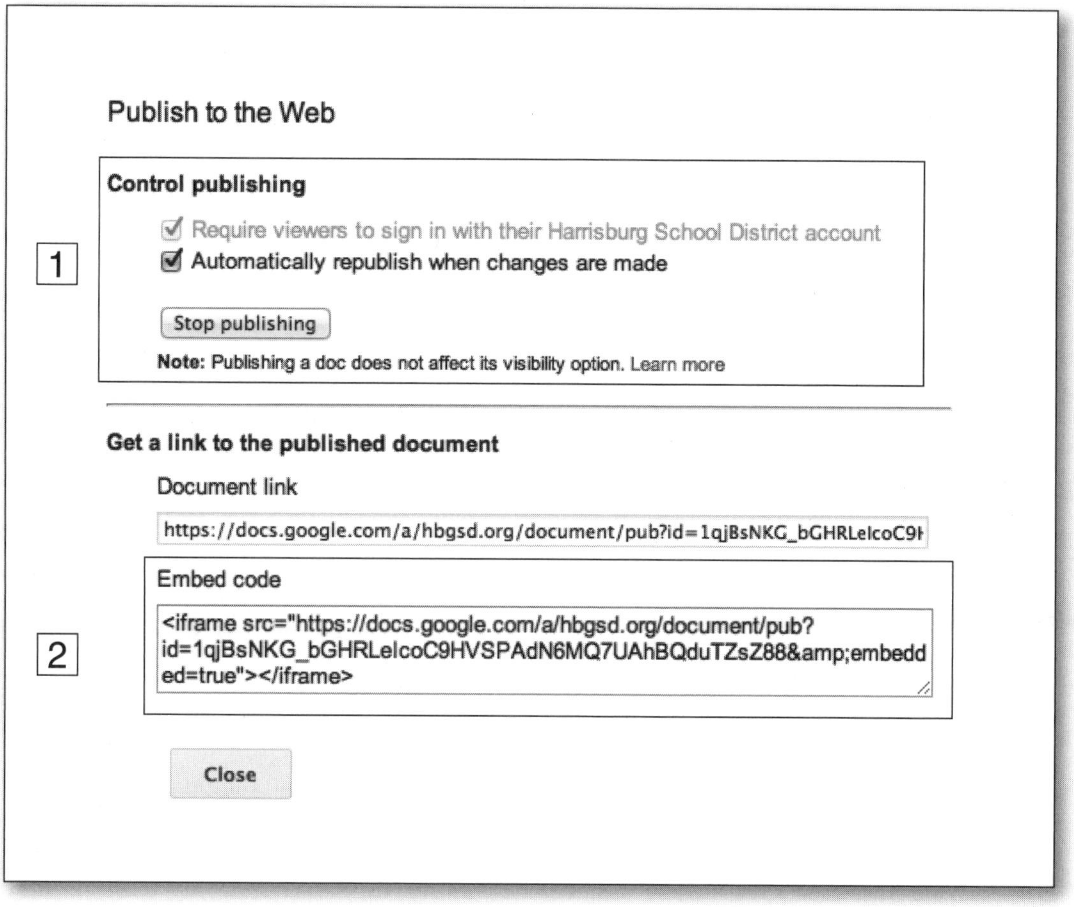

Publish to the Web

Control publishing

1

☑ Require viewers to sign in with their Harrisburg School District account

☑ Automatically republish when changes are made

[Stop publishing]

Note: Publishing a doc does not affect its visibility option. Learn more

Get a link to the published document

Document link

https://docs.google.com/a/hbgsd.org/document/pub?id=1qjBsNKG_bGHRLelcoC9H

Embed code

2

```
<iframe src="https://docs.google.com/a/hbgsd.org/document/pub?
id=1qjBsNKG_bGHRLelcoC9HVSPAdN6MQ7UAhBQduTZsZ88&amp;embedd
ed=true"></iframe>
```

[Close]

Web from the document to anyone, not just collaborators. Publish to the Web if you want others to view the document and see changes through the unique Web address but without inviting them to become a collaborator. Stop publishing any time by selecting the option in box #1 in Figure 4.12. In addition to publishing the document's link, there is also an option that gives the document the HTML embed code as shown in box #2 in Figure 4.12. This code may be placed into websites and modified to fit the user's needs.

TECHNOLOGY-INFUSED TEACHING TIP

Use the publishing features to share student work through social media websites. For example, Harrisburg Middle School has an official Facebook Fan Page located at http://www.facebook.com/harrisburgmiddle. We use this page to communicate with our school community on the Web. Often, we publish examples of award-winning student work or links to student projects that were made with Google Docs. Since each Doc is given a Web address, it is easy to post the link of the work to the page for our community to view.

E-mail Collaborators

Click **E-mail Collaborators** to send an e-mail message to all who are working on the document. In-document chat is also available for instant feedback of student work. Teachers may assign a writing exercise and be online while the students are creating. This allows the teacher to give immediate feedback during the writing process. Common Core Anchor Standard 6 in Grades 11 and 12 wants students to receive ongoing feedback from writing that is collaborative.

E-mail as Attachment

Google Documents lets the user e-mail documents as attachments in a variety of formats (Figure 4.14). Use the e-mail as attachment feature to bypass the old way of attaching documents to e-mails. In the past, people were forced to save the document, open an e-mail, click attach file, find the document, then e-mail it. With Google Docs, click **E-mail as Attachment** under the **File** menu to send it directly from Google Docs as indicated by numeral 1 in Figure 4.13.

Figure 4.13	E-mail as Attachment

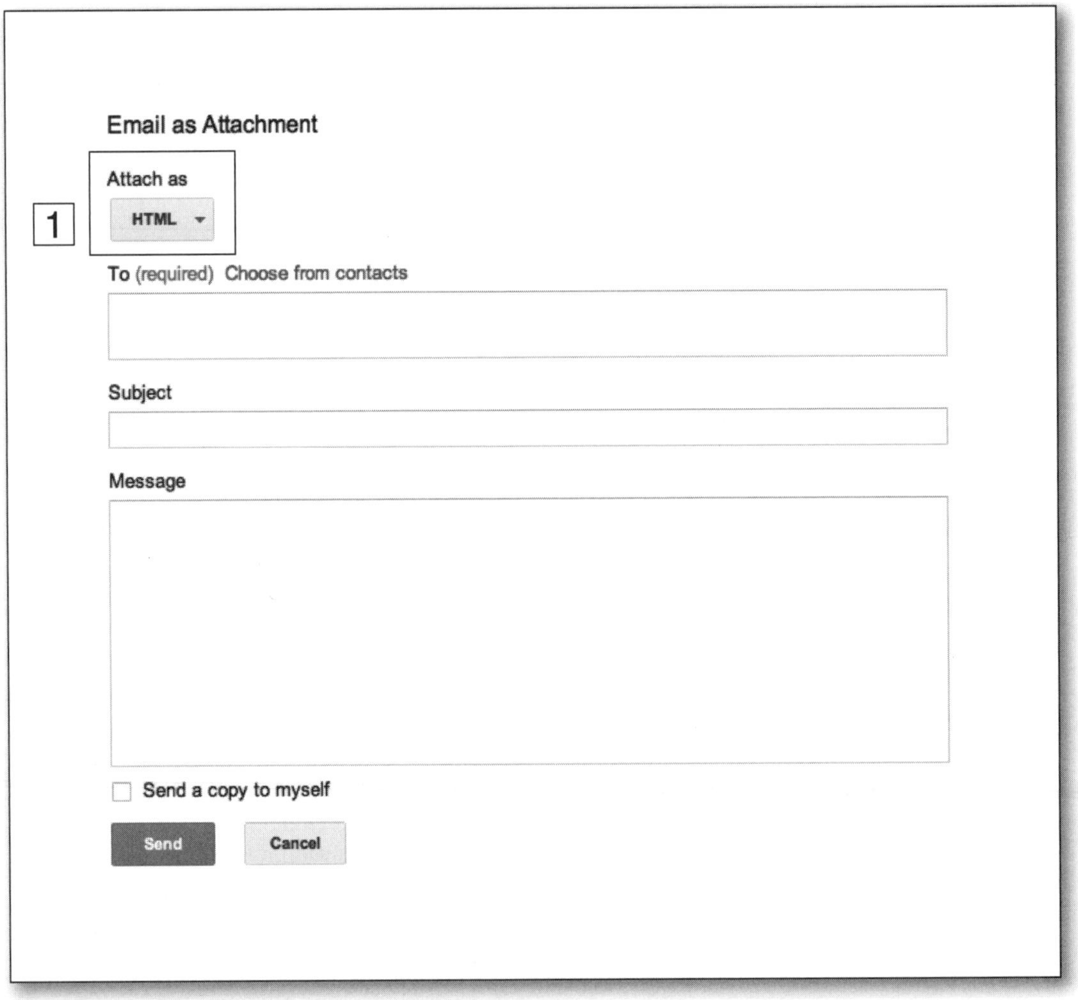

Page Setup

Use the tools in Figure 4.15 to switch to landscape or portrait views as well as manage the margins and paper size. As students start to share their work, this will allow them to use tools that are more creative. Anchor Standard 5 in Speaking and Listening stresses that students use digital tools to express their understanding by enhancing presentations. Adjusting paper sizes, orientation, and page color can make printed or Web-shared documents more visually appealing.

Print

To **Print** a Google Doc, follow these steps:

1. Click **Print** from the **File** menu or press **Command+P** for Mac or **CTRL+P** for PC to bring up the Print menu.

2. Click **Print** as shown in Figure 4.16.

3. Click **Change...** to switch printers.

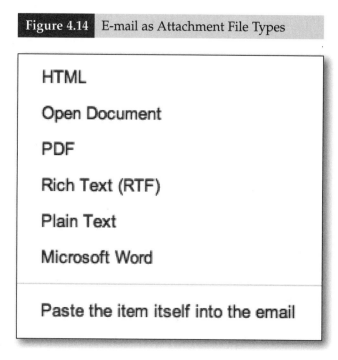

Figure 4.14 E-mail as Attachment File Types

HTML

Open Document

PDF

Rich Text (RTF)

Plain Text

Microsoft Word

Paste the item itself into the email

Figure 4.15 Page Setup

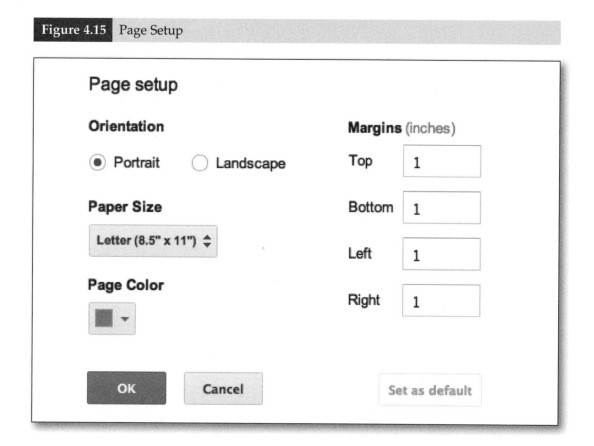

| Figure 4.16 | Print |

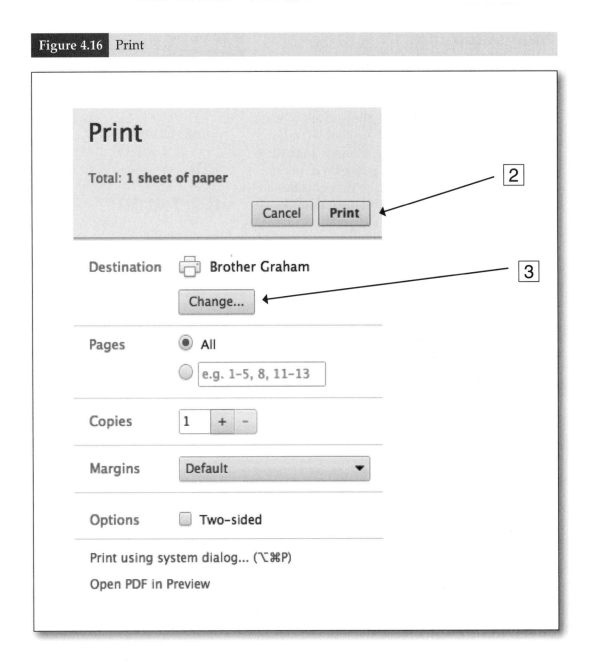

EDIT MENU

The **Edit** menu is very similar to other word-processing programs. See the Google Docs Edit menu in Figure 4.17. Be aware that some Internet browsers do not allow right-clicking to copy and paste in Google Documents. If this is the case, PC users press CTRL+C for copy, CTRL+V for paste, and CTRL+X for cut. Macintosh users press Command+C for copy, Command+V for paste, and Command+X for cut.

VIEW MENU

The **View** menu displays commands to control the way the users visualize the document they are editing. These options are common in various word-processing programs and are easy to understand. Figure 4.18 shows the **View** menu.

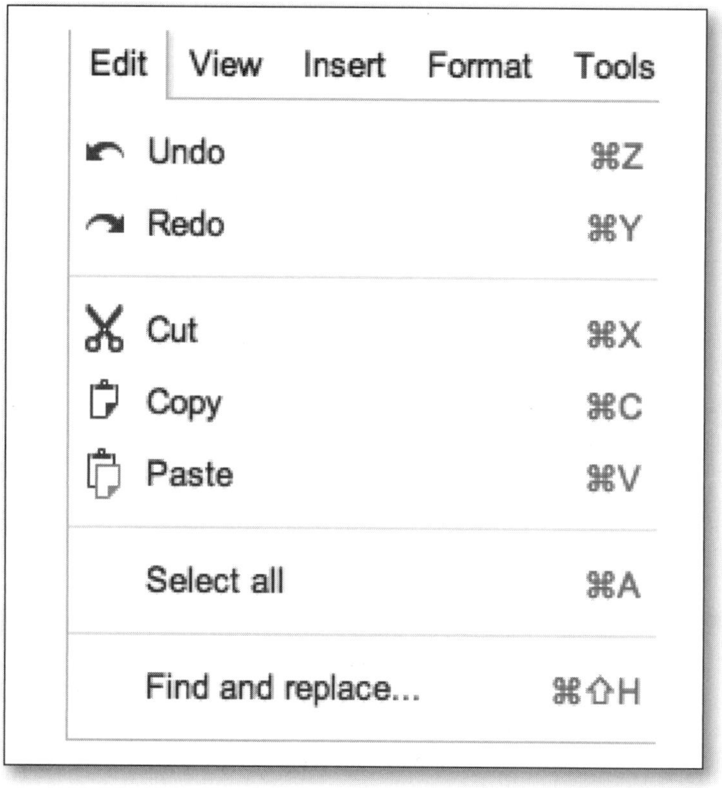

Document View

Document view is a command that lets the user see the document as a paginated format or a continuous view where the pages are not spaced. The continuous view uses less space and displays a thin line where the pages are separated as opposed to a space in the paginated view.

Show Ruler

The show ruler option allows the user to control the margins of the document. Encourage students to bend the rules when displaying informal documents to others in a presentation or when linking to social media. Using innovative ways to display information might spark an artistic flair, making the difference in the document's impact. Instruct students to know when documents should be presented in formal and informal formats to become aware of the audience and to be appropriate to task.

Show Equation Toolbar

With the equation toolbar, teachers and students have the ability to use symbols and other math characters not normally found on the keyboard. Teachers can use this to create assessments, or students can make their own math problems and share with the class. Create shareable math help that can be continually updated and shared with a class or classes anywhere in the world.

Show Spelling Suggestions

Placing a checkmark beside this option will toggle on the red line under words, denoting spelling errors. Students need to be aware of this to take advantage of the spellcheck feature of Google Docs.

Figure 4.17 Edit Menu

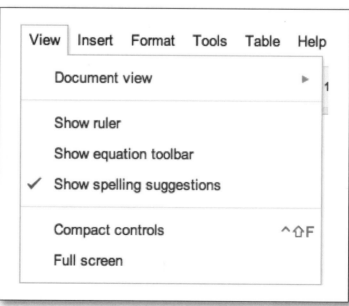

Figure 4.18 View Menu

Compact Controls

Compact controls are used to hide the Google Apps toolbars and the title of the document. This is useful when a user is presenting a document with a projector. More of the document can be seen on the screen without having to scroll.

Full Screen

Full screen allows the user to hide all toolbars and the control panel to maximize space on the screen for the text. Press the Escape key to return to normal view. This may be useful when presenting ideas or taking notes collectively to emphasize the importance of the text. Google Documents lets users take collective notes or brainstorm ideas to a shared document. Follow these steps for an example of a quick lesson idea using full screen.

LESSON IN FOCUS

The teacher will . . .

1. Create a document.

2. Insert a table with the number of cells matching the number of students in the class.

3. Place a number in each cell.

4. Assign a number to students, and instruct them to type only in their cells.

Fifty students may type at once on this document, creating collective notes or ideas for a brainstorming session. Use a projector to show the class the document in real time. The student responses will automatically appear on each student's screen and the projector. Use the full-screen mode to make the presentation visually appealing.

Living Documents

Google Documents provides a way for students to create documents that are adaptable with the rapid influx of relevant information concerning a topic. In the 21st century and beyond, most material that students read will be on a screen, giving the authors the ability to constantly update information as it presents itself (see English Language Arts Standards 11–12.W.6–10). Reading interactive text that contains links to other information will change the way students relate with the written word. Students need to learn how to read informational text that comes from webpages and other online materials to extract meaning and purpose. In addition, students in their careers will be writing in these mediums, creating living documents like blogs, wikis, online news articles, and Twitter posts. Most printed material will rapidly become outdated with the use of cloud-based tools, Web-based writing, and mobile devices that can interact with this content. As soon as the document is printed on paper, new and useful information may become available. Students need to develop skills of writing digitally, and Google Documents provides ways to acquire these skills. Living documents allow the students to be interactive authors with the ability to change their work with new knowledge learned. Students getting ready for college and career need to be exposed to writing text that is changing rapidly. Table 4.2 presents standards of writing that embody living documents. Google Documents provides the platform for which students can achieve these standards. For example, when writing, link keywords or phrases to a Web address to offer more information. The Web address can link to other Google Docs created by the student or link to webpages with more information. Adding hyperlinks to text leads the reader to new or supporting ideas. Follow these steps to add hyperlinks.

TECHNOLOGY-INFUSED TEACHING TIP

Use links in documents that are shared with students. When creating a link in a document, it will turn blue and become live. When you click on the blue word, the Web browser will open a new tab, opening that link to be viewed. Instead of having http://youtu.be/4h1fyDNk6v8 in the document, create a link that packages the entire URL into a descriptive title, such as Harrisburg Middle School Lip Dub (the blue line under text indicates a live URL link). In the Common Core State Standards, students are expected to be familiar with the Internet and how to navigate it.

1. Right-click on any word in a Google Document to reveal the ᴄᴅ Link... button.

2. Click ᴄᴅ Link... to reveal Figure 4.19.

3. Enter text to hide the URL.

4. Enter the URL for the link.

| Figure 4.19 | Link |

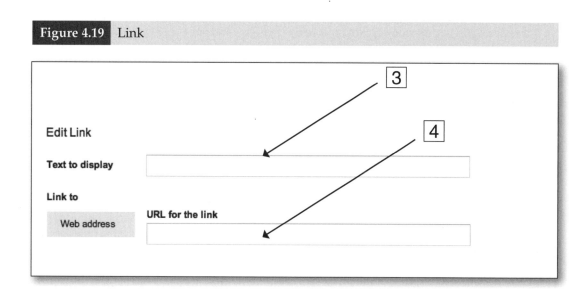

- Link other documents, spreadsheets, presentations, forms, or drawings that the user created. Linking data collected from experiments in math or science into a document is a great way to publish results.
- Link supporting information from websites taken from reputable sources.
- Use Google Forms to collect survey results and add commentary about the study.

Table 4.4 describes Anchor Standard 6 for Writing for Grades 9–12, which directs students to write with "response to ongoing feedback." Google Docs can make this anchor standard come alive with the use of links and living documents.

Table 4.4 Writing Standards for Technology

9th and 10th Grades (9–10.W.6)	*11th and 12th Grades (11–12.W.6)*
Use technology, including the Internet, to produce, publish, and update individual or shared writing products, taking advantage of technology's capacity to link to other information and to display information flexibly and dynamically.	Use technology, including the Internet, to produce, publish, and update individual or shared writing products in response to ongoing feedback, including new arguments or information.

The Common Core State Standards want students to be able to create, collaborate, and share their work as well as be able to update accordingly to accommodate new information. Teaching students to read dynamic information like blogs, Facebook, and Twitter feeds to extract important information while discarding the unimportant will be a significant skill for the digital citizen. Learning to write in these elements and produce high-quality work will be equally important.

TECHNOLOGY-INFUSED TEACHING TIP

Facebook, Twitter, and blogs offer important information as well as traditional media. For example, a student researching the Arab Spring may follow prominent figures of the rebellion on Twitter, gaining very important information in real time directly from the source. Having the courage to explore the benefits and problems new media brings to school settings will have lasting impact on students. Be open-minded to new media.

TECHNOLOGY-INFUSED TEACHING TIP

Use **equation editor** to write math quizzes and share with the students. Students make a copy of the document in the File menu and work the problems on the computer using the editor. Then have the students share them back with you. This creates an electronic database to collect homework. The shared files will appear in the user's Google Drive folder. Make sure the naming convention is properly followed, making for easy searching. An alternative method is for the student to share the document as an attachment through Gmail. Use the Comment option in the File menu to give feedback immediately or at your convenience. See Chapter 3 to learn how to create filters and labels that help collect assignments automatically skipping the inbox, allowing them to be graded when you are ready.

INSERT MENU

The **Insert** menu in the Google Doc's toolbar is packed with features. Google makes it easy to insert graphics, pictures, links, and other important document style options. Many of these same features are offered in the other Google Docs programs.

Image

Insert images from your hard drive, a URL, Google Image Search, or Picasa Web Albums into any Google Doc. The URL import feature is significant because many images that the user would want to use may be housed on the Web. For example, a student may want to drive home his point with a picture from a website taken on a battlefield in Afghanistan. The student may browse websites and copy and paste the URL of the photo, and it will appear in the document. Be particularly mindful of copyright. If the user chooses Google Image Search, he or she can search Google Images directly in the Google Docs program without having to go to another window. Picasa Web Albums are also available. Picasa is Google's photo management and editing software. This program links to the user's Google Account and provides cloud space to store photos. Picasa will create a Web Album associated with the Google Account, giving access to photos wherever there is an Internet connection. For example, a middle school writing assignment asks students to create a narrative story describing details of a family vacation. The student may use photos taken during the trip and insert these images into the document. This is seamlessly accessed from any computer with an Internet connection. As long as the user is signed into her Google Account, Picasa will link personal photos to any document. To insert an image, follow these steps:

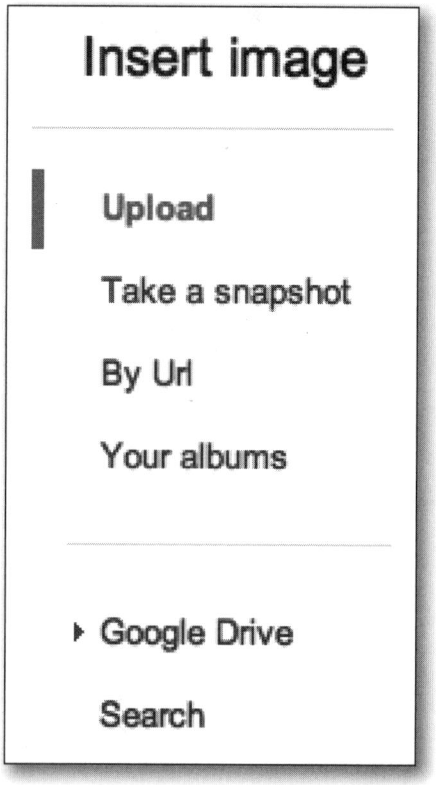

1. Select **Image** from the **Insert** menu in Google Docs to reveal the menu shown in Figure 4.20.

2. Click the desired method to insert the image.

3. Click  Select to insert.

Methods to Insert Image. Use the methods here to insert an image into Google Docs.

- Upload: Click this option to upload an image from your computer's hard drive.
- Take a snapshot: Click this option to take a snapshot from your computer's webcam.
- By URL: Click this option to copy and paste an image URL to automatically insert it without saving the image to the hard drive.
- Your albums: Click this option to upload an image from your Picasa Web Albums.
- Google Drive: Click this option to insert an image from the user's Google Drive.
- Search: Click this option to search photos from Google Image Search, *Life* magazine, and stock photos. All of these images are labeled for reuse. That means that they

Figure 4.20 Insert Image

can be used without permission. Investigate further if you plan to sell work with images from this service in it. Look at Figure 4.21 for more information and how-to steps for inserting Google Images Search.

Figure 4.21   Search Images to Insert

Google Image Search is embedded in Google Documents to insert photos with ease. Type into the bar any search term. After searching, Google displays images according to the query. Students may choose what color is in their photo by selecting the colored boxes underneath the search bar. Look at Figure 4.22, for example; a student searched for frogs, then the student may choose what color of frog to display.

Figure 4.22   Google Image Search Color

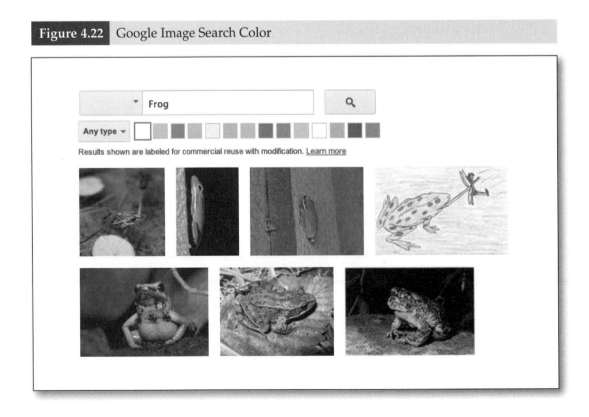

Also, notice that you can choose what type of picture the results will display. Choose from Any type, Face, Photo, Clip Art, or Line drawing. This can enliven any boring document with a picture. Students will be able to craft and express their understanding visually. For example, students may be studying the Bay of Pigs in history class. While writing their review of the incident and its repercussions, students may search for a photo of Castro and Kennedy and insert it directly into the document. Students aware of these tools can start to become digitally fluent, honing much needed skills for college and career.

> *"They need to be able to use technology strategically when creating, refining, and collaborating on writing. They have to become adept at gathering information."*
>
> —Taken from "Commentary of Standards,"
> Common Core State Standards English Language Arts (p. 63)

TECHNOLOGY-INFUSED TEACHING TIP

Be aware of licensing. Some images and videos may need permission to be used. Follow all copyright laws. If you need help searching for more items that may be used without restriction, go to http://www.google.com/advanced_image_search for more information on Google Advanced Image Search. All photos searched in the manner above have permission to be reused.

Drawing

Insert Google Drawings into Documents. For example, students may create flow charts or graphic organizers explaining what they understand graphically and insert them into Documents. Common Core State Standards for Speaking and Listening Anchor Standard 5 says, "Make strategic use of digital media and visual displays of data to express information and enhance understanding of presentations." Insertion of Drawings to documents published to the Web or shared through print or e-mail will meet this standard. See Chapter 8: Drawings for more details on how to create a drawing. To insert a drawing, click **Drawing** from the **Insert** menu.

In Tables 4.5 and 4.6, the standards call for students to enhance meaning through the use and creation of graphic organizers, graphs, tables, and charts. Using Google tools will help the classroom teacher meet this standard.

Table 4.5 Middle School Standards for Writing and Speaking and Listening

Fifth-Grade Speaking and Listening	*Middle School Writing 6–8*
Include multimedia components (e.g., graphics, sound) and visual displays in presentations when appropriate to enhance the development of main ideas or themes.	Introduce a topic clearly, previewing what is to follow; organize ideas, concepts, and information into broader categories; include formatting (e.g., headings), graphics (e.g., charts, tables), and multimedia when useful to aiding comprehension.

Table 4.6	Writing Standards for Literacy in History/Social Studies, Science, and Technical Subjects 6–12

Introduce a topic and organize complex ideas, concepts, and information so that each new element builds on that which precedes it to create a unified whole; include formatting (e.g., headings), graphics (e.g., figures, tables), and multimedia when useful to aiding comprehension.

Consider the standards in Table 4.5 and 4.6. Inserting Drawings into Documents and other programs such as Presentations is a great way to meet these standards. The main idea is to get students to analyze and synthesize information in a way that they can graphically represent the idea. Students must have experience using these tools to be successful on the next-generation assessments and in college and a career.

Comments

Inserting comments is a great way to interact with the content of student writing. As student papers are shared with the teacher, the teacher can give immediate feedback in a comment. Comments are great for revising work and offering suggestions for rough draft corrections. For example, when a student is writing a paper for English class, the student will produce the writing on the computer or other device. During the formation of the paper, the student will share the paper with the teacher, giving the teacher access to the document in real time as the student is typing. The teacher could work with groups of students, providing immediate feedback in the form of comments and in-document chat. Parents, peers, and adults could share the document to help revise guiding the student's writing. An example of what this looks like is located in Figure 4.23. To insert comments, follow these steps:

1. Highlight the portion of text that you wish to leave a comment on.

2. Right-click the text and choose **Comment.**

3. **Or** Click **Comment** from the **Insert** menu.

4. Type the comment in the space provided as shown in Figure 4.23.

Figure 4.23 is an actual piece of student writing from a sixth-grade student. The teacher, Mrs. Betsy Davis, is a veteran educator with more than 28 years of experience teaching writing. She says that using Google Documents has helped her students with organization and revising more than any other method she has seen. This assignment was a part of an interdisciplinary unit between Mr. Steven Cazort's sixth-grade social studies class and Mrs. Davis's sixth-grade English class.

Table 4.7	Common Core State Standards Anchor Standard 5 Grade 6

With guidance and support from peers and adults, develop and strengthen writing as needed by planning, revising, editing, rewriting, or trying a new approach. (Editing for conventions should demonstrate command of Language standards.)

Figure 4.23	Student Writing With Comments

President Barack Obama
The White House
1600 Pennsylvania AV,NW
Washington,DC 20500

Dear President Obama,

   Hey, how are you doing? My social studies class is writing you a letter from Harrisburg Arkansas Middle school.

I think that gas prices are to high and keep going up. So we need to put a stop to it. Maybe it could help some with money.It could also help with people and kids getting to school and to work and to work.

If gas prices were lower then people would travel more places and buy more things which could help the economy. If lower then people could spend their money on other needed things.

I don't believe that gas prices should go up because of hurricanes ,earthquake's ,floods.I believe gas prices should stay at one price.

I hope by writing this letter it will make a change and make life easier for many people . Please help us!

Betsy Davis
12:28 PM Oct 23
The use of to, too, and two are common mistakes. Use this rule: Two is the number, too means also, to means toward something.

Betsy Davis
12:29 PM Oct 23
Space once after a period.

Betsy Davis
12:32 PM Oct 23
Very good point, the more money that people have the more goods

The letter to the president was written in Mr. Cazort's class on Google Documents. Later, the document was accessed in Mrs. Davis's English class to edit and revise. Since this was the first time Mrs. Davis and the students were using Google Docs for the production of writing and editing, she focused on pointing out three revisions at a time. (Yellow) highlights bring attention to the part needing review. Notice timestamps to denote when the revisions were made and the discussion. This is a fun and exciting way to talk about writing and the writing process.

   Also, feedback can be given in the form of the teacher writing directly on the paper with the student. A teacher may choose a different text color than the student and make comments and corrections live in the text.

   The other options in the Insert menu are easy to understand. So, for the sake of brevity, these will be left for the reader to discover.

Figure 4.24	Tools Menu

Tools	Table	Help	Last edit wa:
Research			^⌘R
Define...			⌘⇧Y
Word count			⌘⇧C
Translate document...			
Preferences...			

TOOLS MENU

Figure 4.24 shows the **Tools** menu. This menu option has many features that will be helpful

Figure 4.25 Research Tool

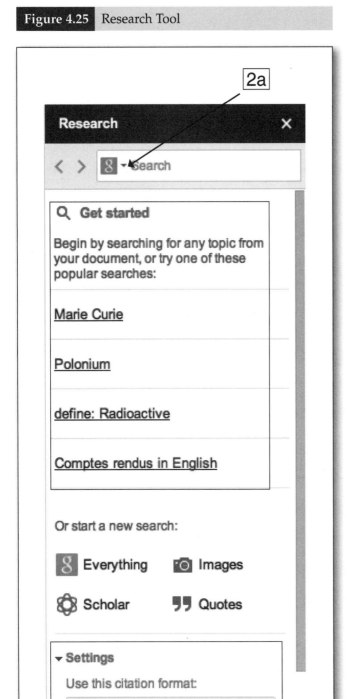

to students and teachers. All are discussed in detail in the following section except word count, which is self-explanatory.

Research

The research tool in Google Documents is great for student research during a writing event. This feature allows the user to search Google directly from the document and add information from the Internet directly into documents. Users can search Google, Google Images, Google Scholar, and Quotes. The research tool will appear on the right-hand side of the document as shown in Figure 4.25. To learn how to use the research tool, follow these steps:

1. Select **Research** from the **Tool** menu as shown in Figure 4.24, or right-click on a word in the document to research it automatically.

2. Type into the search box a search query.
   a. To change the search type, click the drop-down arrow. Choose from:
      i. Google Images
      ii. Google Scholar
      iii. Google Search
      iv. Quotes

3. Results will appear in the research window.

4. Click one of the **Getting started** links in box #1 to get familiar with the research tool.
   a. These are popular searches happening in real time.

5. Click the drop-down arrow in box #2 to change citation format (APA, MLA, or Chicago).
   a. When the user chooses to insert some of the research, the research tool will automatically cite the source.

When searching images in the research tool, insert them by dragging and dropping them into the document.

The research tool is ideal for students. It focuses their searching directly in the document to specifics and that information can be directly inserted into the students' writing. Follow the steps here for a classroom activity using the research tool. This activity is ideal for the beginning of a research project when the students are organizing their research and notes.

LESSON IN FOCUS

The teacher will . . .

1. Share a premade document with the class that contains boxes for students to organize their research in and notes for each main idea of their writing.

2. Instruct students to make a copy of the document, taking ownership and naming it accordingly.

3. Instruct the students to use the research tool to research their topics and make notes in the boxes.

4. Monitor their progress by viewing their shared documents and offer comments and feedback.

Translate

Translate can be used in foreign language classes or with English language learners. Being able to write in their native language and then to translate key sentences or phrases back to English will give the students connection to the meaning and improve their writing skills. The translate tool should benefit the English language learner and help the teacher understand the English language learner. This allows the student to go deeper with meaning by exploring writing in his or her native tongue. Often English language learners receive failing grades because of the language barrier. They may be fantastic writers but struggle with English. Using **Translate** in Google Documents provides a way for teachers to understand what the student is trying to say other than how well they understand English. This tool will help the students learn English by letting the student translate any document that is shared by the teacher or other students to their native language. Follow these steps to translate Google Documents:

1. Open the document to translate.

2. If a non-Google Doc, convert it to the Google Docs format.

3. Select **Translate** from the **Tools** menu as shown in Figure 4.24.

4. Name the new translated document as shown in Figure 4.26.

5. Choose a language from the drop-down menu.

6. Click Translate.

Figure 4.26	Translate Document

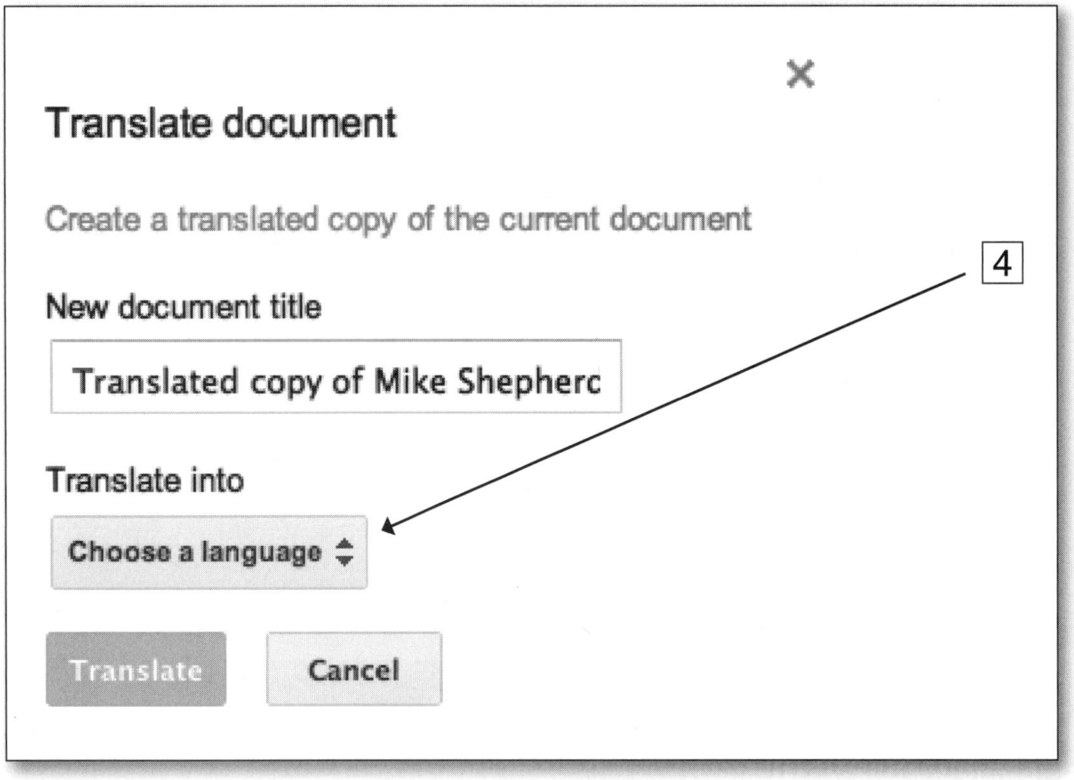

The document is now translated to the language chosen. Be aware that the original document is still in the user's Google Drive and was not altered. A new translated document was created and will appear next to the original in the *documents* list in Google Drive.

Define

Define is a tool that will define words, provide synonyms, and link to other websites to provide extra information about the word. A classroom example for Anchor Standard 2 in Writing, students will be required to give precise summaries of writing across most grade levels. This is a particularly hard skill. Using the define tool, students can look up any difficult words and their synonyms directly in Google Docs. To access the dictionary, follow these steps:

1. Select Dictionary from the Tools menu.

2. Type a word to be defined in the box in Figure 4.27.

3. Click Define .

4. Scroll to find more information about the word, including pictures, alternate definitions, and links to websites.

Figure 4.27 Dictionary

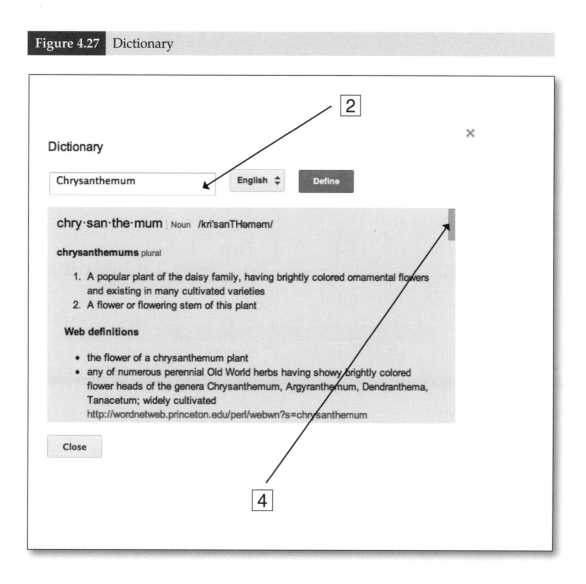

TABLE MENU

Tables are a great way to quickly collect data for elementary mathematics. For example, students studying theoretical versus experimental probability may create a 2 x 10 table to record the results of a coin being flipped. Below the results, students can write about their findings explaining their observations. Share the results of the study with all class periods. Discuss what happens to the percentages of heads and tails as the sample size increases. Follow these steps to insert a table:

1. Select **Table** from the toolbar.

2. Hover and click the mouse over the dimensions of the table to insert as shown in Figure 4.28.

   a. Figure 4.28 only shows a 5 x 8 table, but hover the mouse outside the limits to create a larger table. The largest table in Google Documents is 20 x 20.

Figure 4.28	Insert Table

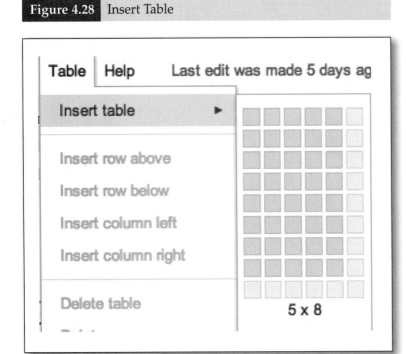

SUMMARY

Documents gives the teacher and students a dynamic word-processing program attached to the Google account. School districts that use Google Apps for Education for their student and faculty e-mail have all of these capabilities built in. With the Common Core State Standards quickly approaching, school leaders, technology specialists, teachers, and students need to be ready for the coming changes in curriculum and technology. Google offers these services and support for free. Documents is just the beginning. The upcoming chapters are full of interesting, engaging ideas and procedures to motivate students to create, collaborate, and share.

RESOURCE LINK

Lesson Plans

Grade Level	Lesson Plan Title	Digital copy found at the link. Lesson plans with numbers are in order in the resource section.	
Elementary School	Reader's Workshop Online Activities by Joseph Hartman	(http://goo.gl/QzOPi)	Only online
Middle School	Jefferson, Adams, and History	http://goo.gl/rHn33	#4
	Choose Your Own Adventure Story by Susan Wells	http://goo.gl/Bbu9c	Only online
High School	Political Campaign	http://goo.gl/rHBmn	#5
	Writing for Context, Audience, and Purpose by Andrea Zellner	http://goo.gl/gQgnt	Only online

For additional resources, including lesson plans, videos, and video tutorials, access this link:

- http://goo.gl/oTUUO

5

Presentations

KEY FEATURES

❖ Collaborative presentations

❖ Cloud storage

❖ Share presentations with teachers, students, and parents

❖ Insert image and video

❖ Publish presentation to the world

❖ Slide transitions and animations

Google Presentations is a powerful presentation maker that is part of Google Apps for Education. Presentations has all of the features users have come to expect with traditional presentation software such as Microsoft PowerPoint and Apple's Keynote. Slide transitions, animations, inserting images, and video are all part of Google Presentations. The difference is in sharing, collaboration, and price. Special features like these will help students and teachers fulfill the requirements of the Common Core State Standards.

Many of the same tools that are used in Documents will be used in Presentations. Sharing, cloud-based storage, and download as other formats are available in the same manner as they were in Documents. For example, each presentation made in Google Presentations is given a unique Web address that when typed into a Web browser can be viewed or edited depending on the share settings. This is great for sharing student presentations. For an example of a collaborative presentation made by students, visit http://goo.gl/GYqTD or snap the quick-response (QR) code in Figure 5.1 to view the presentation on your smartphone or tablet.

Figure 5.1 is a QR code. Using a smartphone or tablet QR code reader application follow the link to view the presentation on a mobile device. Common Core State Standards demand students be ready for college and a career. Accessing information with increased mobility will be a necessary skill. Read more about QR codes in Chapter 11.

Figure 5.1 QR Code Student Presentation

COMMON CORE STANDARDS AND PRESENTATIONS

Presentations are key in communication. College- and career-ready students will present information to classmates and coworkers routinely. Preparing students to make high-quality presentations in the early grades will hone in their skills as they progress in school. In the Common Core State Standards, presenting information in clear, concise ways will prepare students for the rigors of communicating to specific audiences. The Common Core State Standards for Speaking and Listening demand that students have an extensive set of skills in presenting information. The standards on page 8 of the English Language Arts Standards report, "Students must learn to work together, express and listen carefully to ideas, integrate information from oral, visual, quantitative, and media sources, evaluate what they hear, use media and visual displays strategically to help achieve communicative purposes, and adapt speech to context and task."

Google Presentations meets this requirement by allowing collaborative work and the ability to easily share that information with peers, parents, and teachers. The standards say that it is the responsibility of all teachers to make sure students are able to speak and listen with clarity in their particular content areas. Grades K–5 do not separate the speaking and listening standards into content categories like in Grades 6–12. In Grades 6–12, the speaking and listening standards are broken down to English Language Arts and Literacy in History/Social Studies, Science, and Technical Subjects.

Anchor Standard 5 for Speaking and Listening found in Table 5.1 embodies Google Presentations. For example, students may make visually stunning displays that capture the attention of the audience. Animations and video may be added to presentations as well as representations of data such as graphs, tables, or charts. All of this can be done in collaboration and can be shared with the world through share settings. Google Presentations offer a unique opportunity for students to create, collaborate, and share their work. Presenting about concepts studied is one of the best learning strategies. It provides a forum for students to research the content, summarize the information, display data in the form of charts, tables, or graphs, and create visual representations of content with video and images. Making presentations can teach the student how to organize information, letting it flow seamlessly to the viewer. The Common Core State Standards believe that it is an important skill to become ready for life after high school. The Anchor Standard in Table 5.1 addresses digital media and displays of data when making presentations.

Table 5.1 Anchor Standard 5 for Speaking and Listening

Make strategic use of digital media and visual displays of data to express information and enhance understanding of presentations.

Consider the standards in Table 5.2. Each one can be directly linked to Google Presentations. In Table 5.2, the fifth-grade example, multimedia and visual displays are explicitly mentioned. Fifth-grade teachers not only must teach their subject, but also must imbed technology by using presentations to meet the standards.

Table 5.2	Fifth-Grade Speaking and Listening Standard SL.5.5

Include multimedia components (e.g., graphics, sound) and visual displays in presentations when appropriate to enhance the development of main ideas or themes.

Table 5.3	Reading Standard for Literacy in Science and Technical Subjects 6–12

Integrate quantitative or technical information expressed in words in a text with a version of that information expressed visually (e.g., in a flowchart, diagram, model, graph, or table).

Table 5.3 explores the writing standards for History, Social Studies, Science, and Technical subjects for Grades 6–12. These standards increase with complexity over the years, ending with the creation of living presentations in Grades 11 and 12. Creating living presentations requires students not only to use the Internet to produce and publish writing, but also to update individual or shared projects with feedback from teachers, peers, and professionals in the field. Students are no longer expected to turn in a dead assignment that is meant for only the teacher's eyes. Common Core prepares students to create work that matters and that can contribute to the knowledge base of the topic. Graduating seniors who are college and career ready can use collaborative writing and presenting tools like Google Apps for Education to meet the needs they face in the 21st century and beyond.

Table 5.4 displays writing standards for other subjects. The Common Core State Standards hold all accountable for reading and writing. It is clear that using Google

Table 5.4	Writing Standards for Literacy in History/Social Studies, Science, and Technical Subjects 6–12

6–8
Use technology, including the Internet, to produce and publish writing and present the relationships between information and ideas clearly and efficiently.
9–10
Use technology, including the Internet, to produce, publish, and update individual or shared writing products, taking advantage of technology's capacity to link to other information and to display information flexibly and dynamically.
11–12
Use technology, including the Internet, to produce, publish, and update individual or shared writing products in response to ongoing feedback, including new arguments or information.

Apps for Education can meet the challenges set forth in the new Common Core State Standards.

Same Great Features

All of the programs in Google Docs, Presentations, Documents, Spreadsheets, Drawings and Forms have the same great features. This chapter will focus on these programs plus Presentation-specific features that make this software ideal for implementing Common Core State Standards.

- Sharing
- Collaboration
- Publish to the Web
- Embed
- Every Doc has a unique URL
- All Docs are stored in Google Drive cloud-based storage

Accessing Presentations

All of the Google Docs share a common pathway to be accessed. Follow the steps here to start working with Presentations. When the user is logged into her Google Apps account, Figure 5.2 will be at the top left of the page. Alternatively, the user may type in any Web browser's address bar **drive.google.com/a/yourschool.org** (replace yourschool.org with your school's domain address) to access the Documents List without going through Gmail. To access Presentations, follow these steps:

1. Click on **Drive** located at the top of the screen as denoted in Figure 5.2 to access the users Documents List.

| Figure 5.2 | Accessing Drive |

2. Click the red **Create** button on the left-hand side of the page as shown in Figure 5.3 to reveal the drop-down menu displaying all of the Google Docs software.

3. Click **Presentation** to access the presentation editor.

After clicking on Presentations, the next screen will ask the user to choose a theme for the background of the slides. When working collaboratively on presentations, take note that when a theme is chosen, it is applied to all slides. For example, if a group of students is working on a collaborative presentation and each student is responsible for a particular set of slides, then if any of the group members changes or chooses a theme on the shared presentation, it is applied to all slides. Look at Figure 5.4 to see an example of theme choices.

Name the Presentation

The next step in creating a Google Presentation is to give the presentation a name. Students need to be aware that naming Google Docs they create ensures that they can easily retrieve the file. To give a Presentation or any other Google Doc names, follow these steps:

1. Click on the words **Untitled presentation** as shown in Figure 5.5.

2. Type your new title of the presentation in the box in Figure 5.6.

3. Click the box **OK** when finished.

Figure 5.3 Accessing Presentation Editor

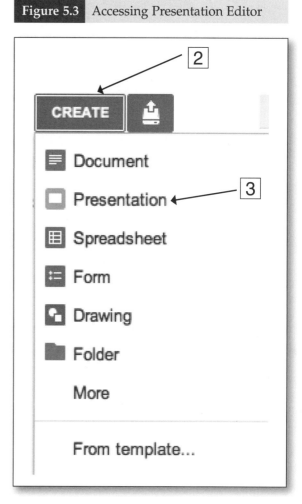

Figure 5.4 Accessing Drive

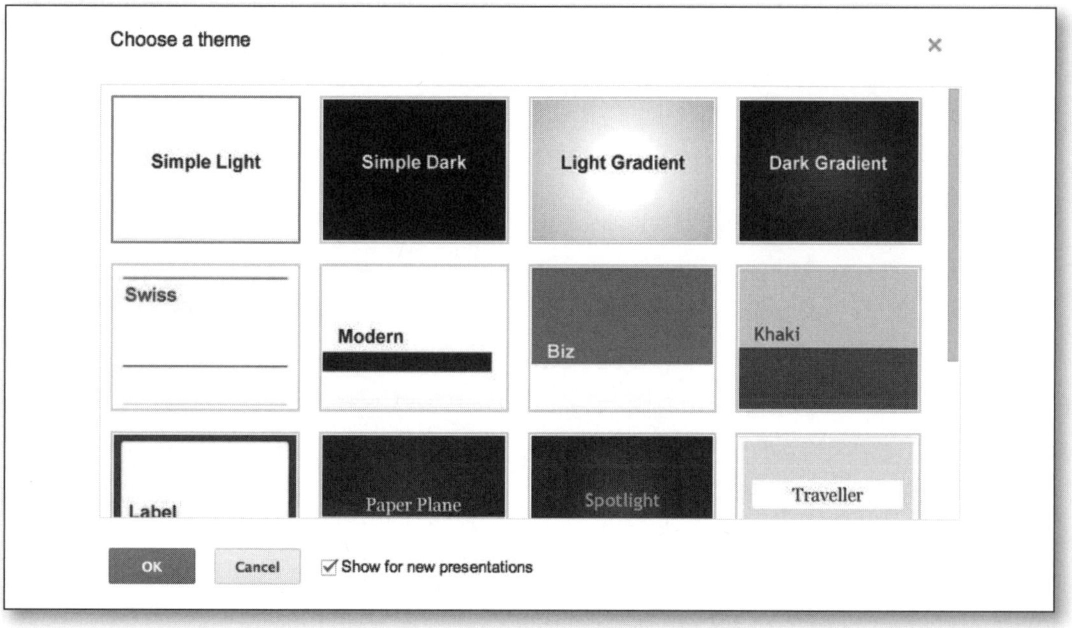

TECHNOLOGY-INFUSED TEACHING TIP

Instruct students to give names to their work based on a predefined formula. Students will create a massive amount of digital content over their lifetimes, and it will most likely be saved in a cloud storage space like in Google Drive. It is important for students to learn how to manage the content they create. Managing student's quality of work over time could be a valuable part of a student's electronic portfolio. It is imperative that the information be easy for the student to recall years later. Giving the documents searchable names that follow a formula will make it easy. For example, the student Marcy Tolbert will name documents she creates by defining what type of assignment and adding her name (e.g., "Marcy Tolbert History of NASA Presentation"). Teachers should require this or a similar naming convention to be able to search for Marcy's documents for grading, and later in her school career, she can access these documents to see her progress over time. Students need to be aware that organizing their digital life is an important task. Students who are college and career ready realize that digital organization will be a skill that is in demand in the professional world. A recent *Time* magazine article on learning reports that when students are asked questions, they tend not to think of a particular class. Instead, they think of where the nearest device is located to search for the information. Students and adults alike are thinking in terms of search rather than being able to instantly recall the fact. Learning to search the massive amount of digital content that the user produces or others produce is more important than the futile attempt to memorize it.

Figure 5.5 Giving the Presentation a Title

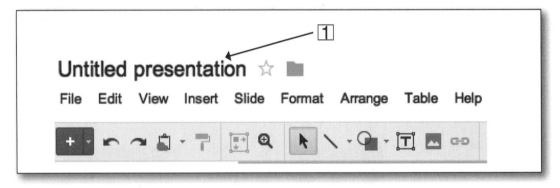

Figure 5.6 Rename the Document

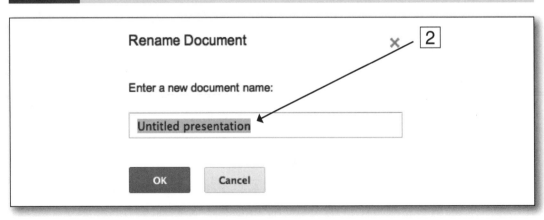

After clicking OK, the file will appear in the user's Drive folder with the appropriate name given to it in the Documents List. Notice the star in Figure 5.5 next to the file name. If the user clicks the star, the document is given special significance and will appear in the starred list in Google Drive. The user could star documents that are important or frequently worked on, making them easier to access. Starring a document is the same as starring an e-mail in Gmail.

Previously Detailed Features

In Chapter 4, many of the same commands were discussed. Please refer back to Chapter 4 to learn how to perform the actions in the following list. This section will focus only on Presentation-specific commands, and some may overlap.

- Share
- New
- Rename
- Make a Copy
- Revision History
- Language
- E-mail Collaborators
- E-mail as Attachment
- Print Options

FILE MENU

The **File** menu is usually the first menu that computer users come into contact with. Most word-processing programs have similar features, but Google Presentations provides some pleasant surprises that other programs can't compete with. Read this section to become familiar with Google's presentation maker.

Import Slides

Import slides is a command that will let the user import slides from any Google Presentation and/or Microsoft PowerPoint files that are located on the user's Google Drive or on the computer's hard drive. Google recognizes the ubiquity of Microsoft Office and wants to make using Google Docs an easy and compatible experience. Teachers will find this helpful with the transition to Google Presentations because, just like with Documents, users can upload any file type to store in their cloud storage space, Google Drive. Teachers may have created many PowerPoint presentations in the past that are useful for their classes. To use them, teachers can convert them to Google Presentations or insert specific slides from Google Presentations or Microsoft PowerPoint into Google Presentations. Remember, working with Google Docs allows the user to store and edit work from any computer with Internet access. Students in the new economy of the 21st century will most likely not be required to learn only one piece of software. The Common Core State Standards or the Next Generation Assessment consortia have not endorsed any software as of yet, and there is doubt that they will. It is key for the college- and career-ready student to be able to be adaptive in any software to do the job. That is why Google Docs is so important. It has all of the basic features of the mainstream office packages, but it has the ability to use the Internet to create, collaborate, and share, plus it is free. If a student can be comfortable with Google Docs' toolbars, then he or she can master any program the testing companies or their future bosses can throw at them.

Follow the steps below to import slides from other presentations, including Microsoft PowerPoint, from the user's Google Drive.

| Figure 5.7 | Importing Slides |

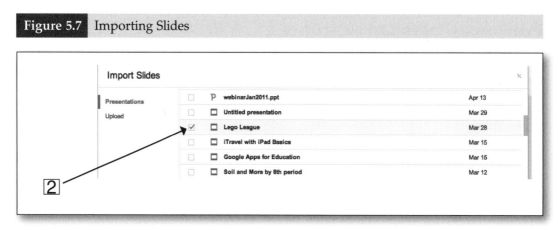

1. Click **Import slides** from the **File** menu in the upper right-hand corner of Presentations to reveal the window in Figure 5.7.

2. Select the Google Presentation ▢ or the Microsoft PowerPoint ᴘ presentation that the user wants to import by placing a check mark in the box as in Figure 5.7.

3. Click on which slides to import as shown in Figure 5.8.

   a. Slides selected will appear highlighted like in Figure 5.8.

4. Select **Keep original theme** to import backdrop, colors, and other features.

5. Click ▰ at the bottom of Figure 5.8.

| Figure 5.8 | Selecting Slides to Import |

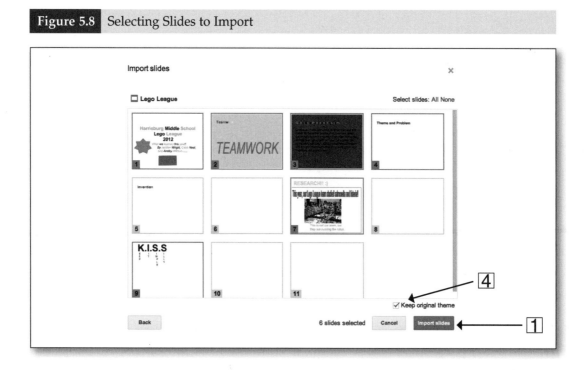

To upload slides from a presentation that is not in the user's Google Drive, but located on the user's computer, follow these steps:

Figure 5.9 Upload Slides From Computer

1. Click **Upload** under Presentations as seen in Figure 5.7.

2. Drag Google Presentation or Microsoft PowerPoint files only from your computer into the box to upload them, or press the [Choose files to upload] button to select files manually from your hard drive to import.

More Reasons Google Presentations Work

Using Google Docs is perfect in a school setting. Google Docs are device neutral. It doesn't matter if the computer lab has iMacs and the mathematics teachers have PCs, no software has to be purchased, and no programs have to be downloaded. Students can move from device to device without the worry of losing information or not having the right program.

Teachers who want to avoid creating "dead" presentations can convert their existing PowerPoint presentations to Google Presentations or at least start making presentations exclusively in Google Docs. A dead presentation refers to the information being locked into one saved file on one storage device like doing a Microsoft PowerPoint. Revive presentations by converting them into a Google Doc. This gives life to the work because the information is stored in the cloud: the user can edit the information from any computer or share it with anyone in the world. No longer do teachers and students have to be chained to a physical hard drive.

If users don't want to convert documents but still want to share them the Google Docs way, they can upload the file and click share just like sharing a Google Doc. This is another way that Google strives to make it easy on users.

Download As

Download as is the command that lets the user download the Google Presentation as any of the supported file formats. Presentations supports the following file types for download.

- PNG
- JPEG
- SVG
- PPTX
- PDF
- TXT

Students who want to submit presentations as part of a science fair or other public events may be required to have specific formats other than the Google Docs format. Some formats such as PDF are very difficult to edit, unless you have expensive software. This would be ideal for teachers and students who do not want their information changed on the presentation when they share a digital copy with the public.

Publish to the Web

Publish to the Web allows the user to publish the presentation directly to the Web, giving it a unique URL. This option will make the presentation easy to share with anyone with Internet access. Teachers may use this option when presenting to a class; they need only to get the presentation's unique URL and copy and paste it into an e-mail to share the presentation with students. When the user clicks on the link, the presentation will appear in the browser. The URL is long and confusing. Use Google's URL Shortener, http://goo.gl, to shorten the link. This makes it easy for the user to share the presentation. This is helpful when the presenter does not have the e-mail of the participants but wants to share the presentation with a group. The participants will type the shortened URL into a browser's address bar to view the presentation.

Another dazzling way to access Google Presentations or any documents created in Google Docs on the Web is through the use of QR codes. QR codes allow the user to access the information on smartphones or tablets without typing in the URL. See QR codes and Google URL Shortener in Chapter 11 for more details.

INSERT MENU

The **Insert** menu gives users many options to make their presentations come alive. Read the next section to become familiar with inserting graphic design elements to make your presentations stand out.

Video

Videos can be uploaded from YouTube into Google Presentations. There is not an upload from hard drive option for videos. Teachers and students could create a YouTube account to upload videos. Some domain administrators allow students and teachers to link their YouTube and Google Apps accounts, allowing them to fully use this feature in presentations. Some districts may not feel that it is in the best interest of their students and faculty to have this option because of inappropriate content. Google owns YouTube, making integration with Google Apps easy. The only problem is that the district domain administrator must allow YouTube for Schools to be turned on in the Google Apps domain. Contact your domain administrator and ask him or her to allow YouTube for Schools. It is understandable that some schools may opt out of giving students access to the YouTube site. Alternatively, there is YouTube for Schools. In this version, all comments and advertisements are taken off the site. If YouTube for Schools is unblocked for students, they can post their own videos into their Google Presentations. If your school has this capability, follow the steps in the following two options to insert existing YouTube videos into presentations.

Option I: Insert YouTube Video From Search

1. Select **Video** from the **Insert** menu in the upper left side of Presentations.
2. Click **Video search** as indicated in Figure 5.10.
3. Enter a search term into the search box.
4. Press the play icon in the middle of the video thumbnail to preview.
5. Click to choose that video to be inserted in the presentation.

Figure 5.10 Insert YouTube From Search

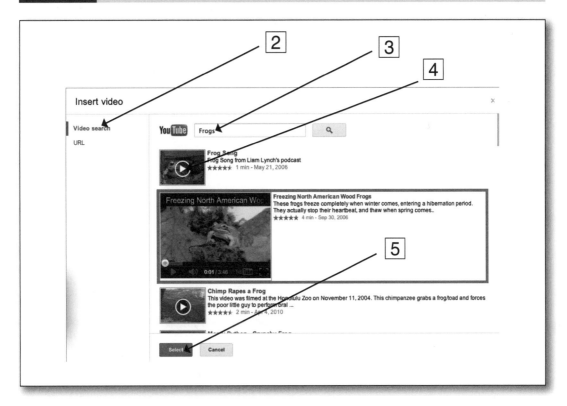

Option II: Insert YouTube Video From URL

Each YouTube video has its own unique URL, exactly like every Google Doc and Google Calendar. To place specific videos into presentations, follow these steps:

1. Select **Video** from the **Insert menu** in the upper left of presentations.

2. Click on the initials **URL** as shown in Figure 5.11.

3. Copy the URL from the YouTube website.

4. Paste the URL into the space provided.

5. Press [Select] to insert the video.

Figure 5.11 Insert YouTube Video From URL

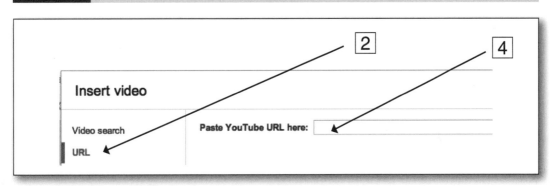

Word Art

Word art is a way for students and teachers to add creativity to their presentations. To insert Word Art into Presentations, follow these steps:

1. Select **Word Art** from the **Insert** menu in Presentations.

2. Enter text into the Word Art text box as shown in Figure 5.12.

3. Enter multiple lines by holding **Shift+Enter**.

4. Press **Enter** when finished to insert the Word Art.

Figure 5.12	Inserting Word Art

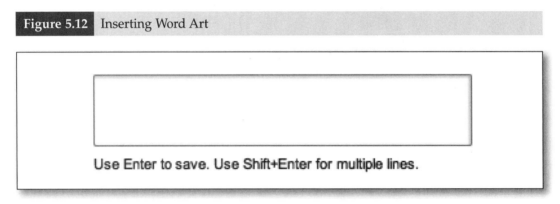

Use Enter to save. Use Shift+Enter for multiple lines.

Word Art can be edited for the following designs by selecting the drop-down menu when the Word Art is highlighted on the slide.

- Fill color .
- Line color .
- Line weight .
- Line dash .
- Font Arial · | 48 · .
- Bold, italic, underline **B** *I* U .

These options allow users to express their unique style. View Google's Demo Slam video at http://goo.gl/Fvsev to see what is possible with presentations with respect to Word Art, lines, shapes, and other media.

Animate

Animations are a great way to give life to a presentation. The Common Core State Standards encourage the use of multimedia as detailed in the fifth-grade standard shown in Table 5.5. This Common Core standard pushes students to use multimedia components to enrich concepts being presented. Teaching appropriate style

Table 5.5	Speaking and Listening Standard 5.SL.5

Include multimedia components (e.g., graphics, sound) and visual displays in presentations when appropriate to enhance the development of main ideas or themes.

is essential for college and career success. Students must recognize audience and present in a style appropriate to the task.

Follow the steps below to add slide transitions in Google Presentations.

1. Select **Animate** from the **Insert** menu in the toolbar of Google Presentations.

2. Select the drop-down arrow next to the word **Slide** as shown in Figure 5.13 to add

Figure 5.13 Adding Slide Animations/Transitions

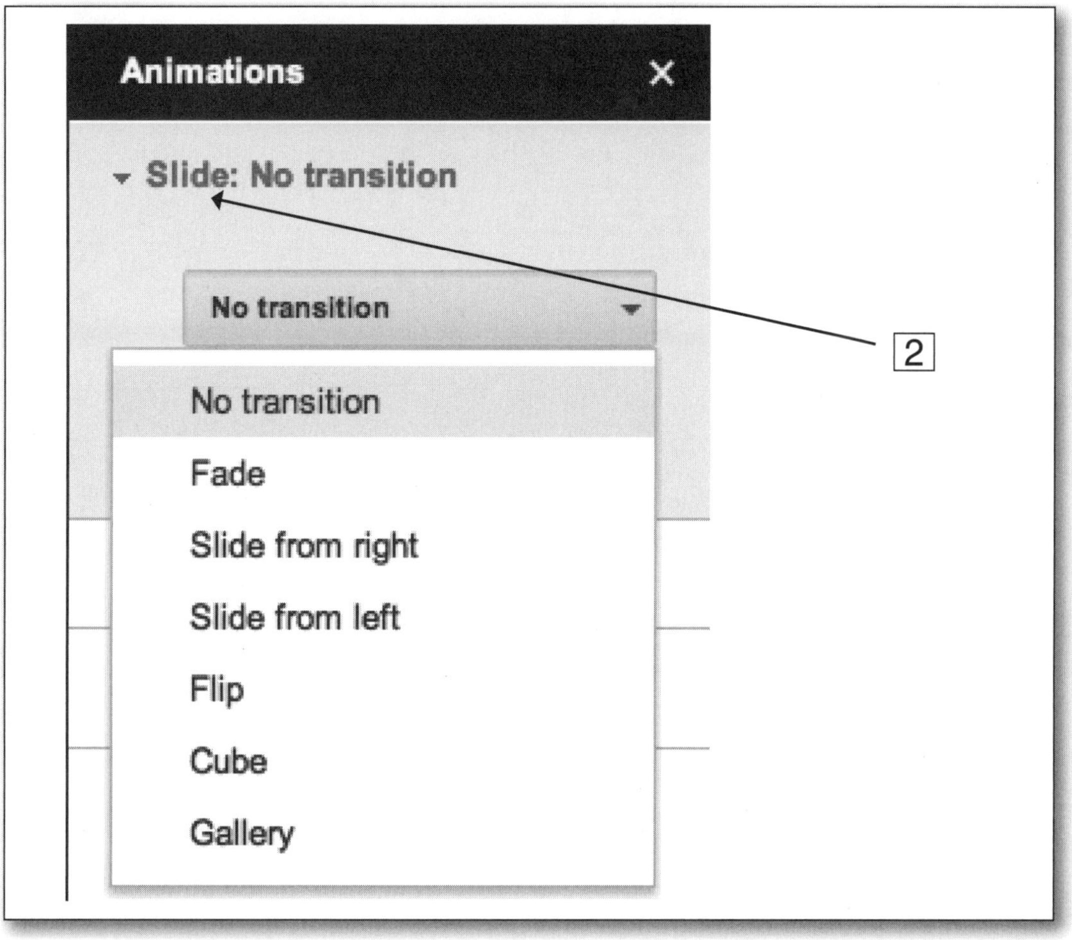

slide transition to the current slide.

3. Choose from the list of animations in Figure 5.13.
   To animate a particular object on the slide, follow these steps:

1. Select **Animate** from the **Insert** menu in the toolbar of Google Presentations.

2. Select an object to animate on the slide.

   - Graphics
   - Images
   - Word Art
   - Text boxes

3. Click **+Add Animation** to reveal the options located in the drop-down menu in Figure 5.14.

4. Choose which animation style and command to place on the object shown in Figure 5.14.

5. Repeat Steps 2–4 to select additional objects for animation.

6. Select <kbd>Play</kbd> underneath **+Add Animation** to preview animations you have selected.

Figure 5.14   Animate an Object

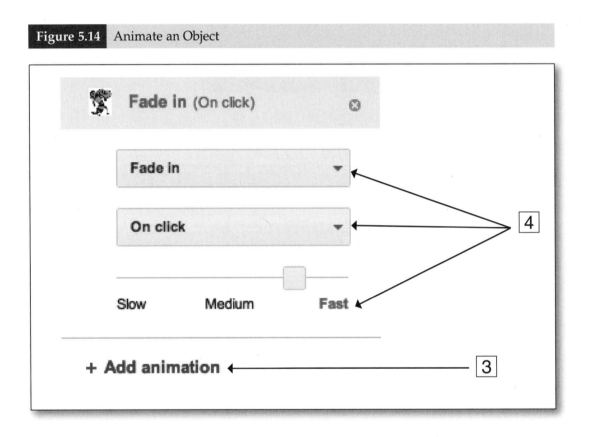

Line

Inserting lines into presentations is a great way for students to express themselves artistically while exploring geometry concepts. For example, the type of line called Polyline is great for learning shapes and their names in early grades math classes. Polylines are used to make polygons. Common Core State Standards for geometry in the third grade directs students to analyze and create shapes. For example, students could draw polygons on their slides, name them accordingly, and share them with other students. One idea is to create databases of study materials organized in folders stored on the teacher's Google Drive. An example of a database would be slides with explanations and drawings of polygons. These databases could be shared with students when studying a particular shape and its properties. This is a great way to review for a test or send home as a study guide. Once the slideshow is shared with the class, students can access it anywhere they have connection to the Internet. In a perfect world, students would study their materials from their smartphone as they ride home on the school bus. Take this idea one step further by collaborating with other classes or other schools. Since

Common Core is a national initiative, sharing relevant materials with classes all over the country could help.

To insert lines into Presentations, follow these steps:

Figure 5.15 Types of Lines

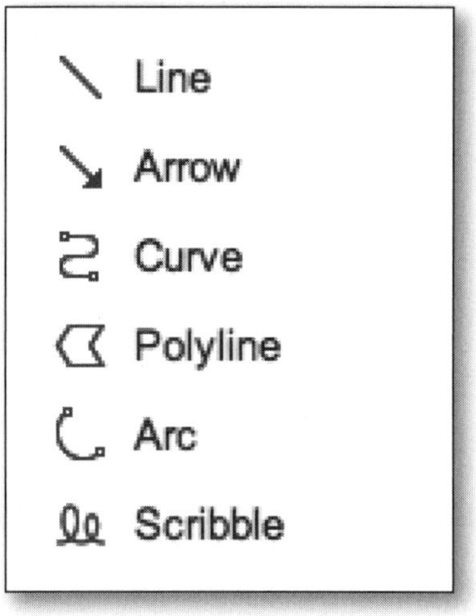

1. Select **Line** from the **Insert** menu at the top of Presentations to reveal the drop-down menu containing the types of lines that may be inserted as shown in Figure 5.15.

2. Click on which type of line to insert.

3. Edit the line.

4. Highlight the line by clicking on it to reveal the toolbar and drop-down menus that can change:

   - Fill color
   - Line color
   - Line weight
   - Line dash
   - Arrowheads ; these are placed at the beginning and end of the line to give it direction

LESSON IN FOCUS

Classroom Activity With Lines

Students in third grade must "reason with shapes and their attributes." This mathematics standard wants students to understand that shapes have similarities and differences. For example, a student learning this standard could make a presentation. The teacher may prepare slides in advance that have the names of shapes on them. Follow the steps laid out here to make the lesson a reality in your classroom.

The teacher will . . .

1. Create a Google Presentation with each slide containing names of various shapes students are studying.

2. Share the premade presentation with the students.

The students will . . .

3. Make a copy of the presentation by selecting **File,** then **Make a copy.**

   This step lets the student take ownership of the shared document. Any further edits that the student makes to the document will not appear on the original.

4. Rename the presentation using the naming convention selected by the teacher.

5. Research on the Internet properties of the shapes and their appearance.

6. Use Polyline to draw the shapes, then name them appropriately.

7. Use the Internet to give research information about the shapes to summarize on the slide.

8. Re-share the new presentation with the teacher for scoring.

TECHNOLOGY-INFUSED TEACHING TIP

Writing on slides in the lower grades is important. It may be difficult for a third grader to write in the large white space of a traditional document. Working with slides gives the students a smaller space with a defined area to work in. This is great way to build skills of producing content with technology using the Internet.

TECHNOLOGY-INFUSED TEACHING TIP

Students who are college and career ready will be prepared to write in many different mediums. Documents such as Microsoft Word, Apple's Pages, or Google Documents are not the only way to present formal writing. Websites, blogs, wikis, Twitter, Facebook, and countless other not-yet-invented formats in which people consume information will be important. Promote other formats; students who are versatile will be college and career ready. The standard in Table 5.6 seeks to expand students' ability to read and write in diverse media.

Table 5.6	Integration of Knowledge and Ideas Anchor Standard 7 for Reading

Integrate and evaluate content presented in diverse media and formats, including visually and quantitatively, as well as in words.

New Slide

To insert a new slide, follow these steps:

Figure 5.16	New Slide Layouts

Title

✓ Title and Body

Title and Two Columns

Title Only

Caption

Blank

1. Click the ⊞ icon in the left side of Presentations.
2. Click the drop-down arrow next to the red plus sign to select from the slide layouts shown in Figure 5.16.

The slide layouts shown in Figure 5.16 pertain to what type of text and object boxes will appear on the slide for the particular layout. For example, the Title and Body slide will have a text box for the title of the slide and a separate text box for the body of the slide. If the user wants to create his or her own text and object boxes select the **Blank** layout.

Concerns With Collaborative Work in Presentations

When working collaboratively, students need to be aware of which slides they have permission in which to work. Many times in collaborative presentations, students will be assigned a specific slide number for their contribution. For example, if a student added a slide to the middle of the groups' presentation and every student was assigned a slide number in which to work, then the slide numbers would be changed, causing confusion. If the teacher predefines the slides and does not allow adding slides to the middle of the presentation, then the confusion can be averted. To help avoid the bewilderment, use the chat feature built into every Google Doc. This helps if a small group is working on a presentation project. Users can chat about whatever they need to on the side. This helps collaborators be organized when unexpected changes occur in the making of the presentation. Google Docs chat is automatically turned on even if chat in Gmail is disabled. This is great because the domain administrator would have to disable all of Google Docs features to keep students from collaborating. Learn how to chat in Presentations by reading the next section.

Chat in Google Docs

Chat in Docs is located in the upper right-hand corner of any Google Doc. When others are viewing, the users can chat with each other. This is helpful when working collaboratively. They are able to talk with each other, discussing the presentation and ideas that they have to make it better. Collaboration is one of the key features of the Common Core State Standards. The word *collaboration* is mentioned 39 times in the Mathematics and English language arts standards. Whether the student is working on a math proof in Presentations or using the space to create online notecards to study with a friend, collaboration is at the heart of Google Apps for Education. The chat feature can make this collaboration a reality. To access chat in Google Docs, follow these steps:

| Figure 5.17 | Chat in Docs |

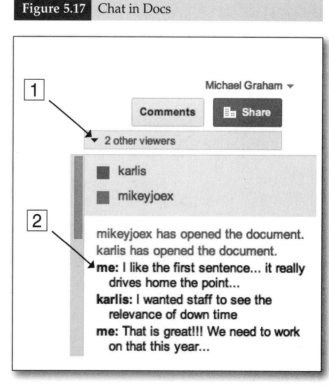

1. Click the drop-down arrow denoting how many viewers are collaborating on the document located under the comments and share buttons as shown in Figure 5.17.
   a. The names of the viewers are located here with a colored box.
   b. The color box represents their cursor color on the document.
2. Type text in the chat box, then press **Enter**.
   a. Chat will automatically pop up in the other viewers' windows.

Google Presentations for Research Notecards

Consider this Common Core State Standard in Table 5.7 when planning long-term or short-term writing projects with students.

Presentations can be used in more ways

Table 5.7   Anchor Standard 10 Writing Standards for Literacy in History/Social Studies, Science, and Technical Subjects 6–12

Write routinely over extended time frames (time for reflection and revision) and shorter time frames (a single sitting or a day or two) for a range of discipline-specific tasks, purposes, and audience.

than a simple performance of conveying knowledge to a formal group of spectators. For example, a student researching information about certain historical figures for a history/social studies research paper would find presentations a useful tool for organization. The student will undoubtedly find many resources in print and digital formats as the Common Core State Standards express routinely. Taking notes on traditional note cards does not pave the way into the 21st century. Using Google Presentations as research notecards is both efficient and convenient. The content created in Presentations is always stored in the cloud and accessed anywhere there is an Internet connection. Students are able to modify their research with their smartphone or home computer. The research will be shared with the teacher so the teacher can give feedback in the form of comments. Comments are used in Documents, Spreadsheets, Presentations, and Drawings as a way for teachers to grade or leave feedback on assignments. Presentations allows the teacher to guide the student in the writing process from research to final draft.

Other Uses for Presentations

- Flash cards
- Note-taking
- Writing projects for elementary students
- Teacher presentations for content
- Student presentations for content

Shapes

In Presentations, users may insert various shapes, arrows, callouts, and equation elements that enhance the presentation. Look at Figure 5.18 for the full collection of shapes that may be inserted into a presentation. Encourage students to use these transitional elements to make eye-catching flowcharts and graphics. To insert shapes, follow these steps:

1. Select **Shapes** from the **Insert** menu located in the toolbar in Presentations.

2. Hover the mouse over the arrow pointing to the right beside **Shape** to reveal the objects available for insert as shown in Figure 5.18.

3. Click the object to insert and edit it accordingly.

Figure 5.18   Insert Shapes

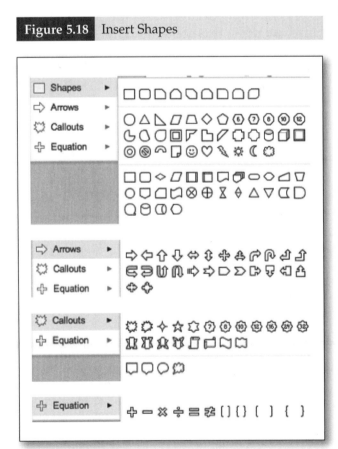

SLIDE MENU

Many of the features in the **Slide** menu are offered in other presentation makers and are self-explanatory. We will learn only about the background option in depth.

Background

Under the **Slide** menu in the toolbar is background. Background is different than theme. The background refers to the color or image on the background of the slide, and it can be applied to all slides or a particular slide. Theme refers to the arrangement of text boxes, titles, and body of the slide. When students are working on collaborative projects, they may change the background color or image to their preference without changing the group's background as a whole. Teach the students to be aware of the **Apply All** button. To change the background, follow these steps:

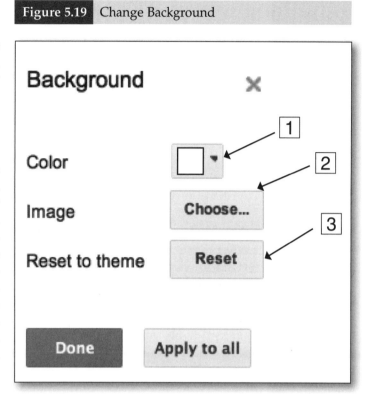

Figure 5.19 Change Background

1. Select **Background** under the **Slide** menu in the toolbar to reveal Figure 5.19.

2. Click the drop-down arrow next to the box to change the color ▢▾.

3. Click Choose... to select an image from your Google Drive, search the Web, or upload from your hard drive.

4. Click Reset to reset the theme to default.

5. Click **Done** or **Apply to all.**

TECHNOLOGY-INFUSED TEACHING TIP

Changing the layout and theme will affect the entire presentation. When working on collaborative presentations, make sure to seek the advice of the group before applying a new motif to the presentation. Use the convenient chat or comment features to consult group members.

FORMAT MENU

Format refers to the style of text, paragraphs, line spacing, and options like bold, italic, and underline. These are common in most office software. One exception in Google Docs that makes it stand out from other presentation- or document-creating software is the **Alt Text** utility. This feature will help students with special needs who have difficulty seeing or reading the text on the presentation. Alt Text works with third-party screen-reader software to deliver text to speech for individuals with text deficiencies. Some of these third-party software programs will work with Google Docs to print in Braille. Google Presentations can help everyone learn regardless of their learning or physical disability. If you have access to the screen-reader technology, try it for your students. To access Alt Text, follow these steps:

1. Select a piece of text on the slide.

2. Select **Alt Text** from the **Format** menu in the toolbar.

3. Title and describe the Alt Text as shown in Figure 5.20.

Figure 5.20   Alt Text

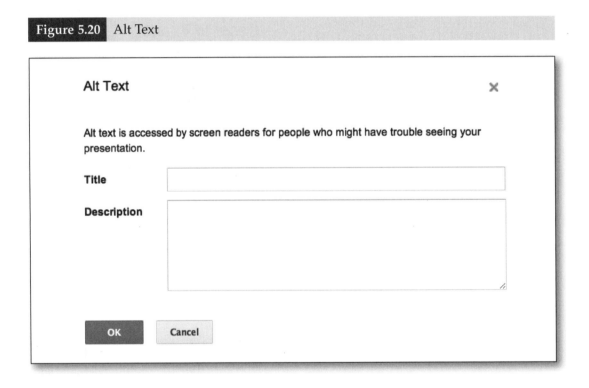

Example of Student Work

In this example, students are using presentations to create collaborative slide shows about soil in eighth-grade science class. The teacher, Ms. Jacquie Dubrava, prepared ahead of time a presentation titled "Soil." The presentation she shared had one title page and one individual slide for each student in the class. She shared the presentation with the entire class period easily by using the share settings and selecting the sixth-period group that she had previously created (see Chapter 3: Gmail). In the first slide, Ms. Dubrava gave directions and slide assignments to the students. Students were assigned to create a slide covering an aspect of what they have learned about soil within the unit of study. Students were assigned which topics to cover in their slide. Each student was given a particular slide number in which to work. All students in the class were working on the presentation at the same time.

By the end of the class period, the students had created a full collaborative presentation covering every aspect of soil that they have learned about. Follow the link http://goo.gl/NJwQ1 to see an example from her seventh-period class.

SUMMARY

Presentations are one more component of Google Apps for Education that will help students and teachers meet the rigor of the Common Core State Standards. The standards addressed in this chapter undoubtedly can be met with the use of presentations. Moving forward, each part of Google Docs will become increasingly familiar. Start to think how you can use these great tools for collaboration in your classroom to exceed the expectations of the Common Core State Standards.

RESOURCE LINK

Lesson Plans

Grade Level	Lesson Plan Title	Digital copy found at the link. Lesson plans with numbers are in order in the resource section.	
Elementary School	Biomes by Ronna Van Veghel	http://goo.gl/ILJ3V	Online Only
Middle School	Peter Pan by Betsy Davis	http://goo.gl/I9XmX	#6
High School	Introduction to the Salem Witch Trials by Heather Eggers	http://goo.gl/wmf7h	#7

For additional resources, including lesson plans, videos, and video tutorials, access this link:

■ http://goo.gl/aFR1q

6

Spreadsheets

KEY FEATURES

- ❖ Collaborative spreadsheets
- ❖ Auto fill
- ❖ Gadgets
- ❖ Insert charts, images, and more

Google Spreadsheets is a fully integrated spreadsheet program that brings data alive in Google Apps for Education. Students and teachers can use it for a range of tasks, from kindergarteners making simple T-charts to master's level statistics. This chapter will cover the basic functions of spreadsheets and how they can be used in the classroom to exceed the Common Core State Standards, particularly math. Keep in mind that any spreadsheet program is difficult to learn at first. Because Google Spreadsheets is complex, it is best to keep trying new features, and, over time, users will gain skills that will help them organize and manipulate data. Google Spreadsheets is the most robust program in Google Docs. The key feature is the collaboration that Google has pioneered. Data collected by Google Spreadsheets users can instantly be shared, modified, and presented in graphically stunning ways with charts and gadgets. Math is the primary focus, but other subjects will use it as well. For example, understanding the 2008 global economic crisis from a history perspective cannot be fully understood if the student has trouble reading graphs, tables, and charts. Furthermore, students need to be able to work with data to convey the information to persuade others of their points of view. This is key in Standard for Mathematical Practice 3: "Construct viable arguments and critique the reasoning of others."

Using Google Spreadsheets to integrate mathematics into other classes is important for learning about decision making. Math examples can explain the most complicated parts of history, science, and behavior with graphs and charts. With Google

Spreadsheets, students can unlock the power of information, giving them a way to compute statistical data, present it in the form of graphs, and share and collaborate with the world or class, making real contributions to the understanding of the subject.

All of the Google Docs programs operate on the premise of sharing. Many of the same great features are included in Google Spreadsheets that are in the other Google Docs programs. This chapter will only cover basic Google Spreadsheets–specific commands.

STANDARDS FOR MATHEMATICAL PRACTICE

The Standards for Mathematical Practice from the Common Core Mathematics Standards are much like the Anchor Standards in the English Language Arts Standards. They guide the teacher throughout all grade levels to instill into the student certain behaviors and ideas that make them develop critical thinking with mathematics. They are meant to capture the "processes and proficiencies" of mathematics, in other words, how the student uses the mathematics and not just what they acquire as far as knowledge and skill. Students must be aware of these ideas to fully become college and career ready for a world full of data analysis and decision making. That is why Standard for Mathematical Practice 5 is perfect for Google Spreadsheets. Google Spreadsheets will allow the student to collect data in cells and manipulate the data to make charts and graphs that the student can use to explain his or her findings with evidence. The software is not doing the "math" for the student; instead, it is a tool that helps the students explore mathematical concepts and models. Students who can choose the appropriate mathematical tool to help interpret results and critical thinking will become college and career ready. Solving problems in college and career will be messy and most likely not look like the problems in many classrooms today. The boss will most likely not say to the employee, "Sally, if two trains are leaving the station and one is going 50 miles per hour. . . ." Instead of this, bosses will have employees working on complex problems that require deep understanding. Teachers must focus on questions and learning experiences that provide a rich and complex set of problems for students to solve. Students must be able to identify their own problems as well as solve the ones that their professors and bosses identify for them. Students who are college and career ready will have sufficient grasp of mathematical concepts and be able to choose the appropriate tool to conceptualize, share, and present their mathematical understanding. Google Spreadsheets does this by giving the students a full statistical package that can help students share, manipulate, and present data.

FILE MENU

The **File** menu gives you access to important commands that will help you create a high-quality spreadsheet. Read the next section to find out some time-savers that will make collecting and sharing data a great experience for you and your students.

Import

Import data sets into spreadsheets from any of the compatible formats.

Table 6.1	Supported Data Formats

Extension	*Program supported*
.xls	Microsoft Excel 2003 and previous versions
.xlsx	Microsoft Excel 2007 and later versions
.ods	OpenOffice
.csv	Comma-separated value—this format is common as an alternative import/export format to go between large databases and propriety formats such as Microsoft Excel and Apple's Numbers.
.txt	Text file—similar as a go-between like .csv
.tsv	Tab-separated values—similar to .csv and .txt
.tab	MapInfo TAB format is a data set that can be used in geographical information systems software.

The user can import all or part of the types of data sets displayed in Table 6.1 into Google Spreadsheets. Students and teachers working in other formats can import them into Google Spreadsheets for easy sharing of data. To import data into Google Spreadsheets, follow these steps:

1. Select **Import** from the **File** menu in the Google Spreadsheets toolbar.

2. Click **Choose file** to upload data from hard drive as shown in Figure 6.1.

3. Choose the appropriate **Import action.**

4. Click **Import**.

Figure 6.1	Import Data

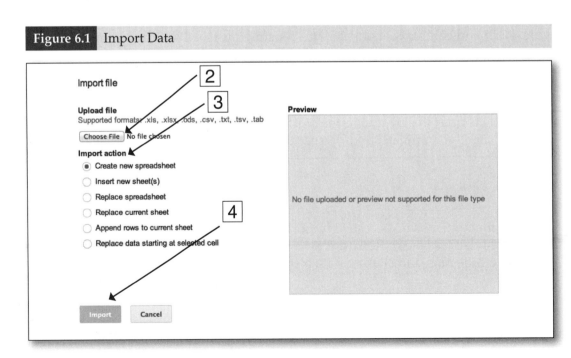

Spreadsheet Settings

Figure 6.2 shows the Google Spreadsheets Settings window. Manipulate defaults for currency, time zone, and more with these settings for the particular file only. Spreadsheet settings will affect formatting defaults such as currency, date, and time settings and other country-specific settings. Selecting the time zone will allow the user to have the revision history displayed in their time zone as well as "affect all time-related functions." There are some time related functions (formulas) that can be inserted into the cells of a spreadsheet. See a full list of functions at http://goo.gl/LBN7R.

Figure 6.2 Spreadsheet Settings

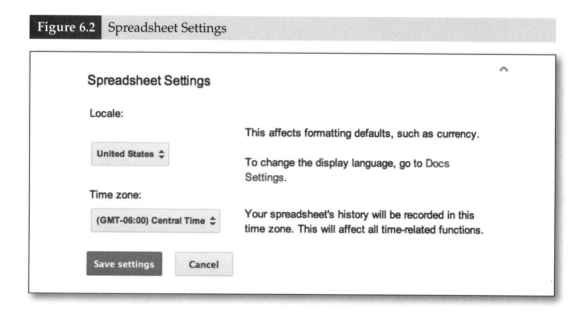

See Revision History

It is important to go over revision history once again because of its usefulness in the classroom and particularly Google Spreadsheets. The Google Docs programs Documents, Presentations, Spreadsheets, and Drawings all have revision history. This is especially important when working with data. Sharing data with other students and teachers presents the possibility of someone in the group making an error that will affect the rest of the data set. Revision history can alleviate the possibility that a member of the group will make a grievous error. For example, if a group of students is working on a high school science fair project and they are collecting large amounts of data, then that data need to be accurate and secure. Each time an entry is made into a spreadsheet, it is saved along with the time and a note on what was revised. At any point in the project, the students can go back in time and see a previous version of the data to find and correct the errors. For a step-by-step process about how to see the revision history, look in Chapter 4.

Importance of Data and Technology

In the Common Core State Standards, students will be expected to work with data to help them make decisions and infer possible solutions to problems that they face. Data-driven decision making is an important skill to acquire. It helps students rely on statistics and data to make informed choices. Much like educators must take data into consideration to make decisions about learning, students need this skill for college and career. Using technology such as Google Spreadsheets can help students and teachers make sense of data and learn how tweaking certain aspects can change the outcomes. Google Spreadsheets is a tool that can quickly generate models for sound decision making. According to the Common Core State Standards, "Technology plays an important role in statistics and probability by making it possible to generate plots, regression functions, and correlation coefficients, and to simulate many possible outcomes in a short amount of time." Tools like this should be used in every class to analyze, predict, and share data that can help mold the understanding of the subject.

Many ideas in mathematics, science, history, and almost every subject taught in school can be explained by observing data and using the data to tell why the event is true. For example, the Common Core State Standards for Mathematics starting in middle school directs students to start to make sense of data and its role in decision making. Consider **Table 6.2** for a sixth-grade Statistics and Probability standard.

Table 6.2 Mathematics Standard Statistics and Probability Sixth Grade
Understand that a set of data collected to answer a statistical question has a distribution, which can be described by its center, spread, and overall shape.

LESSON IN FOCUS

Collecting Data: Heights of Students

The teacher will . . .

1. Create a Google Spreadsheet in advance, naming a column: Height in Centimeters.
2. Share the spreadsheet with the class.
3. Instruct students to make a copy of the spreadsheet, taking ownership and renaming the file.
4. Assign the students a cell number to enter their data.
5. Instruct students to take measurements of group members and place their heights in centimeters into the appropriate cell.

After the data are collected, students can have rich discussions about the variance and recognize clusters of data points by analyzing the data. Going further the students can make a chart explaining their findings and describing the distribution of the curve. Learn how to make charts from simple data sets later in this chapter.

Download As

Download as is a common command in Google Docs. It lets the user download the file being created as a format other than the Google Docs format. The Docs programs

Documents, Presentations, Spreadsheets, and Drawings have this feature. The only difference among the programs is what type of file is available for downloading. For example, in Google Spreadsheets, only some of the compatible spreadsheet file types are supported. If a teacher were making a Google Spreadsheet that she wanted to share with another person that did not use Google Docs, the teacher may **download as** any of the available formats to share with them through an e-mail attachment or other storage device. Being able to **download as** these file formats makes Google Docs easy to share with others. Download as PDF is critical because sometimes users need to share data without the fear of the data being changed. Downloading a Google Spreadsheet as a PDF creates a file that is difficult to edit. Expensive software is required to tamper with the data. See the list below for available **download as** formats.

- CSV
- HTML
- TXT
- Excel
- OpenOffice
- PDF

E-mail as Attachment

The e-mail as attachment feature enables the user to choose the file type directly from the e-mail as attachment window. In other office software, the user must do the lengthy process of downloading the file to the hard drive, remembering where it was stored, opening the e-mail application, drafting the e-mail, and attaching the document to the e-mail. These steps are cumbersome and time consuming. With Google Docs, click **File,** then **E-mail as attachment** to instantly send the file to a recipient. The user can even choose what file type of attachment to send. Notice in Figure 6.3 that Google Docs format is not listed as a file type in which to e-mail; this is because Google uses a different approach to distributing files, called sharing. To refresh yourself on how to share files, review previous chapters.

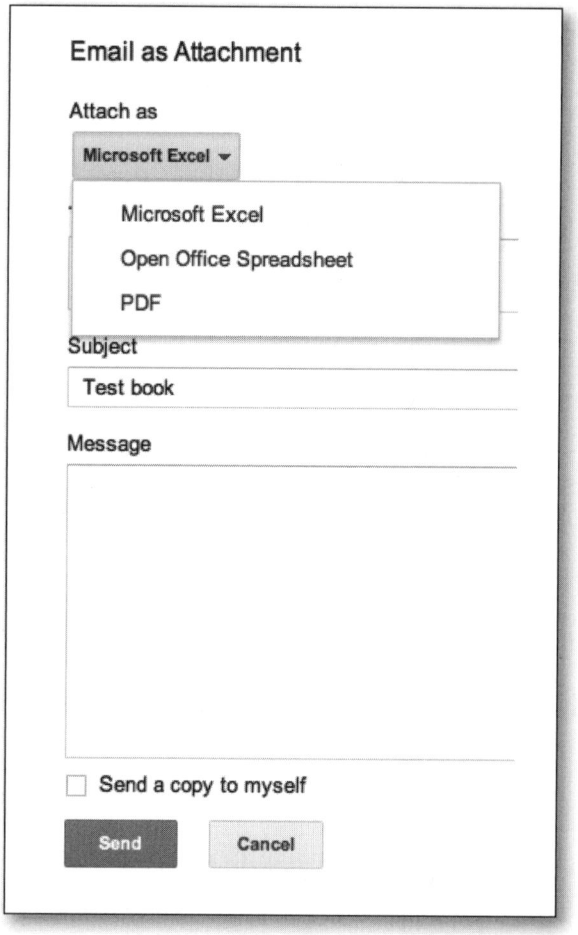

Print

Printing from Google Spreadsheets involves a slightly different procedure than printing from other Google Docs programs. Google Spreadsheets have different print settings. For example, the user can have multiple sheets open in one spreadsheet document and print only from the selected one. Also, there are options for printing gridlines, landscape, portrait, and so on. See Figure 6.4 for detailed printing information.

Figure 6.3   E-mail as Attachment

Email as Attachment

Attach as

Microsoft Excel ▾

Microsoft Excel

Open Office Spreadsheet

PDF

Subject

Test book

Message

☐ Send a copy to myself

Send   Cancel

Figure 6.4	Print Settings

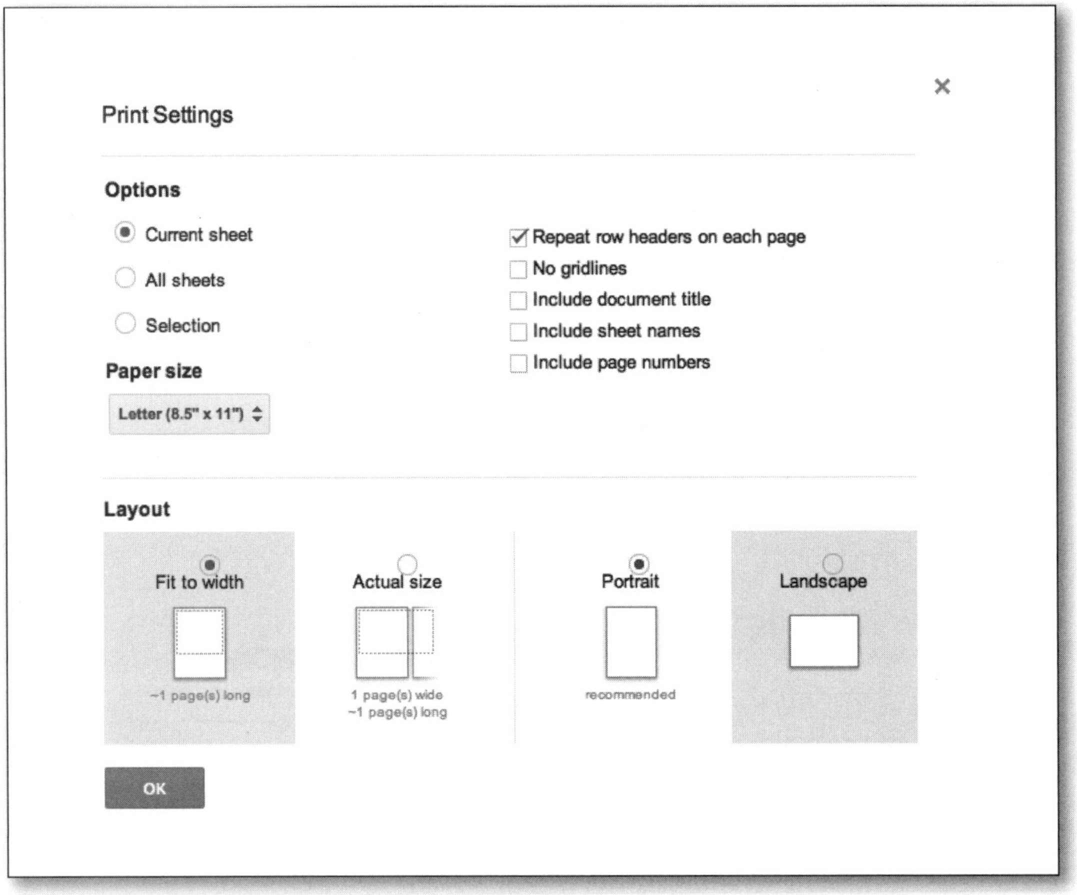

Print Settings   ✕

Options

◉ Current sheet   ☑ Repeat row headers on each page
◯ All sheets   ☐ No gridlines
◯ Selection   ☐ Include document title
                         ☐ Include sheet names
Paper size   ☐ Include page numbers

Letter (8.5" x 11") ⇕

Layout

◉ Fit to width   ◯ Actual size   ◉ Portrait   ◯ Landscape

~1 page(s) long   1 page(s) wide   recommended
                  ~1 page(s) long

OK

EDIT MENU

Edit buttons are available such as copy, paste, undo, and redo. "Chapter 4: Documents" covers these in detail. This chapter will cover the Google Spreadsheets-specific edit commands.

Paste Special

Copying and pasting from cells in a spreadsheet will copy everything in the cell, including text, color, and formulas. Sometimes teachers and students need to copy and paste only particular attributes of cells in a spreadsheet. For example, a student may want to replicate only the cell's background color. To paste special, follow these steps:

1. Copy the cell.

2. Select **Paste special** from the **Edit** menu in the toolbar.

3. Choose which paste special command from the list in Table 6.3.

Table 6.3	Paste Special Explanation
Paste values only	**This option only pastes the text within the cell.**
Paste **format** only	Paste **format** will leave all text and formulas out of the cell. Use this option to paste formatting options like center, left and right justified, as well as bold, italic, underline, color of cell, and borders.
Paste all **except borders**	This option will not paste the borders. It will leave formulas, cell formats, and text in the cell.
Paste **formula** only	This option will only paste formulas and will not paste the outcomes of the formulas.
Paste **data validation** only	Only paste **data validation.** Look for the **Data** section for more on **data validation.**
Paste **conditional formatting** only	Only paste **conditional formatting.** Look at the conditional formatting section for more information.

Delete Rows and Columns

To delete a row or column, highlight the row or column to delete, select **Edit,** then select **Delete row or column**.

VIEW MENU

The **View** menu helps the user control aspects of the spreadsheet making it easy to navigate. Choose from show gridlines, formula, and toggle between compact and full-screen views. Read the following section for ways to improve the user experience.

List View Versus Normal View

The user can choose between two views in Google Spreadsheets. The normal view is the default option. In this option, students and teachers have the full range of tools available. For example, the user can rename sheets, format data, highlight cells, use auto fill, edit functions, add comments, add new collaborators and viewers, or insert images, charts, and gadgets. One drawback to normal view is that it is complicated with many variations and controls that may confuse elementary students. Instead, the users can work with list view. List view offers a much simpler experience with spreadsheets. Data entry is easy and straightforward, making it great for the novice user to enter and sort data. List view also lets the user share the document for collaboration with more than 50 users at a time, and this light version can be loaded quickly with slow Internet connections. It also provides optional data security to protect the data from students and others who may accidently make changes to it. For example, when sharing data with groups of students, the teacher may want to enable the students to sort and filter the data but not allow them to change the data. This is great for teaching elementary students about sorting because no matter what they do they cannot change the contents of the cells. To enable list view, click **List view** from the **View** menu.

List view and mobile devices. List view is also the default view when editing a Google Spreadsheet on mobile devices. This is useful for students who need to collect data on the go. For example, a fifth-grade class studying data collection and measurement has an assignment that requires them to make one-square-meter sampling grids on the school's lawn to collect data about plants found there. Students are able to use spreadsheets to collect their data while outside (as long as the Wi-Fi signal is present) on a mobile device such as iPod Touch, iPad, or Android tablet. Follow these steps to use this lesson idea:

LESSON IN FOCUS

What Grows Where We Play

The teacher will . . .

1. Prepare the spreadsheet ahead of time, making headings for the columns of plants that they may encounter in their class's square.

2. Instruct the students to log in to their Google Docs account on the mobile device and make a copy of the spreadsheet.

The students will . . .

1. Log in to their Google account on their mobile device.

2. Make a copy of the spreadsheet and rename it.

3. Collect data about the plants found in their sampling square.

Properties of List View

- Default for mobile device Google Spreadsheet editing
- Simpler data entry for novice users
- Read-only sharing that can be sorted and filtered. This is similar to **download as** PDF. The PDF cannot be manipulated for sorting, and the data cannot be changed by the person with whom they are shared. List view can prohibit the data from being changed but will allow sorting and filtering.

Early Grade Data Collection

Collecting data using spreadsheets can be a great activity for elementary students. The Common Core State Standards focus in K–5 on the collection and representation of data on line plots and bar graph and on collecting data with the use of a measurement device. Starting in the sixth grade, students will be asked to "develop understanding of statistical variability" and "summarize and describe distributions." The progression for sixth graders is to analyze the data that they learned to collect in K–5 while grappling with measures of center and how different data sets can have different distributions. Using spreadsheets in the early grades will help students become familiar with entering data into cells and help them learn how to draw inference from it. Starting in third grade, students will be asked to draw a bar graph representing data that they have collected. Using Google Spreadsheets can help students represent data with tools as mentioned in the Mathematical Practice Standard 5. It will be good practice to have a mix of bar graphs drawn by hand and made with programs like Google Spreadsheets. The good thing about using Spreadsheets is that the students will be able to correct errors or change their data and see the bar graph change as a result without having to draw it again. For example, a student in the third grade is measuring insects collected on a recent science activity and makes a spreadsheet with the teacher's help. Students can use Google Spreadsheets as a collection place for data that is easily saved into their Google Drive and can use the data to draw their bar graphs and line plots by hand or place the data into charts (see Table 6.4).

Table 6.4	Represent and Interpret Data Third Grade

Generate measurement data by measuring lengths using rulers marked with halves and fourths of an inch. Show the data by making a line plot, where the horizontal scale is marked off in appropriate units—whole numbers, halves, or quarters.

Freeze Rows/Freeze Columns

Users can freeze up to 10 rows and five columns. Freezing a column or row will hold some of the data in place as the user scrolls down the page. For example, headings in a spreadsheet that contain hundreds of rows could be held in place, making it easier for users to input information into the correct column. Select **Freeze** from the **View** menu.

INSERT MENU

Choose **Insert** to place a row, column, a new sheet, or comments about particular cells into a spreadsheet. Comments are an important part of Google Apps for Education. They can be used by collaborating groups to make notes or suggestions to other people managing the spreadsheet and can be used by teachers to give feedback for grading. Teachers that take advantage of comments when giving feedback for grading will decrease the amount of papers to take home. For example, teachers can make comments grading certain aspects of the Spreadsheets from anywhere there is an Internet connection. Open the shared spreadsheet, and begin giving feedback and record the score in the grade book. If your school does not have an electronic grade-book application, create your own in spreadsheets. Using Google Spreadsheets as grade-book software provides powerful sharing capabilities. Parents and teachers can stay in constant contact concerning the students' progress through shared Spreadsheets. Domain administrators may benefit from giving parents school Google Apps for Education accounts so teachers, students, and parents can collaborate on students' progress.

Function

Functions allow for the user to perform calculations of the data in a selected block of cells. For example, if a teacher were using Spreadsheets as a grade book and wanted to quickly find the average of a particular set of grades, then the teacher could choose the function called AVE. Another example for the use of function is performing fast calculations of data that will allow the student to quickly adjust their ideas based on new or updated information. To calculate the data sets, follow these steps:

1. Highlight the block of cells in the sheet in which to perform a function.

2. Select **Insert,** then one of the functions listed in Figure 6.5.

   a. Sum, Average, Count, Max, and Min are listed in the **Insert** drop-down menu. However, this is not near the end to the function list. Click on **More . . .** as seen in Figure 6.5 to see descriptions of the hundreds of functions available.

Figure 6.5 Function List

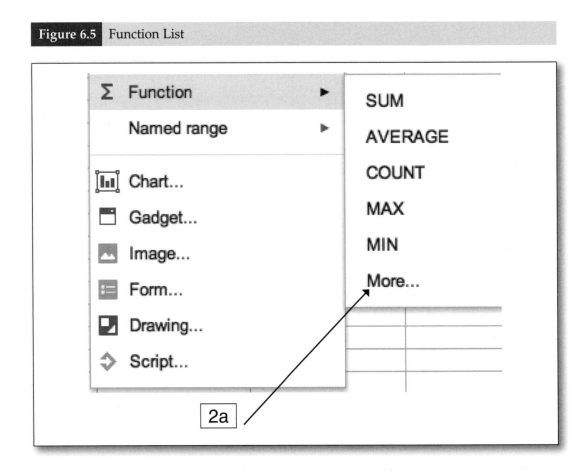

An alternative way to insert functions is to place an equals sign in the cell followed by the first few letters of the function's name as shown in Figure 6.6. For a more detailed list of functions and their descriptions, click on **complete list of functions** or go to http://goo.gl/CwEKL in a Web browser. Many high-level mathematics functions are located in this menu.

| Figure 6.6 | Inserting a Function Directly in a Cell |

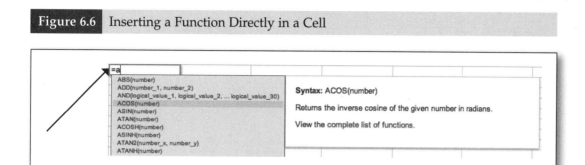

Chart

Inserting charts is one of the most used parts of any spreadsheet program. Taking the data and displaying it graphically can help the students and their audiences conceptualize the data. The Common Core State Standards have a lot to say about data representations. For example, according to the Standards for Mathematical Practice 5 concerning modeling and data, "When making mathematical models, they know that technology can enable them to visualize the results of varying assumptions, explore consequences, and compare predictions with data." Teaching students how to use spreadsheets can help them organize and model their data sets.

To insert a chart, there must be data in the spreadsheet. To create charts, follow these steps:

1. Collect data to display in a chart in a Google Spreadsheet.

2. Highlight the data to be displayed in a chart.

3. Select **Chart** from the **Inset** menu to reveal Figure 6.7.

4. Click on the recommended charts Google provides based on the type of data, or click the **Charts** tab to reveal more types of charts.

   a. Spreadsheets automatically recognizes the data in the sheet and gives the user suggestions for what type of chart may be most appropriate for the data.

5. Click the **Customize** tab to give the chart a title, name the x and y axes, and changes color options.

The box in Figure 6.7 displays the chart preview. The editor will automatically select all cells that contain data and make a preview of the graph. There are currently 26 chart types but more are added periodically. Chart types range from bar graphs to maps. If cities or addresses are in the spreadsheet, they can be mapped along with the data accompanying them in the adjacent cell. For example, an elementary class studying weather in science can understand the tendency of temperatures to be cooler in the northern latitudes. Students can create these data sets and make the graph themselves, and overlay that into a map directly in Google Spreadsheets. The student now has an interactive map that contains data about temperature. This map could be exported as a picture file or be embedded live in a website. When embedded, the information is updated or added to the graph or map and will change accordingly. See an example of this interactive map at http://goo.gl/vw8x8.

Figure 6.7 Insert a Chart

When the chart is finished, it is inserted on the sheet containing the data it was made from. After the chart is inserted, it can be manipulated further by choosing the options located in Figure 6.8.

Figure 6.8 The Inserted Chart

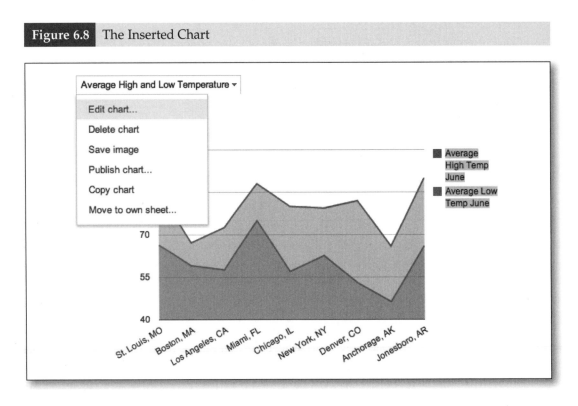

Figure 6.8 highlights what the user can do with the chart after it is inserted. The commands in the drop-down list in Figure 6.8 are common and need little explanation,

except **Publish chart.** Publishing a chart is a great way to share the information collected by the students.

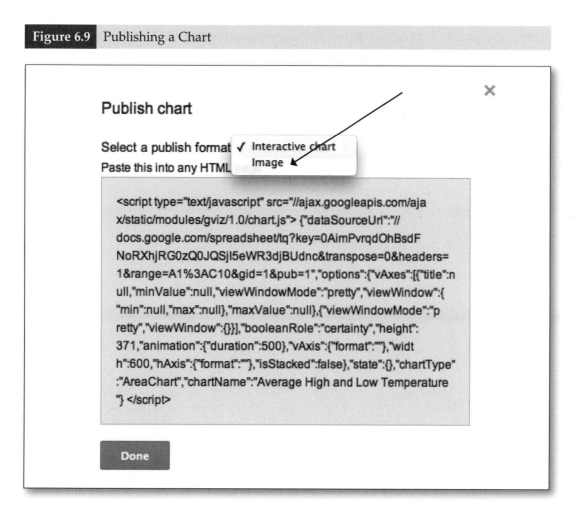

Figure 6.9	Publishing a Chart

Figure 6.9 gives the option to publish the chart as an interactive chart or an image. Interactive charts will change depending on the data entered in the spreadsheet in which it is attached, and the user can hover over data points and see more information. Embed code looks complicated, but all the user has to do is copy and paste it into a webpage's HTML box. If this is too complicated, choose to publish the chart as an image as shown in Figure 6.9. That image may be inserted into Google Presentations and Google Documents.

Gadgets

Gadgets are similar to Gmail Labs. Google maintains most, but third-party companies operate some gadgets so they may be unstable or may not work exactly as advertised, but this rarely is the case. Gadgets are used to display data differently than charts. The traditional charts and graphs offered by traditional office software are mostly available within Google Spreadsheets, but Google Spreadsheets makes the data come alive with sharing and collaboration. Gadgets offer exciting new ways to display information that are dynamic and eye catching.

Gadgets and interactive charts fit perfectly into the Common Core State Standards for mathematics. Much like living documents talked about in Chapter 4, interactive gadgets and charts allow the information from ongoing experiments to be continuously published. There is no need to repeat the creation of the charts and gadgets when new information is available or is edited. The Mathematical Practice Standard 5 says, "When making mathematical models, they know that technology can enable them to visualize the results of varying assumptions, explore consequences, and compare predictions with data." The main idea in this standard is that students need technology to compare their results depending on the data that are generated. Students will need the ability to quickly reproduce and compare data with models that change over time and be exposed to different types of graphs and charts that can take data representation to the college and career levels. To insert a gadget, follow these steps:

1. Select **Gadget** from the **Insert menu gadget** to reveal the gadget list.

2. Choose which data representation best fits the needs of the user.

To see a complete list of Google Spreadsheet gadgets, go to http://goo.gl/ AADA6 in a Web browser. Gadgets can be published just like publishing charts.

Drawings

Drawings can be used to create flow charts and other graphic organizers to help explain the data on the spreadsheet. Drawings are virtually unlimited in their creative capacity. Encourage students to draw or create graphical representations of the data that are not part of charts or gadgets. Students can benefit from expressing the data in their own creative ways.

Consider this excerpt from the Common Core State Standards: "When reading scientific and technical texts, students need to be able to gain knowledge from challenging texts that often make extensive use of elaborate diagrams and data to convey information and illustrate concepts." Use spreadsheets in conjunction with drawings to create and share information in creative ways.

Scripts

Scripts are automations that can be inserted into Google Spreadsheets to make mundane tasks operate on their own. For example, the script Flubaroo can automatically grade a Google Spreadsheet that has been generated from a quiz created in Google Forms. To learn more about forms and self-grading quizzes, see the next chapter. To install scripts, follow these steps:

1. Click on **Tools,** then **Script gallery** in the toolbar to reveal Figure 6.10.

2. Choose from the list of categories to find scripts that fit your needs.

3. Search scripts with the search bar.

Figure 6.10 Script Gallery

FORMAT MENU

The Format tab in Spreadsheets has many of the same commands as the other Google Docs programs. The exceptions are **Number** and **Conditional formatting.** Number relates to how the numbers are displayed in the cells. Look in the box in Figure 6.11 to see the different ways numbers can be recorded in cells. For example, users can choose to have their data be reported in scientific notation using options in the number command. Upon typing in 93,000,000 miles (the distance from Earth to the Sun), the cell would automatically display 9.3E+7 if the number command were invoked. Look at the eighth-grade standard in Table 6.5 to gain insight about scientific notation and technology.

Pay close attention to the last sentence in Table 6.5 about scientific notation that is generated with technology. Students in the digital age will be increasingly reliant on computer technology to display and help interpret data. Students must realize that writing scientific notation with the "E" representing the phrase "times ten to the" is equivalent to the written form of 9.3×10^7. Google Spreadsheets uses the form 9.3E+7 to report scientific notation.

Table 6.5 Expressions and Equations Eighth Grade

Perform operations with numbers expressed in scientific notation, including problems where both decimal and scientific notation are used. Use scientific notation and choose units of appropriate size for measurements of very large or very small quantities (e.g., use millimeters per year for seafloor spreading). Interpret scientific notation that has been generated by technology.

Figure 6.11	Displaying Numbers

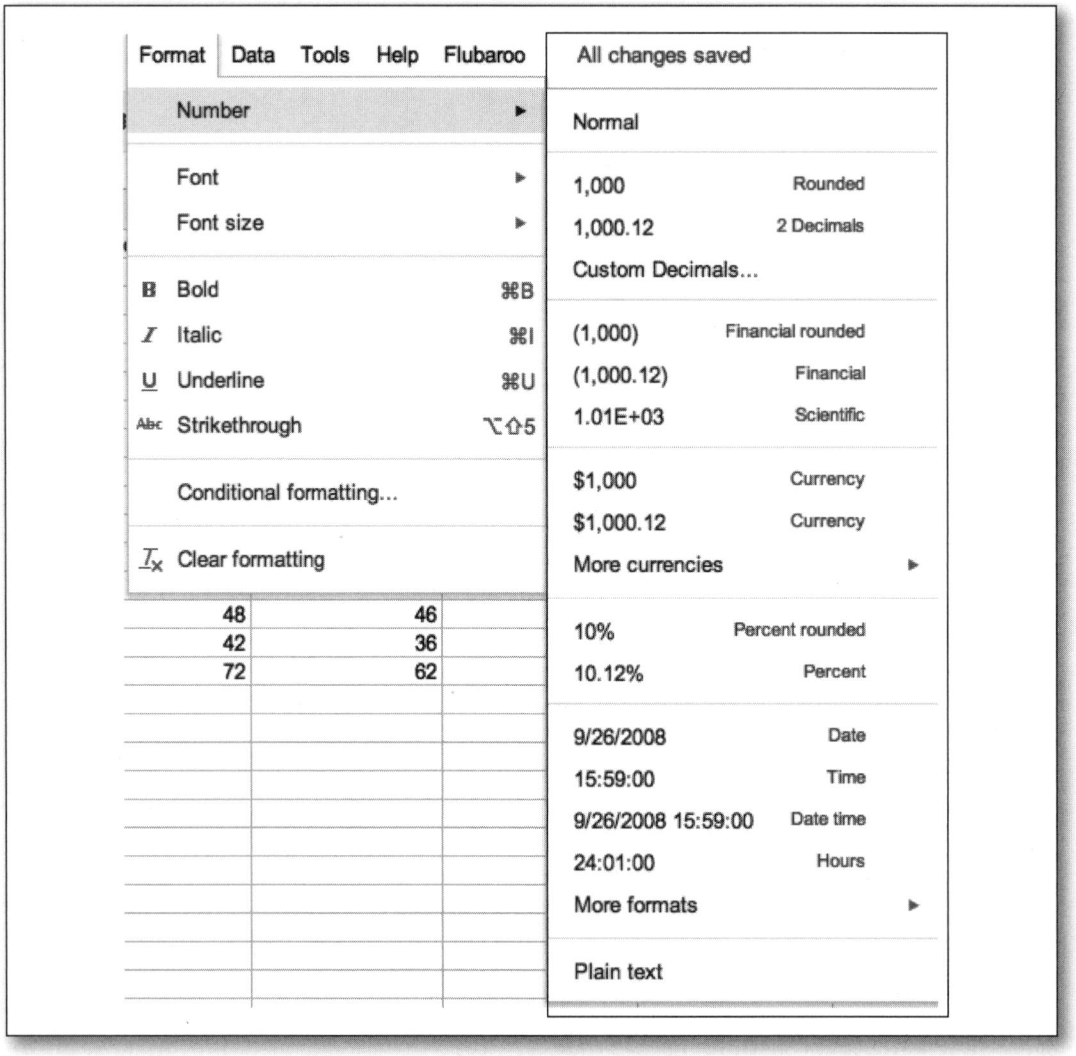

Format	Data	Tools	Help	Flubaroo		All changes saved

Number	▶	Normal
Font	▶	1,000 — Rounded
Font size	▶	1,000.12 — 2 Decimals
		Custom Decimals...
B Bold	⌘B	(1,000) — Financial rounded
I Italic	⌘I	(1,000.12) — Financial
U̲ Underline	⌘U	1.01E+03 — Scientific
A̶b̶c̶ Strikethrough	⌥⇧5	$1,000 — Currency
Conditional formatting...		$1,000.12 — Currency
*I*ₓ Clear formatting		More currencies ▶

48	46
42	36
72	62

10%   Percent rounded
10.12%   Percent

9/26/2008   Date
15:59:00   Time
9/26/2008 15:59:00   Date time
24:01:00   Hours
More formats ▶

Plain text

Conditional Formatting

Conditional formatting lets the user apply background and text color rules to cells. If the cell contains a particular text or number, the cell background or text will change color.

For example, a math teacher who has assigned homework to be entered into a spreadsheet can look for certain answers in the sheet by applying conditional formatting. Highlight the cells that the user wishes to check with conditional formatting and put in the parameters. Choose a background or text color to make the answers standout. For example, a math teacher can create self-checking homework assignments by creating a spreadsheet where the students will place their answers to their homework problems. The conditional formatting will be set ahead of time for the correct answer. If the cell matches exactly as the predetermined formatting set by the teacher, the cell will turn a particular color, denoting the answer is correct. If the cell does not turn color the answer is wrong and the student needs to try again. Assignments like these could be used as guided practice for homework. Students are using this as a self-check only. In this example, students will be required to turn in their written work along with their shared spreadsheet.

It is important to set the master sheet made by the teacher as a view-only file in share settings; this will force the students to make a copy of the file so their answers do not appear on the master sheet. This way, students can't edit it until they make a copy and name the file accordingly. Teachers of other subjects can use this feature to create self-grading quizzes. To explore conditional formatting, follow these steps:

1. Select **Conditional formatting** from the **Format** menu in the toolbar to reveal Figure 6.12.

2. Click the drop-down menu to reveal formatting options.

3. Click the check boxes next to **Text** and **Background,** and choose a color to display these settings.

4. Click **Save rules** or **Add another rule.** The rules are applied for the particular cell only.

Figure 6.12 Conditional Formatting

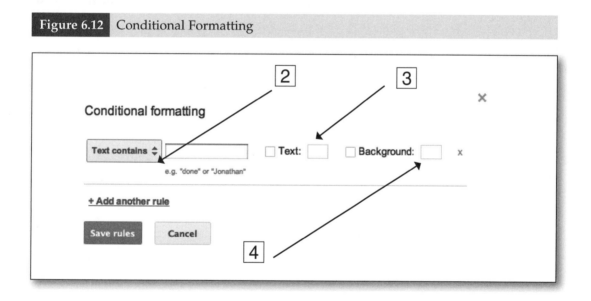

DATA MENU

The **Data** menu holds commands that let the user manipulate data. Sort, Pivot tables, and data validation are discussed here. Use the **Data** menu to make sense of data.

Sort A to Z and Sort Z to A

Sorting by alphabet and reverse alphabet is available. Remember that the cells must be highlighted to sort or filter the data. To sort the data, click **Data** from the toolbar, then click **Sort** as shown in Figure 6.13.

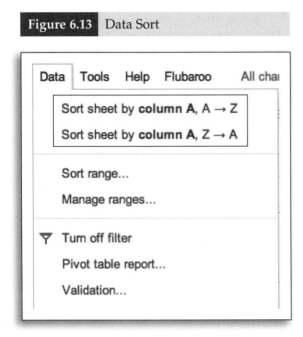

Figure 6.13 Data Sort

Pivot Tables

Pivot tables allow the user to pull a quick summary from a huge data set. They are ideal for dealing with large amounts of data and picking out certain aspects to focus on. Teachers and administrators could use pivot tables to disaggregate testing data. See more about pivot tables at http://goo.gl/A5Mqy.

Validation

Validation controls what data are entered into spreadsheets by the collaborators and the user. Validation can help users avoid entering text or numbers into cells that do not match the predefined criteria. Using this tool can allow for a comment to pop up when entering data, reminding the user what type of data are appropriate for the cell. For example, teachers can set validation on cells when assigning students to make spreadsheets. Giving hints to students about what data type to enter can help them feel more comfortable with spreadsheets.

TOOLS MENU

Spelling, notification rules, and protect sheet are the most used **Tools** commands used by educators. Notification rules may be enabled to alert the user when changes are made to a spreadsheet. For example, in large districts a spreadsheet for technology inventory may be maintained by the building instructional facilitators. The district technology coordinator will need to be made aware of changes to the inventory and manage users' rights to edit. Collaborative spreadsheets are a great way to keep everyone informed. Follow these steps to activate notifications:

1. Select **Notification rules** from the **Tools** menu in the toolbar to reveal Figure 6.14.

2. Choose the parameters that will notify the owner and collaborators of the sheet.

   Use **Protect sheet** to determine who can edit the data (Figure 6.15). Follow these steps to protect the sheet:

1. Select **Protect sheet** from the **Tools** menu to reveal Figure 6.14.

2. Select who is allowed to edit the sheet.

3. Type e-mail or names in the box to allow only those people to edit.

4. Click [Done] to set the rules.

| Figure 6.14 | Set Notification Rules |

Set notification rules   ✕

Help

Notify me at mikeyjoex@gmail.com when...

☐ Any changes are made

☐ Anything on this sheet is changed: Sheet2 ⬍

☐ Any of these cells are changed:

cell range   ▦

☐ Collaborators are added or removed

☐ A user submits a form

Notify me with...

☐ Email - daily digest

☐ Email - right away

[Save]   [Cancel]

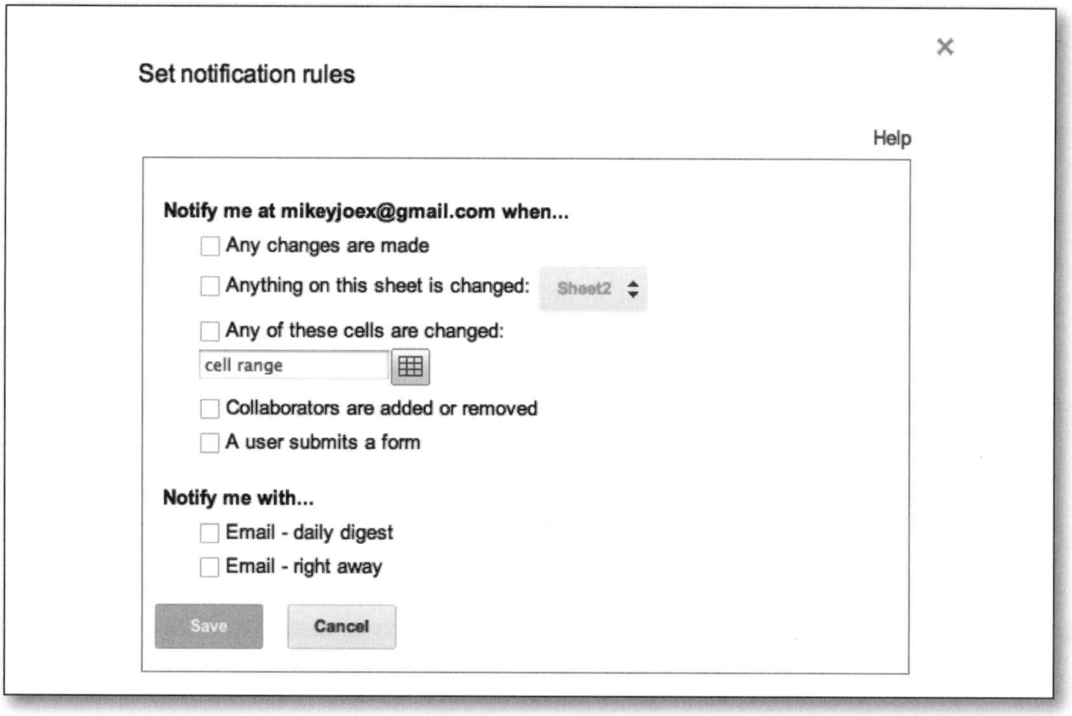

| Figure 6.15 | Protect Sheet |

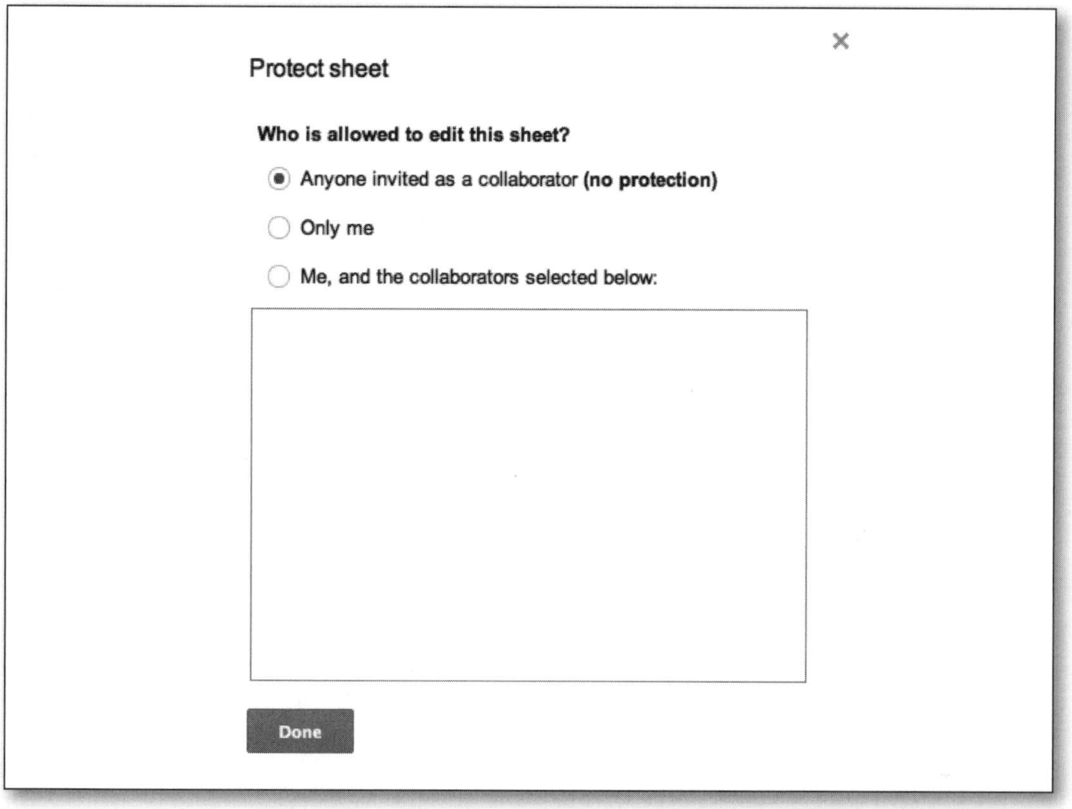

Protect sheet   ✕

Who is allowed to edit this sheet?

◉ Anyone invited as a collaborator **(no protection)**

○ Only me

○ Me, and the collaborators selected below:

[Done]

AUTO FILL

Auto fill lets the user repeat the contents of a cell and can complete a pattern in the subsequent cells highlighted. This feature uses Google search to find patterns in the cells highlighted and will automatically fill in the cells with the pattern. For example, a teacher in fifth-grade social studies class may be studying states and their characteristics. Teachers and students can quickly make lists of common information. Follow these steps to see the magic of auto fill.

1. Type at least three similar items such as states in a column of separate cells like in Figure 6.16.

2. Highlight the text and then click the small blue square in the bottom right-hand corner while holding down **Option** for Mac and **Alt** for PC.

3. Select the cells that you would like to populate and then release the buttons.

Figure 6.16	Auto Fill

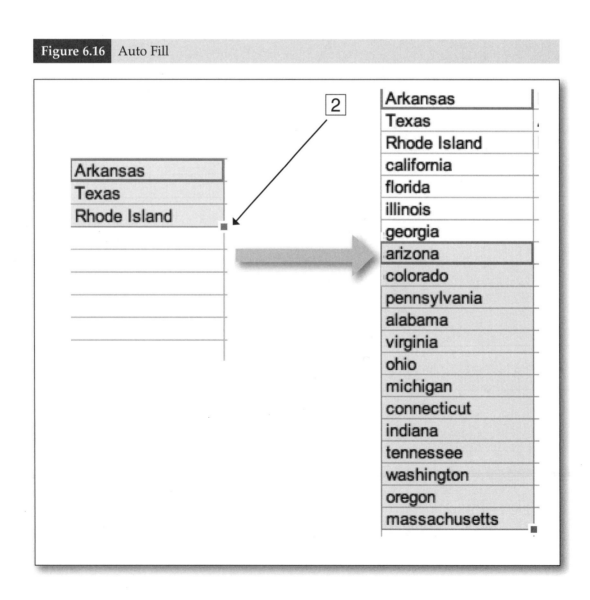

The result is that the list is automatically populated within the cells that were highlighted. If the user does not hold down **Option** or **Alt,** the contents of the cell are repeated for the selection. The pattern will not appear.

SUMMARY

Google Spreadsheets is the most complex program in Google Docs. It houses a powerful spreadsheet program that can rival any statistical package with user-friendly tools that people have come to expect from traditional office software. The difference is in the collaboration. Spreadsheets can share and collaborate on data projects from within the room or around the world. Use tables, charts, and gadgets to publish real-time data to websites and other spreadsheets to make student findings real and authentic in purpose. The Common Core State Standards pushes students to use appropriate tools when thinking mathematically. When students take the time to collect, analyze, and report findings with data, they become better decision makers. Google Spreadsheets gives the student one more tool to become college and career ready. Keep reading to explore another data collection device: Google Forms.

RESOURCE LINK

Lesson Plans

Grade Level	Lesson Plan Title	Digital copy found at the link. Lesson plans with numbers are in order in the resource section.	
Elementary School	Introduction to Scientific Method Mary Fran Lynch	http://goo.gl/WtCm6	Online only
Middle School	iTravel Vacation	http://goo.gl/KZuI5	#8
High School	Collaborative Lab Experience Cheryl Davis	http://goo.gl/LzaTz	Online only

For additional resources, including lesson plans, videos, and video tutorials, access this link:

■ http://goo.gl/QNVzT

7

Forms

KEY FEATURES

❖ Collect data from community and students

❖ Students collect data for projects

❖ Data are automatically sent to a Google Spreadsheet

❖ Gadgets and Charts of data

❖ Share with anyone through e-mail, URL, or social media

Google Forms is a Google App that can deliver data for decision making. This tool is ideal for gathering data from students and the community as well as delivering online assessments to students. Google Forms can collect any type of information electronically by being given access to the form's unique URL. The link may be shared through social media, e-mail, or embedded in a website. The data collected from Google Forms goes directly into a Google Spreadsheet, where it can be analyzed, organized, and displayed in Gadgets and charts. Choose from many themes to create a professional looking form with seven question types:

- Text
- Paragraph Text
- Choose From a List
- Checkboxes
- Multiple Choice
- Scale
- Grid

In this chapter, we will discuss Google Forms and its ability to gather information efficiently. The information collected can be anything that the user needs to know. Review the following for example form types:

- Self-grading student quiz
- Student survey for use in data collection
- Beginning of the year student information form
  - Collect interests, phone numbers, addresses, and other information that may help the teacher

- Faculty meeting sign-in form
- Discipline form that automatically e-mails parents, team teacher, and principal

ADVANTAGES OF FORMS

Google Forms offers an easy way to connect with the public's concerns by gathering relevant data from the community. School administrators can create questionnaires and surveys to obtain information about the community to inform decisions made by school officials. For example, many schools send home a parent survey to gather information from the parents about certain aspects of school life. A Google Form could be created and posted on the school's Facebook, Google+, or Twitter page. Posting these forms on public virtual spaces allows for easy data gathering. If the parents do not have access to a computer, provide it at school or suggest that they access the Google Form from their mobile device or direct them to the local public library.

Teachers are also in need of gathering data but in different ways. Educators in the classroom are bombarded with collecting data concerning student performance. For example, teachers are responsible for managing parent contact logs, students' grades, and teacher documentation about discipline and good behavior. Google Forms can be created to easily capture data about students. For example, teachers can create forms that will track specific students' grades, behavior, and assignments. This information can be e-mailed directly to the parents and shared with other teachers. The data collected in Google Forms give teachers and parents powerful insight about how their student is performing. Start by focusing on struggling students. Create forms that can track concerns raised by parents, teachers, and other school professionals, and share the information with other teachers on the team to craft a better educational experience for the child.

TECHNOLOGY-INFUSED TEACHING TIP

For advanced users, research Google Apps Script and Google Apps Script Gallery to find out how to automatically e-mail the parent the information gathered by the teacher. Every time the form is submitted, the program will automatically e-mail parents or anyone who might find the information useful from the user's school Gmail.

Managing Forms

Every Google Form is given a unique URL. When the URL is typed into any Web browser, the live form is ready to be taken. Save the URL as a bookmark or a favorite in your Web browser to get access to forms that are frequently used. Another option is to create a desktop icon linked to the form that automatically opens the form when clicked. For example, at my school, teachers have icons on their computers, smartphones, or tablets that are linked to the discipline referral Google Form. Another example is Mrs. Casey Kocher, a special education teacher. She uses forms to track her students' progress. She has eight special education students that she teaches all day. She is very busy throughout the day with her teaching duties, and she wants to collect data on her students' progress on certain skills. She has created a personalized Google Form for each of her students so she can track their progress daily. Instead of filling out the form on a laptop or desktop computer, she uses her iPhone. She has made a folder on her home screen that contains an app icon with the students' names that when tapped, opens the particular student's form using the Web browser on the iPhone. She is able to quickly collect students' progress with the mobile smartphone because all Google Forms can be taken anywhere there is an Internet connection. Android phones have the same shortcut feature. The data are automatically populating a Google Spreadsheet, where they are kept safe and ready for review.

Use Form Data in PLCs

Monitoring students' progress and collecting data with Google Forms is ideal for professional learning community (PLC) meetings. PLCs need this information to accurately assess problems and successes students are facing. Use the time to accurately discuss student's strengths and weaknesses and to formulate a path for success with other teachers on the team. A PLC without data is less effective. Use data from forms like in the example of Mrs. Kocher to talk about the student objectively based on the data and to make better decisions to improve the child's educational experience.

Students and Forms

The Common Core State Standards provided in Table 7.1 and Table 7.2 are good examples of why forms are important to get students college and career ready. According to the standards, students will "present information, findings and supporting evidence." They can authentically gather real information from peers, parents, and the community using Google Forms and use that information to make decisions and form conclusions about a given topic.

Gathering the information about real events and attitudes and presenting it making "strategic use of digital media and visual displays of data" is vital for college and a career. For example, high school student Ryan is working on a joint research project for English and mathematics classes. Ryan wants to research school safety. In addition to using appropriate print and digital sources such as primary sources of informational text, Ryan needs information from his peers and teachers to compare with his research. He wants to investigate how local attitudes of school safety compare with the nation as a whole. Ryan should use Google Forms to create an attitudes survey to collect real data from his school community. After the information is collected, Ryan can draw inferences with his knowledge of statistics and spreadsheets learned in mathematics class. This is done without printing one sheet of paper or counting tally marks of responses from paper forms. After the form was created, Ryan e-mailed his participant sample the link to the form. After the participants took the survey, all of the responses were collected in the attached spreadsheet. Giving students assignments that use technology will prepare them for life after high school.

College and career professionals are asked to perform analyses like this in their work or place of higher learning. Society asks these skills of the citizen. For example, choosing political candidates to support requires analysis of primary sources and the ability to make sense of peer's opinions to help form their own. The technology in Google Apps for Education connects information and people in a way that allows for deeper understanding of what is learned. That is one of the most important challenges the Common Core State Standards pose to educators. Teachers must have the courage to slow down, delve deeper into understanding, and explore concepts thoroughly.

Table 7.1	Presentation of Knowledge and Ideas Anchor Standards 4 and 5
4. Present information, findings, and supporting evidence such that listeners can follow the line of reasoning and the organization, development, and style are appropriate to task, purpose, and audience.	
5. Make strategic use of digital media and visual displays of data to express information and enhance understanding of presentations.	

Table 7.1 displays two Anchor Standards for Speaking and Listening. Using digital data-gathering techniques can save time and prepare students for college and a career.

In addition to the Anchor Standards in Table 7.1, consider Table 7.2 standards for high school writing in Ryan's scenario. To become college and career ready as defined by the Common Core State Standards, Ryan will need to focus on research projects and data gained through them to aid in making assertions in writing. In addition, data management that he will learn through the use of Google Forms and Google Spreadsheets can help him with his writing. Citing relevant data in writing only improves the work. The standards push students to take lessons from all disciplines in the completion of a project. The standard in Table 7.2 could be tackled in mathematics, science, or English language arts. Seek out ways to bring in other disciplines when planning projects.

Table 7.2	High School Writing Standard 11–12.W.7
7. Conduct short as well as more sustained research projects to answer a question (including a self-generated question) or solve a problem; narrow or broaden the inquiry when appropriate; synthesize multiple sources on the subject, demonstrating understanding of the subject under investigation.	

CREATING A GOOGLE FORM

The previous sections contained some ideas about how to start thinking about forms and how they could be used with students, faculty, and the community. The next sections are devoted to learning the processes to create forms and distribute them. To create a Google Form, follow these steps:

1. Open Google Drive.

2. Click the [CREATE] button to reveal the list of Google Docs.

3. Choose **Form** as shown in Figure 7.1.

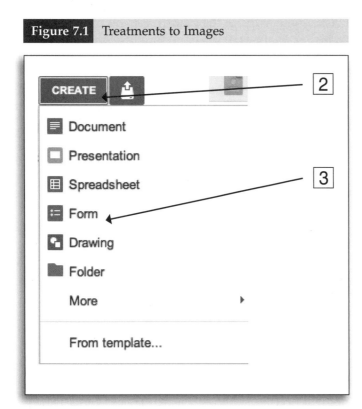

Figure 7.1   Treatments to Images

Theme

After creating a Google form, the next screen will ask the user to choose a theme for the background of the form. Google Forms gives the user many themes to choose from to make the forms look professional or fun. When a theme is chosen, it automatically changes the font, colors, and style that the live form will display. After the theme is chosen, the user will get a chance to preview the theme by clicking on 🌐 **View live form** located under the toolbar. While the user is editing the form, it will look plain with no colors or font changes, but when the form is viewed live, the theme will be displayed. Make forms stunning by choosing an appropriate theme to drive home your point.

EDITING A GOOGLE FORM

After the theme is chosen, the form is ready to edit. Start creating questions immediately using the steps in the following section. This is where the user can create the form and customize it to meet the needs of the project.

To create a Google Form, follow these steps:

1. Title the form by clicking on **Untitled form** like in the box in Figure 7.2. Underneath the title box, include any directions or help statements that will guide users to provide relevant information.

2. Type a question into the **Question Title** box.

3. Provide any **Help text** that will guide the response.

4. Select an appropriate **Question type** from the drop-down menu.

5. Click **Required Question** to force the user to answer the question. When this is checked, the user will not be able to submit his answers to be collected if he has not marked an answer.

6. Click **Done** to finalize the question.

7. Click **Add item** to add another question.

| Figure 7.2 | Edit Form Window |

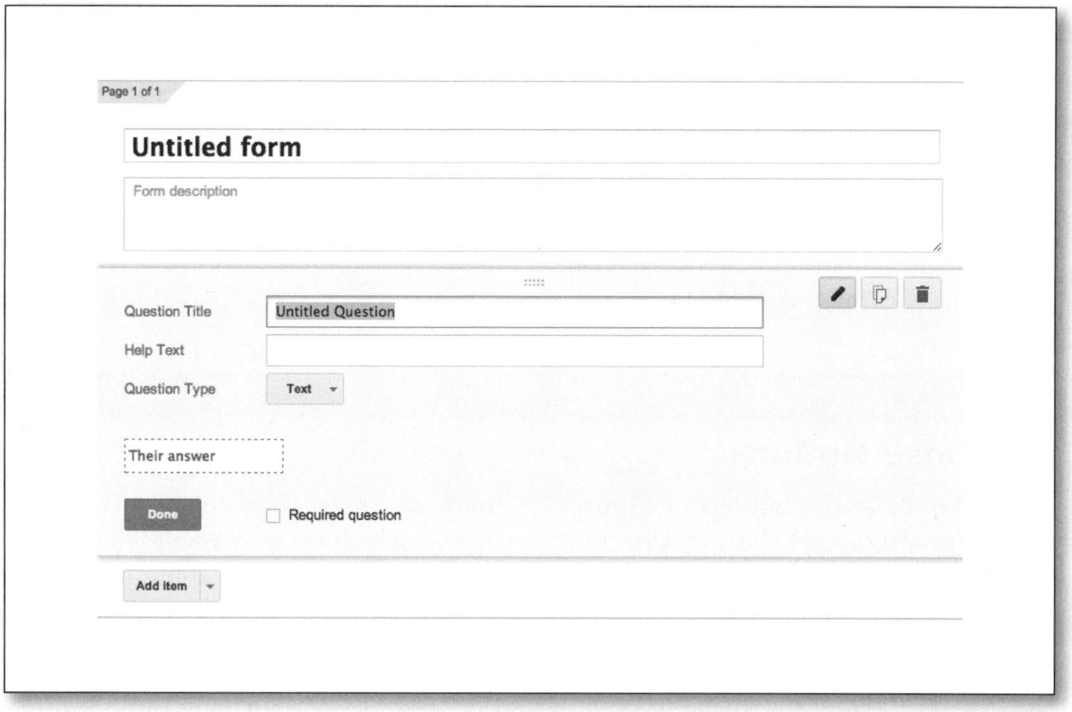

TECHNOLOGY-INFUSED TEACHING TIP

Copy long lists of multiple rows of text or answers to a form question, and paste them into the first box of the possible answers. This will automatically make each line of text a possible answer to a form question. Teachers use this when converting old quizzes to Google Forms. Watch the video found at this link to see it in action: http://goo.gl/Eoa1s.

CONFIRMATION PAGE

The confirmation page contains options that allow the user to choose how to collect and display the information gathered by the form. It is found below the question-editing boxes.

Confirmation Message

The confirmation message box shown in Figure 7.3 will allow the user to write a message that will appear after the user has submitted the form. This is helpful to the people taking the form because it assures them that someone has received their submission. Change the text in the confirmation box to thank the user for completing the form or to offer words of encouragement to students after a test or quiz.

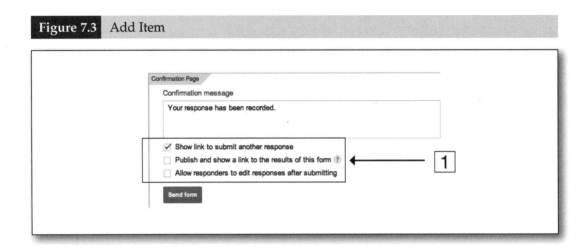

Figure 7.3   Add Item

Response Options

In box #1 at the bottom of **Figure 7.3,** there are three check boxes. These are important options for sharing. Checking or unchecking these boxes will have different effects on the way the data are collected. See the following explanations to get a better understanding of response options.

- Show link to submit another response
  - If checked, this will give the option for the respondent to submit another form. This is useful when students or teachers are engaged in collecting data. For example, students collecting data about heights of students in the classroom need to submit multiple entries to the form. Conversely, if the form is used for assessment, the teacher would make sure the box is unchecked to prevent the student from submitting multiple tests or quizzes.
- Publish or show a link to the results of this form
  - Check this box to show the response summary to the people who have completed the form. Be careful about selecting this option if usernames are automatically collected because some data might need to be confidential. This would most likely not be checked if the form is being used as an assessment for grading because all students' names and responses would be viewed by the whole class. However, if the teacher is using an informal assessment to review material, it may be appropriate.
- Allow users to edit responses after submitting
  - If checked, this will allow users to change their responses to an already submitted form. Teachers who are assigning quizzes with Google Forms would probably want this option unchecked because at any point after the students submitted the form, they will be able to change their answers to the quiz. Conversely, teachers can allow students to change their answers as an ongoing learning activity. Students and teachers can use revision history in the associated spreadsheet to see a timeline of responses, gaining insight on concepts learned.

More response options for students and teachers. In Google Apps for Education, teachers and students may require respondents to sign in to view the form and may require them to collect the usernames of respondents to the survey. These options are not available for regular Google Accounts. See Figure 7.4 and the following descriptions for more information.

- Require *yourschool.org* sign in to view this form
  - If checked, the form will not be accessible without first logging in to the user's school Google Apps for Education account. This prevents unwanted viewing and completion of the form by people outside the domain. This box is checked by default. If the user wishes to send surveys to parents or to community members who do not have a school Google Apps for Education account given by the domain administrator, uncheck the box. That way, anyone with the URL to the form can take it without having to sign in.
- Automatically collect respondent's school district username
  - If checked, the spreadsheet attached to the form will automatically collect the respondent's username. This option is great for teachers when using forms as assignments because it eliminates no-name papers. Every time a student submits a form, her username will appear in a column of cells on the accompanying spreadsheet. Use sort features to order the students' usernames alphabetically. The default sort is by timestamp; the first responses appear first on the spreadsheet. Sorting by username will help grading go smoothly because teachers can match the order of their grade book. When taking surveys that should remain anonymous, make sure the box is unchecked.

Figure 7.4	Sending Form to Others With E-mail

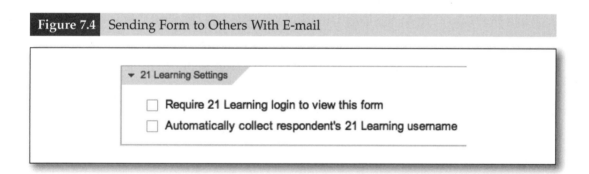

Send Form

The send form button is located at the bottom of the confirmation page as shown in Figure 7.3. Clicking the **Send form** button will reveal Figure 7.5, showing the different options for how the forms link will be distributed to users.

Link to Share

The link in the **Link to share** box is the unique URL for the form. Anyone who has this link may take the form (unless the user has checked the *require user to sign in to view the form* box like in Figure 7.4). Copy and paste the link in an e-mail, social networking site, or any place where it can be clicked on, and the user will be taken automatically to a webpage where he can complete the form. Use Google's URL Shortener, http://goo.gl, to shorten the link into a manageable URL to be shared

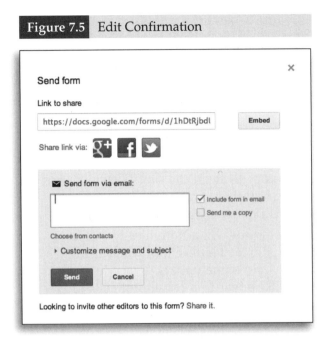

Figure 7.5   Edit Confirmation

with anyone. For example, a teacher could create a quiz and shorten the URL, then write the URL on the board for the students to copy into the address bar of their browsers. Shortening the URL is ideal any time a person must physically type the URL into the address bar in a Web browser. Learn more about http://goo.gl and shortening URLs in Chapter 11.

Send the Form Through E-mail

Sharing the form with people is easy with Google Forms. The user can e-mail the form to any e-mail address regardless of whether or not she uses Google. The recipient of the form is not required to have a Google Apps account unless the user checked the box *Require School District sign-in to view this form.* For example, a teacher who wants to assign a quiz to particular classes will create and e-mail the form to the student groups. Choose which class periods to e-mail the form to and click **Send.** Follow these steps to share the form by e-mail:

1. Click **Send form** from the **Confirmation page** box as shown in Figure 7.4.

2. Add e-mail addresses into the box as shown in Figure 7.5.

    a. Separate multiple e-mail addresses with commas or click the **Choose from contacts** option to select groups or other contacts.

3. Click **Customize message and subject** to give the message a subject and body.

4. Place a checkmark in the box **Include form in e-mail.**

5. Click **Send.**

TECHNOLOGY-INFUSED TEACHING TIP

Quick-response (QR) codes work well with Google Forms. Create the form and shorten the URL with http://goo.gl. Click on **Details** after it is shortened to reveal the QR code for the link to the form. The uses are limitless with the QR code. The code is an image file that can be copied, e-mailed, faxed, or printed on anything. When the code is read by a smartphone or tablet, the user will be taken directly to the live form. Print the code on T-shirts, coffee mugs, or letters to parents. Get the word out with QR codes!

When using e-mail to share the form, there are two ways for students to take the quiz following the previous example. In the first option, if the teacher checked the box **Include form in e-mail** like in Figure 7.5, the quizzes' questions would be embedded in the body of the e-mail. The student would take the quiz directly in the e-mail and submit the responses back to the spreadsheet that the teacher is maintaining for grading. Forms taken in the e-mail will not have the theme displayed. The second option allows the teacher to e-mail only the link to the form by unchecking the box **Include form in e-mail.** After the student has received the e-mail, the student will click the link opening a new Web browser window. In this option, the student will see the theme associated with the form.

TOOLBARS IN GOOGLE FORMS

Most of the toolbars in Google Forms are the same ones found in the other programs in Google Drive. The menus File, Edit, View, and Insert are easy to understand because of discussions in previous chapters. The unique menu in Google Forms is **Responses.** Responses manages how the information is collected using Google Forms. Look at Figure 7.6 and the description for more information.

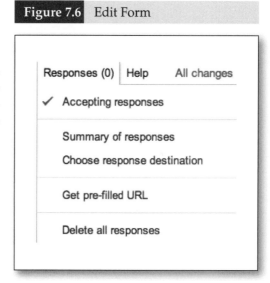

Figure 7.6 Edit Form

Accepting Responses

If Accepting responses is checked like in Figure 7.6, then the form will allow respondents to submit data. If this is not checked, the respondent will get a message saying that the form is no longer accepting data.

Summary of Responses

Responses from participants who completed the form are continuously being collected into the form in real time. Click **See responses** to view the responses to the form. Summary view automatically creates simple charts and graphs that describe the data in the spreadsheet. Students and teachers do not have to learn how to create charts and graphs in spreadsheets to see the data graphically. This is great for elementary students who need immediate results without having to learn complicated spreadsheet commands. To see the data in the spreadsheet, open Google Drive and search for a spreadsheet that has the same file name as the form. Use the commands learned in Chapter 6 to create visually stunning Gadgets and charts. The Common Core State Standards Mathematical Practice Standard 5 calls for students to use appropriate tools wisely. Also, Anchor Standard 7 for Reading states that students should "integrate and evaluate content presented in diverse media and formats, including visually and quantitatively, as well as in words." Standards in this anchor starting in Grade 4 specifically call for students to "quantitatively" use "charts, graphs and information on webpages" to understand what is going on in the text. Using forms and spreadsheets is good practice.

Choose Response Destination

Data collected by a Google Form will be automatically collected and stored in two ways, depending on the user's choice. The user may choose for the data to be automatically collected in a new Google Spreadsheet so he may manipulate the data and create charts and graphs. The user may also choose to keep the data in the form without migrating it to a spreadsheet. This option will keep the data gathered in the **Summary of responses** section for review. Figure 7.7 depicts the options.

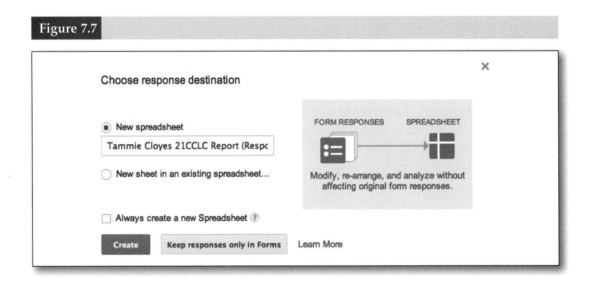

Figure 7.7

Get Prefilled URL

This option allows the user to pre-answer form questions. Choose this and a message will appear on the live form asking you to do the following: **Answer questions you want to pre-fill, then press submit.** This is helpful for a study guide.

Delete All Responses

This option will clear the form responses from the spreadsheet and summary-of-response report. This is great because when teachers are giving the same test or quiz to multiple class periods, the teacher can make a copy of the accompanying spreadsheet, saving those answers as first period's, then clear the form for second period's answers. This scenario only works when the user chooses to have the data go directly in a spreadsheet as shown in the first option in Figure 7.7.

USES FOR FORMS

Forms are especially useful in the day-to-day management of school information. Once the user is comfortable with the creation and deployment of Google Forms, it becomes easy to collect and sort data. Use the next section as a starting point for form creation, but remember Google Forms can collect any information you need.

Special Education

Collecting data and making them work for the teacher is one of the best strategies that special education educators can employ to identify weaknesses and find solutions. Knowing the difference between incremental changes in ability to comprehend are great indicators of successes. Teachers have a hard time objectively knowing without measurable data. Forms could be created to include certain skill sets desired by the successful special education student. It may be hard to define goals for the students with special needs, but it is imperative to actively assess where they are and where they are going skillwise. Forms can make tracking students' progress a reality. For example, a teacher could create a form that is designed with the particular student in mind. Review individualized education plans, accommodations, and other learning goals before creating the form. Begin with the end in mind. Ask these questions when making forms for student skill data:

- What benchmarks should this individual student strive for?
- What is appropriate developmentally for this particular student?
- What skills are coming soon in the teaching plan that will help students reach their specific goals?

Create a form that assesses this information so that it is easily discussed in meetings and that has the validity of data to back up the assertions made by the educators. An example form is located at http://goo.gl/ebSXe.

Dean/Disciplinarian/Assistant Principal

Discipline forms are perfect for Google Forms because they reduce cost of paper, time, and clutter. Create teacher-friendly discipline forms that can expedite the process. All data are secure and are immediately incorporated into a spreadsheet for easy data analysis by the person who created the form. The spreadsheet is safe and data are secure because, unless told otherwise, forms do not let participants see the results. Depending on the contents of the form, disciplinarians can filter or sort offenses by time, class period, teacher, and student. Use your knowledge of spreadsheets to make data color-coded for easy viewing. Take a look at a sample lunch detention form from Harrisburg Middle School located at http://goo.gl/nISg5. Encourage teachers to make shortcuts to forms for discipline and other types. You can even make shortcuts on mobile devices like those that Mrs. Kocher did earlier in the chapter.

Counselor

Counselors need to be contacted by students for a variety of reasons. Counselors could create forms that are accessible by students. For example, the counselor will create a form in Google Docs, copy the link, and shorten it using http://goo.gl. Students need easy access to important forms that they are required to use. The principal or their designee should be "keeper of the forms." In this role, the keeper of the forms will create a Google Document that has the links displayed under a heading for the purpose of the form. Share the document with every student, keeping it in his or her documents list. When students need a form, they are able to log in to their account, find the forms list, and fill out the form. For examples of forms, go to http://goo.gl/8NyVq. This link provides a sample of what a Student Form Bank would look like. Feel free to take and modify the forms to make them appropriate for your school. Find the forms and more at the book's companion website, www.21learning.net.

Response to Intervention Progress Monitoring

Monitoring student progress is an important part of a teacher's role in differentiating instruction for the individual student. Forms are an easy way to collect such data that could make a difference in the way a student is taught. For example, students identified as performing below expectations should be monitored. PLCs that meet during or after school could look at the data and help teachers make better decisions about instruction or remediation. Data should drive decision making, and Google Forms can provide a modality for collecting and sharing that data.

Test or Quizzes

Google Forms is perfect for assessment. Ask questions pertaining to the subject in a form and wait for the responses to fill into the spreadsheet for grading. Students will be engaged while taking the quiz because of the use of technology. Teachers will be happy because the responses do not have to be printed. No more carrying home stacks of papers to grade. To grade the assessments, log on to Google Drive and grade from anywhere there is an Internet connection.

Self-grading quizzes are also a possibility using the free script Flubaroo. To learn more about Flubaroo, go to www.flubaroo.com to see a short demonstration.

Other Ways to Use Google Forms

- Getting-to-know-you first day of school icebreaker
- Maintenance request forms
- Computer technician request
- Teacher evaluation
- Principal can gather data about classroom during a class visit

SUMMARY

Forms are great at gathering and organizing data into spreadsheets. Students can create surveys gaining authentic data they can use in research, math class, or for organizing a club event. Teachers can create self-grading quizzes and monitor student progress with ease, making real impacts on students during PLC meetings. Google Forms supports the effectiveness of the Common Core State Standards by getting technology into the hands of students, allowing them to analyze their world and help them make better decisions. In the next chapter, find out how Google Drawings can help students be creative to explain what they are learning in the form of art. Also, students can organize information in show-stopping drawings that can be inserted into any of the Google Docs or simply shared online.

RESOURCE LINK

Lesson Plans

Grade Level	Lesson Plan Title	Digital copy found at the link. Lesson plans with numbers are in order in the resource section.	
Elementary School	About Us	http://goo.gl/zIFu0	#9
Middle School	Slow Down!	http://goo.gl/XnXki	#10
High School	Attitude Survey	http://goo.gl/2Zfx3	Online Only

For additional resources, including lesson plans, videos, and video tutorials, access this link:

- http://goo.gl/unjoW

8

Drawings

KEY FEATURES

- ❖ Design organizational charts, flow charts, and graphic organizers
- ❖ Publish work directly to the Web or insert into other Google Docs
- ❖ Work collaboratively on drawings
- ❖ Chat in the margin to guide collaborators
- ❖ Express what is learned visually

Google Drawings offers something Microsoft Office cannot compete with. Google Drawings makes it possible to share real-time creations that connect meaning visually. Use drawings to create flow charts, custom graphs, informational posters, and graphic designs to publish online using the document's unique URL. Insert these creations into presentations, spreadsheets, or documents to make connections to text and meaning visually. Add images to drawings from your hard drive or the Web adding text and other annotations. Google Drawings has "snap-to" alignment guides and auto distribution to keep objects placed on the drawing canvas precisely spaced. These features make it easy to create professional looking graphic designs with this free Google App.

Google Drawings can help students with writing by helping them organize their ideas. Students can make their own graphic organizers, use templates found online or in a book, or use a specific teacher's template. For example, a teacher could create a custom graphic organizer designed for organizing ideas obtained from text. The Common Core State Standards Anchor Standard 1 for Writing wants students to "read closely" to understand the text and make analytical conclusions from it. This type of close reading should be taught throughout the reading standards as well as Reading in the Content Areas. Teachers who create graphic organizers give students a chance to organize their thoughts and facts gathered from text to prepare for writing. The teacher may create the graphic organizer and share it with the class. The class will make a copy of the organizer and use it to prepare for their writing about the text. Table 8.1 provides the standard that fits this example.

Table 8.1	Anchor Standard 1 for Reading

Read closely to determine what the text says explicitly and to make logical inferences from it; cite specific textual evidence when writing or speaking to support conclusions drawn from the text.

GRAPHIC ORGANIZERS

Use the graphic organizer in Figure 8.1 made for organizing complex text. The reader can have full access to this graphic organizer by going to http://goo.gl/zt3UY.

Creating graphic organizers that are saved in the user's Google Drive account will help the students and teachers transition to a paperless classroom. The standards are clear that college- and career-ready students will need to be organized when writing. Take advantage of Google Drawings to provide digital organization that can be accessed by any Internet-ready device.

Figure 8.1	Graphic Organizer for Writing

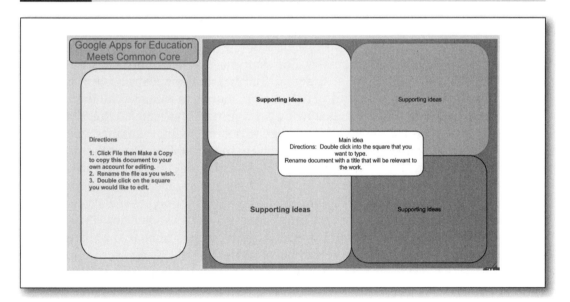

Follow the directions in Figure 8.1 to make a copy of this drawing. Once a copy is made, rename it to become the owner and then edit or share the document with anyone. Readers can have full access to this graphic organizer for use with their students by going to http://goo.gl/zt3UY.

> ### TECHNOLOGY-INFUSED TEACHING TIP
>
> Notice in Figure 8.1 that the drawing has objects (directions) outside the canvas area. Use the whole area to create the drawing. When publishing the drawing, only the objects on the canvas will be seen. However, objects outside the canvas will be seen during sharing. Teachers can create objects off-screen for students to use while making a drawing; sometimes limiting their options increases their creativity.

SHARE VERSUS PUBLISH

Sharing a Google Drawing allows it to be viewed, edited, or commented on by the person it is shared with. Collaborative drawings shared with students allow them to create the work together in real time like any of the other document programs. They can work on it at the same time, or they can contribute at any time they choose and the work will be saved along with the revision history. Publishing the drawing, conversely, will publish the work that is on the canvas only. That means if the user has placed directions or other objects off the canvas, then that content will not show up in the published version. When publishing drawings, the URL given to the drawing will automatically download the drawing as a .PNG picture file. This downloaded file will not change with subsequent versions of the work. However, if the user clicks on the published link again, this will download the new and most current version of the drawing.

Using Google Drawings for Exploration of Math Concepts

Look at Table 8.2 to see an appropriate Common Core State Standard for using Google Drawings to explore geometry. For example, teachers who want students to investigate shapes could create a drawing that has the shapes placed outside the canvas region. The students would click on the shapes to manipulate them on the canvas. Shapes can be edited by clicking and dragging, rotating 90 degrees, and flipping horizontally and vertically (also great exposure to mathematics vocabulary words). Have them add color and text to liven up the drawings. Share them with the teacher and class and have the students explain their understanding of their drawing. Navigate your Web browser to this link to see an example of this lesson. Make a copy of this drawing to use it in your own class: http://goo.gl/xAP4W.

In addition to exploring shapes, the drawings app can be used to create puzzles. For example, teachers can create a set of digital tangram shapes to be manipulated in the drawing. Instruct students to explore the shapes using flips, slides, and turns in a variety of activities. Freely use the premade tangram set at this link: http://goo.gl/Wml6A.

Table 8.2	Draw, Construct, and Describe Geometrical Figures Seventh Grade

Draw (freehand, with ruler and protractor, and with technology) geometric shapes with given conditions. Focus on constructing triangles from three measures of angles or sides, noticing when the conditions determine a unique triangle, more than one triangle, or no triangle.

Exploring shapes and using lines to make triangles with technology can help students understand how graphic design could be used as a career.

FILE MENU

The **File** menu in Google Drawings contains commands that will help the user with the creation of the drawing. The following section only describes Drawing-specific commands. For more on the other **File** commands, see previous chapters.

Download As

Download as will download the file that the user has created in another format other than a Google Docs format. Each document type has its own set of *download as* options (see Figure 8.2). The least common of the file types in this figure is .SVG. That extension is used in high-end graphics. PDF, PNG, and JPEG are very common image filetypes and will work on any platform (PC, Mac, iOS, or Android).

Figure 8.2 Download As

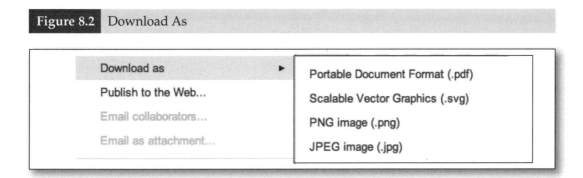

TECHNOLOGY-INFUSED TEACHING TIP

The default canvas size can be changed to form any rectangle. Click and drag the lower right-hand corner of the canvas to make it a different size and shape. For example, to make a square canvas, click on the sizing handle and shrink it to its smallest size, then hold down shift and enlarge it to make a square. Holding down shift while sizing objects keeps the proportions of the sides the same. For example, if the default canvas ratio is 4:3, then holding down shift while resizing will keep the 4:3 proportion no matter how large or small the canvas is resized.

VIEW MENU

The **View** menu is pictured in Figure 8.3. It has some of the same features as other **View** menus in previous chapters. Read the next section to see Drawing-specific commands.

Figure 8.3 View Menu

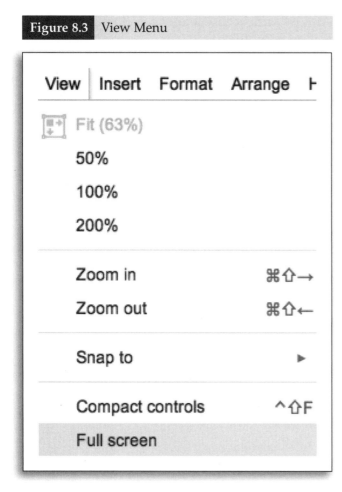

Fit Zoom

Fit zoom fits the drawing to the size of the screen. While editing a drawing, the user may zoom in many times to get a detail just right. Click **Fit zoom** to go back to show the entire drawing. For example, a student making a flowchart for chemistry class explaining how to balance a chemical equation may need to add specific detail in certain parts of the drawing. Use the zoom feature to zoom in on a particular part of the equation, then click **Fit zoom** to go back to see the whole drawing.

Snap To

This feature helps align objects to the canvas of the drawing. Choose from snap to grids or snap to guides. Snapping to grids aligns the objects to the coordinate plane. For example, objects such as squares will appear straight forming 90-degree angles with the borders of the canvas. The downside to this is that having to align two shapes in similar size proportional distances from the vertical and horizontal will be difficult because it will have to be done by sight. Snap to guides align objects to guide lines that keep objects equidistant from each other and from the canvas borders.

FLOWCHARTS

Creating flowcharts in science and math is a great way to take the information of processes and make it graphically appealing. This is a great differentiation tool for students. Have students use Google Drawings to take a complex set of steps and make a flowchart. For example, students studying the scientific method could create a custom graphic organizer outlining the steps. See an example of the scientific method flowchart at this link: http://goo.gl/qkCMb. In Table 8.3, the Common Core State Standard that describes the importance of understanding charts, graphs, and diagrams is displayed. Students can use drawings to make timelines or animations to explain text or gain information from these informational objects. Using technology can improve the access of these visual displays because they can be shared with the class or the world using share settings.

Table 8.3 Literacy in History/Social Studies, Science, and Technical Subjects Fourth Grade

Interpret information presented visually, orally, or quantitatively (e.g., in charts, graphs, diagrams, time lines, animations, or interactive elements on Web pages) and explain how the information contributes to an understanding of the text in which it appears.

TECHNOLOGY-INFUSED TEACHING TIP

While making drawings, especially flowcharts, use copy and paste to make copies of the shapes. In some flowcharts, it is great to have the same size shape for each of the objects in the flowchart. Use copy and paste instead of inserting a new shape and trying to draw the shape the exact size.

DRAWINGS AS ASSESSMENTS

Teachers can use drawings as an assessment tool. For example, use drawings to assess what the student knows about the scientific method. Assign students to create a flowchart of the scientific method and then share it with the teacher for grading. Another way Google Drawings can be used as an assessment tool is by creating posters. Common Core State Standards for Mathematics eighth grade address the Pythagorean Theorem. Students should be able to "Explain a proof of the Pythagorean Theorem and its converse." Use drawings to create an informational poster describing the proof of the theorem and its converse. Students should be graded on presentation of the poster for speaking and listening standards as well as the mathematics content. Insert drawings into presentations to give students the valuable experience of presenting to groups. Raise the ante by inviting mathematics experts to grade the posters and the presentation along with the teacher's rubrics. Use Gmail's video chat feature to let experts chat with students from far distances. Exposing students to professional science, technology, engineering, and mathematics careers and having them interact will have a positive impact on them.

GRAPHICAL TOOLBAR

The graphical toolbar featured in Figure 8.4 is located at the top of the screen in Google Drawings. The commands listed here are also available in the **Insert** menu. Google places them at the top with graphics to make them easier to access.

| Figure 8.4 | Insert Menu |

Undo and redo. ↶ ↷ Undo and redo are familiar commands. Keyboard shortcuts for these commands are **CTRL/CMD+Z** and **CTRL/CMD+Y**, respectively (CMD for Mac, CTRL for PC).

Copy to Web clipboard. ▣ Web clipboard is an innovative feature Google has developed. Instead of using the computer's clipboard that allows users to copy and paste only on the physical computer, Google Docs can copy and paste from computer A to computer B. This is done by using Google's cloud technology. With Google Docs Web clipboard, students are becoming device neutral even with copy and paste.

Paint format. ⊤ This feature is much like conditional formatting used in spreadsheets. The command will copy the formatting rules for the selected region and paste them in a particular area on the drawing. The word "paint" is used figuratively to describe pasting the formatting. For example, select a region that has a particular style or font and paint format that style or font into another region of the drawing without pasting the content.

Zoom fit and zoom. ⊞ ⌕ This is detailed in the Insert section.

Select. ⬉ This icon is important because it allows the user to grab and move objects on the drawing. The icon must be selected before the user clicks on the drawing to perform a task. If this is not done, then whatever command is selected, such as insert a line, will be performed. Avoid making unnecessary errors by being aware of select tool. Students new to drawings will be inclined to not pay attention to which icon is selected and will most likely become frustrated not knowing why there is a problem.

Select line. ⬊ This icon is a shortcut to inserting lines. Click the drop-down arrow to choose from six line types to give the drawing a unique presence. Look at Figure 8.5 to see what line types are available.

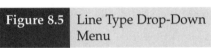

Figure 8.5 | Line Type Drop-Down Menu

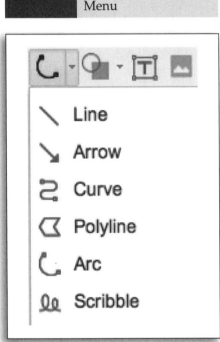

Shape, Arrows, Callouts, and Equations

Click the drop-down menu to insert a shape, arrow, callout, or equation symbol. Add text to any of these by double-clicking inside the object. Students can create graphic designs that aid in their understanding of the concept. Creatively exploring concepts is an important differentiation tool and should be used with students of all ages. For example, when using shapes, students learning early grade geometry lessons could practice manipulating shapes in the drawing program. To manipulate shapes, follow these steps:

1. Insert a shape by clicking on the drop-down menu ▣ in the toolbar.

2. Resize the shape by clicking and dragging one of the white, square resizing handles.

   a. To maintain proportion, hold down **Shift** while resizing.

3. Rotate the object about its axis by clicking on the shape's white, circular handle above the object as shown in Figure 8.6.

Figure 8.6	Rotate an Image

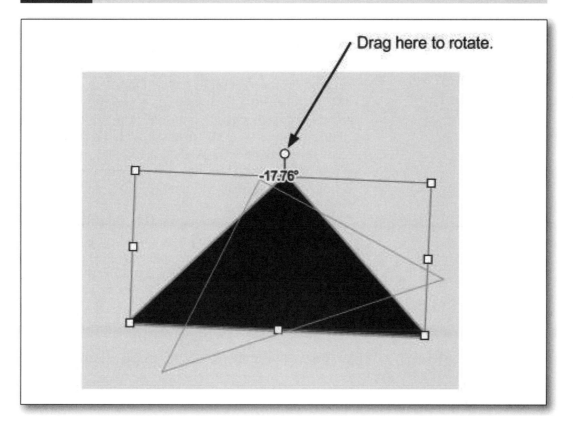

Callouts. Make it possible for students to construct comics with their drawings by inserting callouts. Use callouts to give inanimate objects a voice. For example, when explaining the layers of rock in a photograph, insert callouts to make the rock "say" something clever about its composition. Create comic strips by inserting comics made in drawings into presentations; set the timing of slide transitions to create animation.

Equations. Equations are perfect for math. Create easy-to-read equations that can help students understand a particularly hard concept. For example, create a flowchart on how to use the distributive property. In each object, insert equation symbols showing the steps in order.

INSERT MENU

The **Insert** menu has many of the same commands as other programs as seen in Figure 8.7. Insert will be the most used feature but also remember to use many of these same commands from the graphical insert menu located in Figure 8.4.

Text Box

Insert text boxes into drawings by following these steps:

1. Click **Insert,** then **Text box** or select the ⊞ icon in the toolbar menu.

2. Size the text box accordingly by clicking and dragging the white resize boxes.

Figure 8.7 Insert Menu

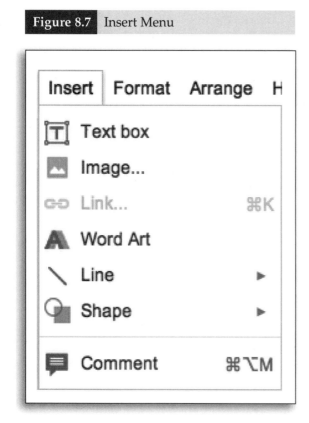

3. Fill the text box with color or change the color of the font using the edit buttons shown in Figure 8.7.

Image

Insert images exactly like previous chapters by clicking on the ▨ icon in the toolbar menu. Inserting images into the drawings apps gives the user more creativity. For example, students can insert images that they have taken themselves or have permission to use to explain a set of ideas. Students can edit the photo by annotating with text, adding arrows, shapes, callouts, and equation symbols to add meaning. Creativity is up to the student. Insert these modified images into Presentations, embed in a website, or publish them with the unique URL. Students can tell a story about what they are learning with their artwork, meeting vital speaking and listening standards.

Link

Insert live links to drawings by following these steps:

1. Select a portion of text to be linked with a Web address.
2. Click on the ⊖ icon to reveal Figure 8.8.
3. Type the URL for the link into the box.
4. Click ⏹ OK ⏹ to link the object.

Figure 8.8 Linking Objects in Drawings to Web Addresses

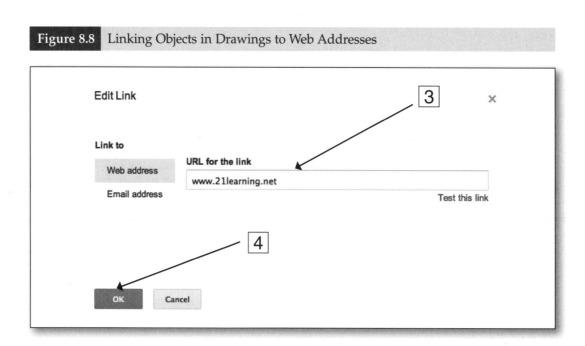

When a user clicks on the link, a Web browser will open, directing the user to more information about the object. For example, a flowchart describing the scientific method could have links directed to more information on the hypothesis step. Students can create Google Documents that are linked to the drawing, detailing the concepts within the flowchart for further study. Create living drawings.

Word Art

Inserting word art gives an artistic feel to text in drawings. Inserting text boxes alone is limiting because the font cannot be changed. With word art, users can select fonts from among the other edit options, including color fill, line color, bold, and italic. Insert word art by following these steps:

1. Click **Insert,** then **Word art** to reveal Figure 8.9.

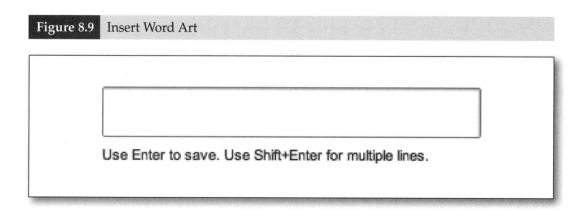

| Figure 8.9 | Insert Word Art |

Use Enter to save. Use Shift+Enter for multiple lines.

2. Type text in the box.
3. Use **Shift+Enter** to insert multiple lines of text.
4. Press **Enter.**

Comments

Comment on certain aspects of the drawing by right clicking on the object you want to comment on. This is great for grading students' work. Insert comments that will be constructive and make the students' project better. Grade for content and style from any Internet-connected computer. Comments will be seen on the drawing, but will be off of the canvas region and will not be published. Click the object that the drawing is attached to resolve. Use the comment stream to review conversations about aspects of the drawing. Also, use the chat feature to collaborate on drawings. To insert comments, see that section in Chapter 4.

EDIT ICONS

Edit icons become visible when the user clicks on an object. If the object can hold text like shapes, callouts, arrows, and equation symbols, then the text edit buttons will appear. If the objects cannot contain text, only the fill color, line weight, and so on will appear. Look at Figure 8.10 to see the edit icons as they appear in the graphical toolbar in Google Drawings.

| Figure 8.10 | Edit Icons |

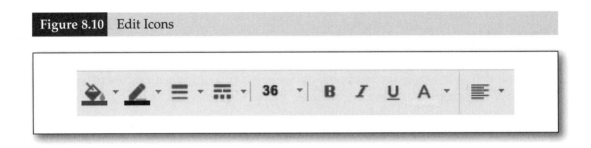

Adding Text

To add text to any drawing, use text box, word art, or double-click a shape, callout, arrow, or equation symbol. Click the object, and edit buttons will appear.

- Color fill and color lines of any object in the gallery.
- Choose font size for any object.
- Choose font style for word art only.
- Change the color of text, underline, make bold, or italicize.

For an example of actual student work from fifth-grade student Fallan Harper, look at Figure 8.11. In this example, Fallan has used all elements of adding text to a Google Drawing to create an infographic to help younger students learn how to open their lockers. Fallan shared this Drawing with the entire middle school as part of a school community service project. Students now have this information in their Google Drive.

| Figure 8.11 | How to Open Your Locker |

60

The right way to open your locker!

You get a locker combonation which is three numbers, example: 12,40,18

You first twist the knob right two whole times and land on the first number. Which in this case is 12.

Next, you twist the knob left one whole time on the second number and land on it the second time around. Which in this case is 40.

Last you twist the knob right until you land on your last number. In this case it is 18.

If you do all the steps right your locker should open easily.

... and thats how you properly open your locker!

SUMMARY

Google Drawings is a dynamic graphic design program that uses Google Apps for Education signature collaborative features. Students and teachers can create collaborative drawings that explain meaning in visually stunning ways. Students are able to express their learning in creative ways using art while learning an important skill of graphic design. Insert drawings into other Google Docs to add creativity to presentations or documents. Teachers are able to assess Common Core State Standards of speaking and listening by allowing students to present their ideas depicted in their work. Students are able to create informational posters, flowcharts, and custom graphs that can be published to the Web that can contribute to the worlds' understanding of the topic in new ways.

Google Drawings is a great differentiation tool that can urge students to create, collaborate, and share their work with parents, peers, or the world. Google Drawings is the final app in the Google Docs suite, but the collaboration is not over. Read the next chapter to learn how college- and career-ready students and teachers organize their busy schedules with Google Calendar.

RESOURCE LINK

Lesson Plans

Grade Level	Lesson Plan Title	Digital copy found at the link. Lesson plans with numbers are in order in resource section.	
Elementary School	Exploring Shapes	http://goo.gl/rgg4U	#11
Middle School	Tangram Square	http://goo.gl/ehls8	#12
High School	Graphic Design in Science	http://goo.gl/4mgU9	#13

For additional resources, including lesson plans, videos, and video tutorials, access this link:

■ http://goo.gl/d4Qrl

9

Calendar

KEY FEATURES

- ❖ Live online calendar
- ❖ Create multiple calendars to manage different parts of your busy life
- ❖ Access and edit calendars anywhere there is an Internet connection
- ❖ Manage resources on calendar

Organization of time is one of the biggest hurdles students and teachers face. Planning due dates, turning in assignments, and accessing coworker and peer schedules is difficult with paper calendars. Paper calendars in date-books or on teachers' desks are not practical because they are not collaborative and can only be accessed if the person is in the room. Life is not static, and your calendar should not be either. Google Calendar is an application embedded into the Google Apps for Education account to provide students and teachers with a live online calendar that is dynamic and easy to use and share.

In this chapter, we will discuss how Google Calendar can be a support system for learning and working with the Common Core State Standards. Google Calendar supports the standards by offering ways for students, teachers, and parents to manage their work and learning. The reader will be introduced to Google Calendar, learn how to create, share, and collaborate, and be given practical advice that can help organize time.

ACCESS THE DEFAULT GOOGLE APPS CALENDAR

When the domain administrator creates the users' account, a Google Calendar is created. This is the user's default calendar. The calendar is titled with the name of the user. Any additional calendars that are created or shared with the user will overlay onto the default calendar. Events from different calendars will be shown in different colors. For example, Mrs. Doyle, a science teacher, wants to create a class calendar. She would create the new calendar, as shown in Figure 9.1, and name it accordingly. In this calendar, Mrs. Doyle could set assignment due dates, lab schedules, weekly quizzes, and schedule presentation times for a group project. This calendar can be shared with each student in the class, and this information will appear on the students' calendars in a different color than their default calendar.

To access the default calendar, follow these steps:

1. Sign into your Google Apps for Education account.

2. Click **Calendar** at the top of the screen as seen in Figure 9.1.

Figure 9.1	Calendar Image Treatments

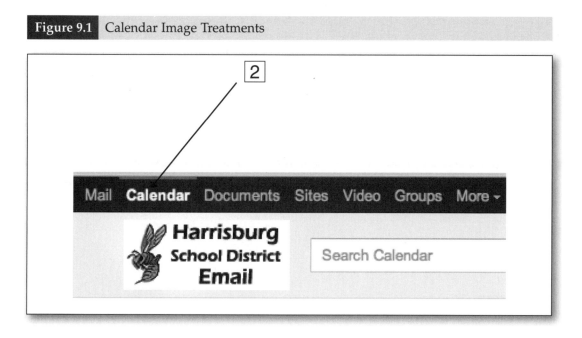

ADDING EVENTS

Events can be anything from regular calendar entries to more specialized forms of record-keeping. Be creative about what is placed as an event on your calendar. Nothing is out of bounds. Some teachers use the calendar as a behavior log. For example, the teacher would create a calendar dealing with behavior and each time a student has a success or failure that warranted a note the teacher would create an event. The incidence would be recorded in the calendar on the date and time it happened along with a description. This creates an ongoing behavior log that can be accessed anywhere. Be specific and create a calendar for a particular student and then share the calendar with the parents. It would be difficult to manage every student's behavior in this manner, but in certain circumstances this could be useful.

Other event types include the following:

- Schedule meetings
- Assignment due dates
- Official school calendar
- Community calendar
- Principal's calendar
- Sports schedules

TECHNOLOGY-INFUSED TEACHING TIP

Google Calendar works with mobile devices. Teachers can sync their Android or iOS device (iPad, iPhone, iPod) with their Google Calendar. Every time an entry is placed on the device, it automatically appears on the Google Calendar on the computer and vice versa. Quickly manage your busy schedule on the go with mobile applications.

To add events, follow these steps:

1. Click on any day on the calendar (if in month view) or any time interval (if in other views).

2. Name the event as shown in Figure 9.2 in the **What:** box.

3. Choose which of the **Calendars** the event will be assigned to from the drop-down box.

   a. The calendar event in Figure 9.2 will be placed on **Michael Graham's** calendar. Because that calendar is chosen from the drop-down menu (follow arrow 3a), other calendars that Michael has created or has been given access to can be chosen from the drop-down menu.

4. Click Create event to add it to the calendar.

5. Click **Edit event** to add more details (see Figure 9.3).

Figure 9.2	Add Event

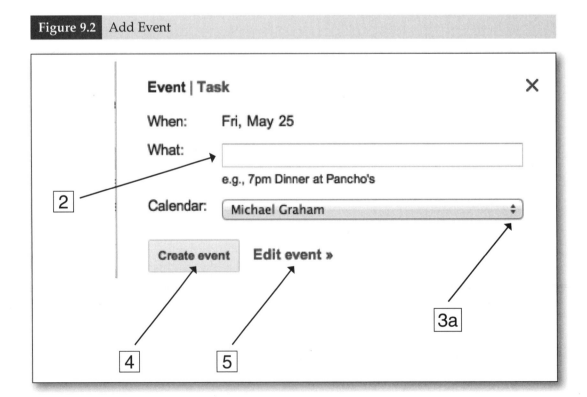

Many times a simple title and time will be enough information when adding an event to a calendar. But, sometimes users need more specific information or they have a need to share the event with others. Look at Figure 9.3 to learn more about adding calendar events.

Figure 9.3 Edit Event Details

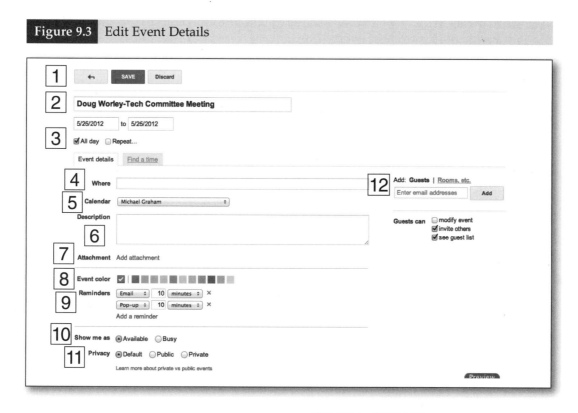

1. Previous Screen, Save, and Discard icons ← **SAVE** Discard .

2. The title of the event is prefilled into the title box; click to change.

3. If **All day** is checked, then the event will be recorded as lasting all day. If not checked, the user may choose a time interval for the event.

4. **Where** gives the option of the user to provide a location (e.g., Central office, Room 601).

5. **Calendar** asks which of the calendars to place the event in.

6. Add a **Description** to the event to give details.

7. Selecting **Add an attachment** lets the user upload a file from the computer or attach a file from the user's Google Drive. This would be useful when scheduling meetings with other faculty members. For example, attach an agenda made with Microsoft Office or a Google Document. When the user invites others to the event using the **Add guest** options, people can download the attached agenda for review during or before the meeting. In addition to meetings, a teacher at my current school, Ms. Jacquie Dubrava, uses the attachment option to give students access to documents that are needed for class during that day. This helps each student keep up with makeup work and if the calendar is shared with the parents, then they have access to class materials.

8. Add an **Event color** to differentiate one event from another on the same calendar.

9. Set a **Reminder** through e-mail or a popup on the computer screen. If popup is chosen, the notification will appear no matter which computer the user is logged in to at the time of notification.

10. **Show me as** available or busy will let others who have access to your calendar know your status for that event time.

11. **Privacy** settings

   1. Default will set the calendar's privacy setting to imitate the particular calendar's setting.

   2. Public will set this particular event's privacy to public even though all of the other events will be private.

   3. Private will set the privacy setting for the event on a public calendar to private. Only the owners of the calendar will see the event details for the specific event.

12. **Add guest/Rooms, etc.** option allows the owner of the calendar to invite other people to see the event and participate. Give a guest the option to modify the event, invite others, and see the guest list. Calendar will notify their Gmail account reminding them of the event and providing details such as description and attachment of documents. See more in the **Schedule a Resource** section.

TASKS

Tasks is a feature built into Gmail and Calendar to manage the user's to-do list. Users may create tasks attached to days in calendar and add notes. The user can check off tasks as they are completed directly in calendar or in Gmail. Event and Tasks are accessed by the same procedure. Instead of creating an Event, create a task by clicking on **Task** as shown in the oval in Figure 9.3. To create tasks, follow these steps:

1. Click on any day in the calendar to create the due date for the task and to reveal the task name and notes boxes as seen in Figure 9.4.

2. Click in the **Task:** box to give the task a name.

3. Add notes if necessary to describe the task.

4. Click a   Create task .

The create Task and create Event boxes appear in the same menu by clicking on any date in the calendar. To create a list of tasks make sure to toggle from Event to Task as shown in the oval in Figure 9.4.

When tasks are created, they appear on the right-hand side of the calendar. Place check marks in the boxes as tasks are completed. Future tasks are shown in the calendar on their due date. If the due date of tasks or events change, drag and drop the task to the appropriate date or time. See Figure 9.5 for a view of the task list. If Figure 9.5 does not appear on the right side of your Google Calendar, then click the box next to **Task** under **My calendars** list. See Figure 9.2 to see where to turn off or on the task list located on the right-hand side of the calendar.

Figure 9.4 Creating a Task

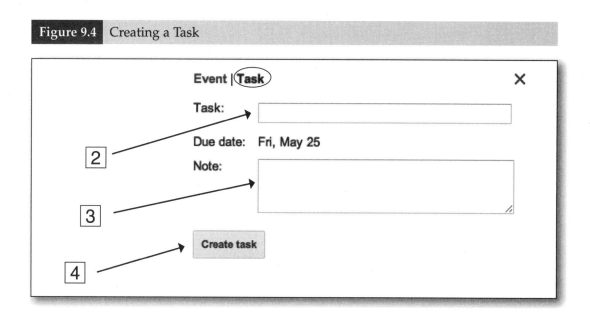

CREATING A CALENDAR

Adding another calendar to the default calendar is a great way to differentiate among groups of events. For example, teachers could create individual class calendars. This ensures that teacher's personal and professional calendars are separated. Teachers can select which calendar to share; this makes sure that students or parents do not have access to other events that do not relate to class. Share the class calendar with the appropriate groups of students or individuals to allow them access to view the class schedule. Each new calendar created by the user will be displayed in a different color. If the user creates multiple calendars and the calendar page is cluttered, the user can click on the colored box next to the calendar's title to hide these events as shown in the circle in Figure 9.6. Create an additional calendar by following these steps:

1. Click on the drop-down menu next to **My Calendars** like in Figure 9.6.

2. Select **Create new calendar.**

3. Fill out the information on the next screen like in Figure 9.7.

4. Click the colored box next to the calendar title to clear the events from the main calendar. Notice in Figure 9.6 that the Task box is not colored. This denotes that task are not visible on the calendar.

Figure 9.5 Task List

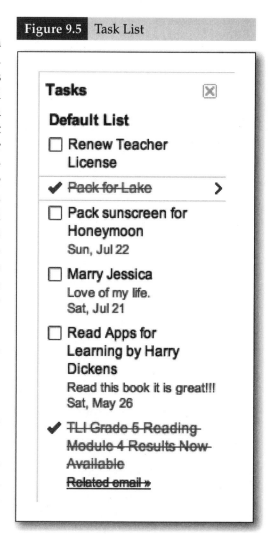

| Figure 9.6 | Create New Calendar |

| Figure 9.7 | Create New Calendar, Continued |

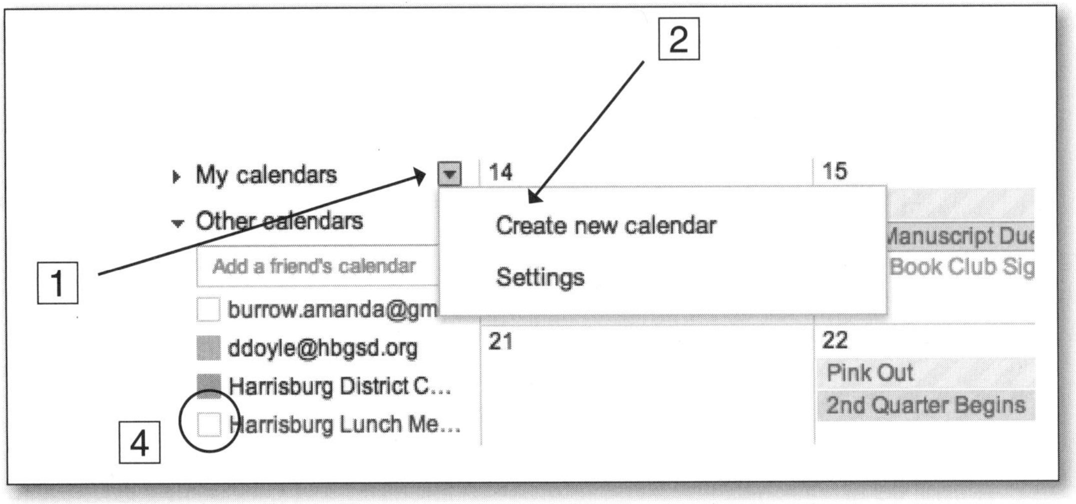

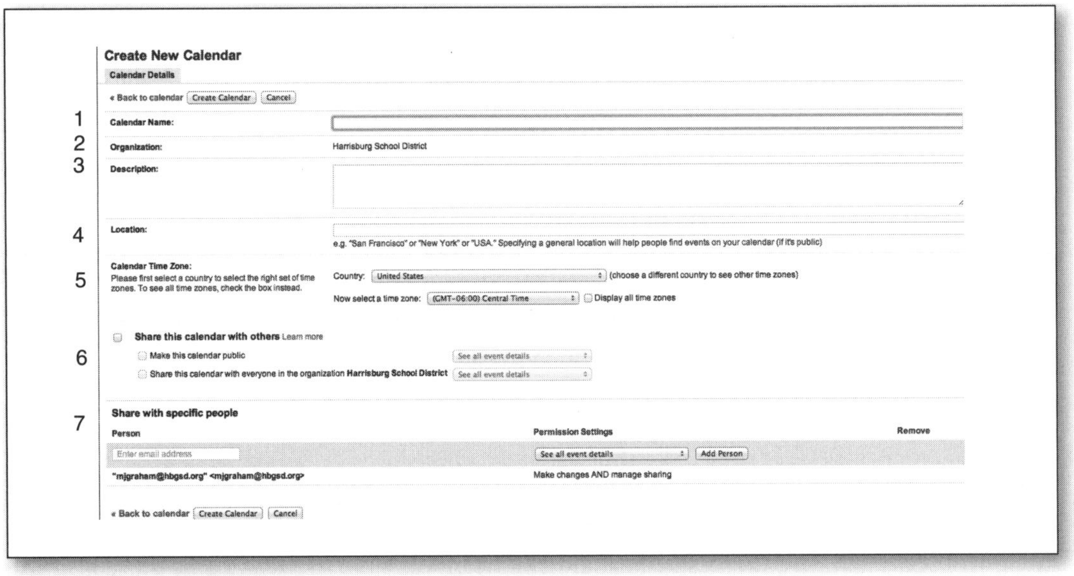

1. **Calendar Name** gives the calendar a title—for example, Mrs. Doyle's First Period Science.

   a. Give the calendars you create specific names. If these calendars are shared with students or others, then the calendar will appear in their **Other calendars** list as shown in Figure 9.8. See the section My Calendars and Other Calendars for more explanation.

2. **Organization** denotes the domain in which the calendar was created.

3. Offer a **Description** to provide users a detailed purpose of the calendar.

4. Add a **Location** to let people search for events located in the area if the calendar is public. This is important for large districts. For example, students and teachers may be interested in events at the school's fine arts center. By adding locations, interested parties can search for events at specific locations. The district could even create a public calendar describing the events that are upcoming and share the calendar with the entire domain. If the domain administrator allows out-of-domain sharing, then share the calendar with the public. This makes the calendar events searchable in Google Search.

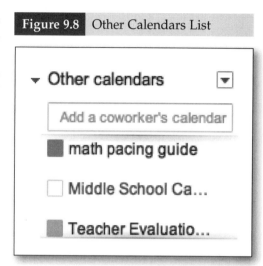

Figure 9.8 Other Calendars List

5. Provide the **Calendar Time Zone** information to accurately schedule events.

6. Check the **Share this calendar with others** box to select the calendar's share settings.

   a. Check the **Make this calendar public** box to set event details options.

      Choose **See all event details** to get descriptions of the event.

      Choose **See only free/busy** to hide event details, only giving the person being shared with access to only free or busy information.

   b. Check **Share this calendar with everyone in the organization** to make the calendar public. This option will display the calendar in all users' **Other calendars** list shown in Figure 9.8. Use this option for domain-wide events such as sports schedules, community calendars, or band concerts.

7. To share with specific people:

   a. Enter an e-mail address into the box in the **G** section of Figure 9.7.

      This address does not have to be in the domain. For example, teachers can share calendars with parents that may not have an e-mail address under the school domain.

   b. Click on the **permission settings** drop-down menu to manage what users can see or manipulate on your calendar. See Figure 9.9 for a list of options.

   c. Click on the **Add Person** button in Figure 9.9.

   d. Add additional e-mails to this list by repeating these steps.

   Add groups of people to the calendar. For example, the domain administrator may have placed faculty of Trumann Middle School (TMS) in a Google Group named tms@trumannk12.org. In this example, everyone belonging to the group will be able to access the calendar. This is done instead of typing in each name individually. Using Google Groups create a group by class period to share calendars with students while giving them proper access permissions. When a calendar is shared with a person or a group, the calendar will appear under **Other calendars** list automatically (see Figure 9.8).

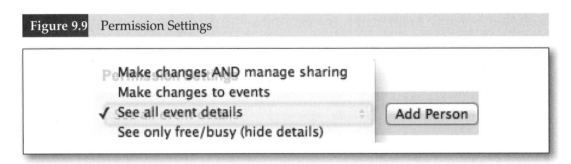

Figure 9.9   Permission Settings

- **Make changes AND manage sharing** allows the person being shared with to add, edit, or delete events on the calendar and add or delete people from calendar access.
- **Make changes to events** only lets the person being shared with to add, edit, or delete events from the shared calendar.
- **See all event details** and **See only free/busy (hide details)** are described earlier.

TECHNOLOGY-INFUSED TEACHING TIP

Encourage students to create calendars for group projects. In college and career, collaborating duties and deadlines can make or break a project's success. The Common Core State Standards' main goal is to prepare students for college or career. Managing time wisely while adding collaboration can help students produce high-quality work in an increasingly complex world.

MY CALENDARS AND OTHER CALENDARS

Calendars that are owned by the user will appear under the **My calendars** list. This means that the user has created the calendar or was given permission to edit event details. Calendars that are under the **Other calendars** list are calendars that have been shared with the user, but they do not have editing access; they are view only. Users may choose to create as many calendars as they wish and likewise they can subscribe to as many or as few calendars as they choose. Students and teachers having many different colors on their calendar denoting a multitude of events from different calendars may have a hard time making sense of the clutter. To combat this clutter, click the colored box next to the calendar's name. This will hide the calendar from view and its colored events will disappear. Click the box again to turn it back on. Another tip is to experiment with different views like these Day | Week | Month | 4 Days | Agenda . Selecting a different view will organize events or tasks into manageable parts.

Managing Calendars

Google provides easy ways to manage calendars that the user has created. For example, Google allows the user to quit sharing a particular calendar that they own with a person or group. This is helpful as students are promoted to the next grade:

The teacher can quit sharing the class calendar with the students so they will not see events for a past class. At the end of the year, teachers should drop students' access to their class calendars. Follow these steps to manage settings like this example.

1. Hover the mouse over the calendar that you want to modify.

2. Click the drop-down arrow as shown in Figure 9.10.

3. Click an option from the following list to modify the calendar, or check a different colored box to display this calendar as that color.

Figure 9.10 Modify Calendar Settings

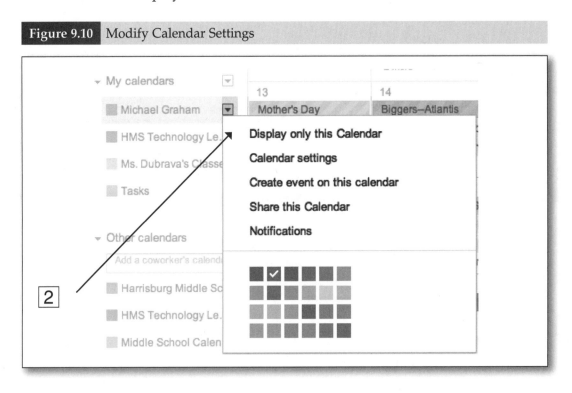

- **Display only this Calendar** removes all other calendars and their color-coding from view. In effect it removes the colored boxes next to all the other calendars.
- Click on **Calendar settings** to:
  - Change the title of the calendar
  - Add a description
  - Add a location
  - Access HTML embed code for this calendar to embed it in websites
  - Access the unique URL to the calendar so it may be shared with anyone with the link

Anyone with the link can access the calendar from any Web browser. This is important for sharing the calendar with parents and the community because they most likely will not have a school e-mail address that gives them access to the school domain. E-mail the link to non-Gmail users or print it on fliers or quick-response (QR) codes. Copy the URL and paste the calendar to Facebook or Twitter for the community to access. For a link that is long and hard to remember, use Google's URL

Shortener located at http://goo.gl to make the link more manageable. Use http://goo.gl to shorten the link as described in Chapter 11. Follow these steps to access the unique URL for each calendar the user owns.

1. Click **Calendar settings** as displayed in Figure 9.10.

2. Look for **Calendar address** in Figure 9.11.

3. Click on the blue HTML icon **HTML** to reveal the calendar's URL.

4. Copy the link to paste it into an e-mail, or post it to a social networking site to display the calendar for public view.

Figure 9.11	Calendar Address

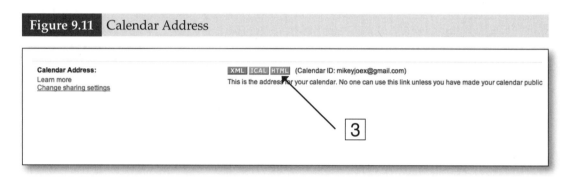

- Create event on this calendar is described earlier.
- Share this calendar is described earlier.
- Click Notifications to set reminders or e-mail collaborators of changes made to the calendar by any of the editors.

Search Calendars

Use Google's massive search power to search all calendars. The search bar is located at the top of Google Calendar and is shown in Figure 9.12. Every part of Google Calendar is searchable. Think of search terms that the user would use to describe the calendar, including:

- Title of calendar, event, or task
- Location of calendar, event, or task
- Description of calendar, event, or task

Click on **show search options** in the box in Figure 9.12 to display a more detailed search as shown in Figure 9.13.

Figure 9.12	Search Calendar

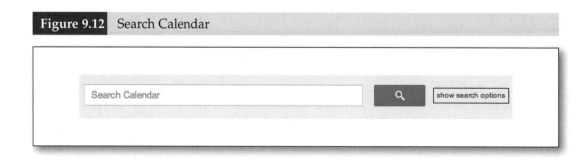

| Figure 9.13 | Search Options |

Search options

What		Search	All Calendars
Who		Date from	to
Where			
Doesn't have			

CALENDAR IDEAS

Calendar is a great way for students and teachers to communicate their schedules. The Common Core State Standards urge students to become ready for college and career by exposing them to learning that is collaborative just like the work environments in college and career. Living and working in this century requires people to become excellent time managers. Our society is more complex than in previous times, and students will require excellent time-management skills to thrive in school and business. Google Calendar can provide a solution for students who struggle with time management, making it easier for them to accomplish their assignments and activities.

The Common Core State Standards do not directly address time management and organizing events, places, and tasks. However, most teachers would argue that these are important skills that must be mastered to become successful in college or a career. The standards quietly address these themes in other ways. For example, commentary located in the notes sections of the English Language Arts Common Core State Standards speaks of complexity in writing and communication. In addition to complexity, knowing audience and understanding how to communicate with it is an important part of writing. The same can be said with Google Calendar. What is more complex than managing a high school student's social, sports, academic, and family life? This information can be shared with multiple audiences to inform. It is important for the teacher to see the importance of complexity and design lessons that incorporate these skills students can use in college and career. Giving them access to Google Calendar can help students learn how to manage complexity.

Student Calendar Ideas

It is important for teachers to give students advice about how to manage their time. Teachers can begin by using Google Calendar to set reminders about due dates and organize group project meetings. Teachers need to be aware of this ability not only to better organize their teaching practice but also to offer students real-world ways to collaborate using a shared calendar. Use the ideas in the following list to help students better organize time.

- Club meetings
- Afterschool activities (band, choir, and athletics)
- Group project meeting times
- Homework due dates
- Class pacing guides
- Skills help time
- Attach documents, videos, and other materials to events in calendar for extra help on a particularly hard concept

Faculty Calendar Ideas

Scheduling the faculty's time for meetings and other events is a challenging task no matter how large or small the size of the district. Often principals and other managers find it difficult to oversee the constantly changing schedules of school employees. Google Calendar can help. With Google Calendar, teachers and administrators can share school related calendars and easily keep up with each other's schedules. For example, scheduling teacher formal observations can be a breeze with Calendar. In the past, our school has had a paper sign-up sheet for preconference and postconference discussion times relating to teacher evaluation. Professional development, fire drills, and emergency parent meetings can throw a monkey wrench into any schedule. Minimalize the damage with Google Calendar. Now teacher evaluations scheduling is easy. To set up evaluations or other similar meetings, follow these steps:

1. Create a new calendar using the steps outlined earlier.

2. Share the calendar with each staff member or the staff group as stated earlier.

3. Set permissions to **Make changes to events** as shown in Figure 9.9.
   a. This allows each person who the calendar is shared with to edit, add events, and change events on the calendar. This feature is needed because the teachers can sign up for their preferred time slot. But they are limited to only editing this particular calendar.

4. Share the evaluator's calendar along with any other calendar that might interfere with the scheduled event.
   a. Select the **Free/busy details only** option so the calendar will not reveal any details of what the scheduled time is for. This allows the viewer to know if a certain block of time is free or busy without giving away why the time is allocated.

After the calendar is shared, the teacher can see on his or her calendar the events of the principal, school, and the teacher's personal calendar simultaneously. The teacher can select the appropriate day and time to schedule the evaluations. Attach any documents that are relevant for the conversation such as class roster, lesson plans, or any other document to facilitate discussion.

Schedule a Resource

Google Calendar can do more than schedule meetings and remind users of events. It also can be used as a resource manager. Resources are plentiful in the school setting, and managing their use can be a challenge. Google Calendar allows users to schedule the resource and invite people to use it; the notification goes to their Gmail. The domain administrator must set resources to be allocated through calendar. For example, the domain administrator for my district set up the Center for the Fine Arts, the gymnasium, and the middle school cafeteria as possible resources to manage and schedule using Google Calendar. Buildings and rooms are not the only possible resources that can be listed. The domain administrator can set any object as a resource. For example, Harrisburg Middle

School has seven computers on wheels carts (COWs) that the teachers may check out with preapproval of a Technology-Infused Lesson Plan. The domain administrator has these resources listed in the resources tab (Figure 9.14) and when approved for checkout, the teacher schedules the resource on the school's Technology Checkout Calendar. Doing this places an event reminder on the shared calendar, alerting other teachers that a particular computer cart is checked out and not available for use. The teachers add the instructional technologist as a guest to the meeting, alerting him or her by Gmail of the intent to schedule the resource. It works well that the domain administrator or his or her designee is the only person who can set resources in Calendar. The list needs to be an official account of the resources available for the district. Users should e-mail the domain administrator to suggest adding resources to the calendar list. Learn how to schedule resources by following these steps:

1. Add an event to the calendar as described in Figure 9.2.

2. Click on **Rooms, etc**. as shown in Figure 9.14 to see the list of resources available. Figure 9.14 is a close-up shot of Figure 9.2; this portion is on the right-hand side of the page.

3. Choose the resource that the user wants to add to the event.

4. Click **Add: Guests** to alert others of the meeting to reveal Figure 9.15.

5. Click the **Suggested times** link, shown in Figure 9.15, to see a list of times guests are available for the meeting using the resource. This option reads the calendars of the potential guest, suggesting times that everyone on the guest list is free for the meeting.

Figure 9.14 Schedule a Resource

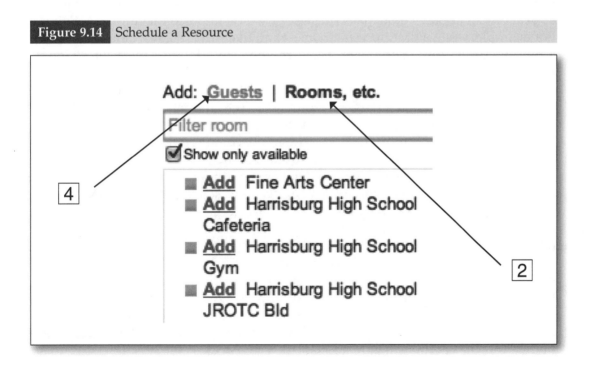

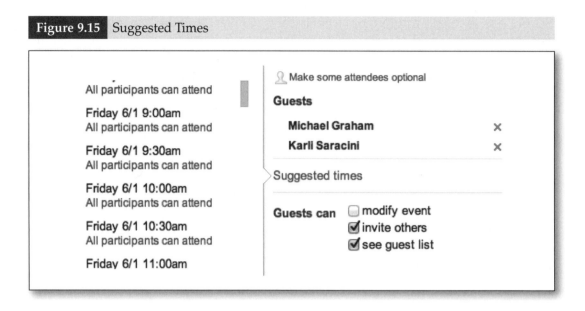

Figure 9.15 Suggested Times

SUMMARY

Google Calendar gives users an experience that paper and other noncollaborative calendars cannot compete with. The ability to share and collaborate meeting times and other parts of a person's busy life is a great way to communicate. Students and teachers can now look at the same calendar at the same time and make edits automatically, changing the events from anywhere an Internet connection is available. Students and teachers who use Google Calendar will have all of their personal and school-related events stored in one place that is easy to share with others. Google Calendar even reads Gmail. When a date sequence appears in an e-mail, Gmail asks if the user wants to place the date in Calendar. For example, when a date appears in an e-mail like July 21, 2012, Gmail will place a blue underline under the date. Click the date to add it to the user's Google Calendar.

Google Calendar can be more than a scheduler. Users can add guests, schedule meeting rooms, and manage resources of the district or building. Adding attachments to events is possible, providing notes and other materials pertaining to the meeting. It is important that students become familiar with applications like Calendar because they are widely used in college and career. The Common Core State Standards recognize the challenges students must face after high school. The world is becoming more complex, and scheduling time is one of the hardest skills to manage during school and work. Google Calendar gives users an opportunity to collaborate and share time more effectively, leading to more productivity.

In the next chapter, Google Drive is introduced. Google Drive is a cloud-based storage platform that can be accessed from anywhere there is an Internet connection. Drive will store unlimited Google Docs and up to 5 gigabytes of other file formats, including Microsoft Office and video files. Drive is full of features that will want to make you throw away your portable storage devices and embrace cloud-based computing. It is the backbone that makes Google Docs work.

RESOURCE LINK

Lesson Plans

Grade Level	Lesson Plan Title	*Digital copy found at the link. Lesson plans with numbers are in order in the resource section.*	
Elementary School	Telling Time and Google Calendar by Caitlin Kelly	http://goo.gl/1Ya5x	Online Only
Middle School	History of Life on Earth by Jason Borgen	http://goo.gl/gWF0k	Online Only
High School	Great Moments in Art	http://goo.gl/oSc2J	Online Only

For additional resources, including lesson plans, videos, and video tutorials, access this link:

- http://goo.gl/M3ynD

10

Drive

KEY FEATURES

❖ Store up to 5 gigabytes of files

❖ Access your files from any Internet-enabled device

❖ Share any file type with anyone

❖ Connect with collaborators to edit and view Google Docs

❖ Create, upload, and share folders and files

Google Calendar, Google Docs, and Gmail all have collaborative power to help students become ready for college and a career. Google Calendar organizes time, Gmail communicates, and Google Docs provides a world-class office suite for users to create, collaborate, and share. The last piece of the puzzle is storage. Google Drive is a cloud-based storage solution that gives access to all of the user's documents in an online drive that can be accessed from anywhere there is an Internet connection. This means that students and teachers can store unlimited Google Docs in their My Drive folder and have up to 5 gigabytes of storage space for any other file type. Google Drive lets users upload files or whole folders and gives the option to share any file type with others. Access Google Drive on tablets or smartphones, including Android, iPhone, and iPad.

Google Drive is important to the Common Core State Standards because it moves students into the cloud for working and learning using technology. It is imperative that students have access to their files and creations across many devices. Device-neutral learning and working environments are everywhere in the 21st century. Many schools and businesses rely on a wide variety of devices to access the Internet and their work. For example, my school has a mix of Apple, Microsoft, and mobile devices that are all compatible with Google Docs and Google Drive. Google works on any device. When students are exposed to the tools that are used in college and in a career, they will be better prepared when they are thrown into that world. In this chapter, we will learn how Google Drive supports the Common Core State Standards, unifies the Google Apps, and can increase digital literacy across grade levels.

ACCESSING DRIVE

Google Drive simplifies storage. For example, a student no longer has to be on the same computer that he or she started working on to access a file. Storage becomes easy because files are stored in the cloud on Google's Drive servers and can be accessed, edited, or shared with anyone in the world from almost any device. For example, as soon as a student creates a Google Doc, the Doc is saved every two seconds in the user's Google Drive. To access the file after the user has finished working, follow these steps:

| Figure 10.1 | Accessing Google Drive |

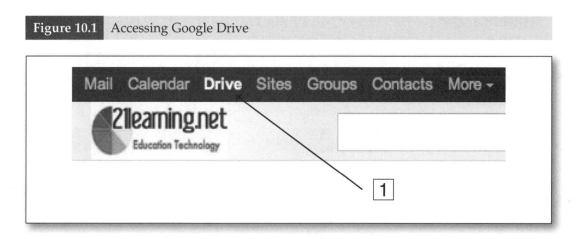

1. Click on **Drive** at the top of the navigation bar shown in Figure 10.1.
   a. This will open the Drive documents list, which is where all of the Google Docs and other file types are stored.
2. Manage My Drive to perform tasks such as:
   a. Create a new Doc CREATE .
   b. Upload a file 🔼.
   c. Create a new folder 📁 .

MANAGING DRIVE

Google Drive gives users access to all of their Google Docs and any other file types they have uploaded to the drive. It is like the documents folder that is stored on a computer, but it can be accessed from anywhere. Files can be stored, shared, and organized in the cloud, giving the users the ability to have their files on demand no matter where they are. Students and teachers will find that managing their files in the cloud-based storage platform will greatly increase their productivity. For example, students may create folders for each class and place documents, research, or other classroom materials into the specified folder for easy retrieval and sharing.

TECHNOLOGY-INFUSED TEACHING TIP

Students live in a mobile computing world. It is natural for digital natives to share photos and ideas using other cloud-based social media platforms such as Facebook, Twitter, and Google Plus. Look for ways to incorporate sharing and communicating ideas about classroom topics on social media. Teachers can use Facebook and Twitter as discussion forums. Google Drive makes it easy to supplement the conversation with class materials such as links to documents and videos because it allows the user to share files easy. Share a file about a classroom topic copying and pasting the unique URL that Google Drive gives every uploaded file. This is the new lifelong learning. Give them opportunities to engage in conversations that will inspire learning in online spaces that they already are involved in.

Click on the red **Create** icon 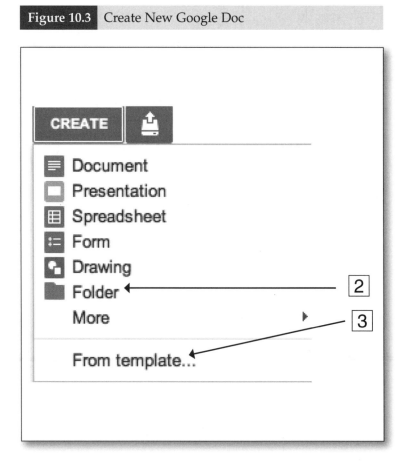 to reveal a drop-down menu that the user will select to create a new Google Doc. See Figure 10.3 for more details.

Figure 10.2	Drive

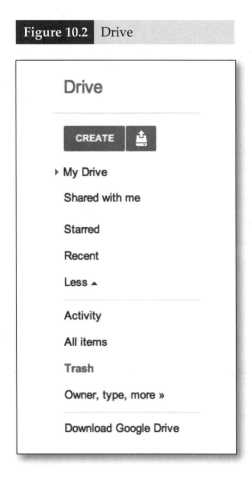

Figure 10.3	Create New Google Doc

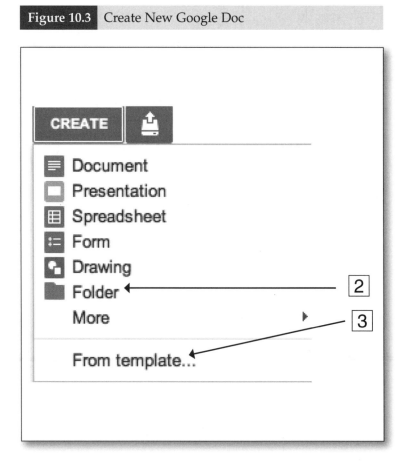

1. Click on any of the document types to create a new Google Doc.

2. Click on **Folder** to create a new folder in My Drive.

3. Choose **From Template** to access documents created by others that may serve your purpose. Explore templates later in this chapter.

- Click the red upload icon 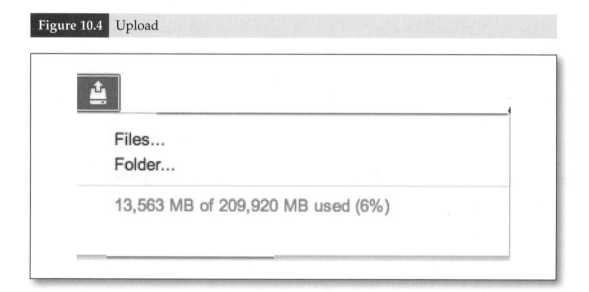 to reveal a drop-down menu that allows the user to upload individual files, complete folders, and manage storage (Figure 10.4).

Figure 10.4   Upload

Files...

Folder...

13,563 MB of 209,920 MB used (6%)

- Under the **My Drive** section in Figure 10.2, click the down arrow to show folders that the user has created. The **My Drive** parent folder stores all of the files that the user owns, created, or uploaded in addition to the subfolders. See how the folders are displayed in Figure 10.2. Look at Figure 10.5 to see how the files look in the documents list.
- The **Shared with me** option in Figure 10.2 displays the documents list items that are shared with the user. These files are not part of **My Drive** because the user does not own them. If the name of the file being shared with the user is bold, then the document has been edited or changed by one of the collaborators much like an unread e-mail in the Inbox label.
- When **Starred or Recent** options are selected, documents that the user has given a star or documents that have been accessed recently will be displayed in the documents list like in Figure 10.5.
- The **Less** option hides the Activity, All items, Trash, and Other, type, more links.
- Click on the **Activity** option to see in the documents list a group of files that have been edited recently by the user or have been edited by collaborators.
- The **All items** option displays all of the files owned by the user and documents shared with the user. This action combines My Drive and Shared with me folders.

Figure 10.5	Documents List

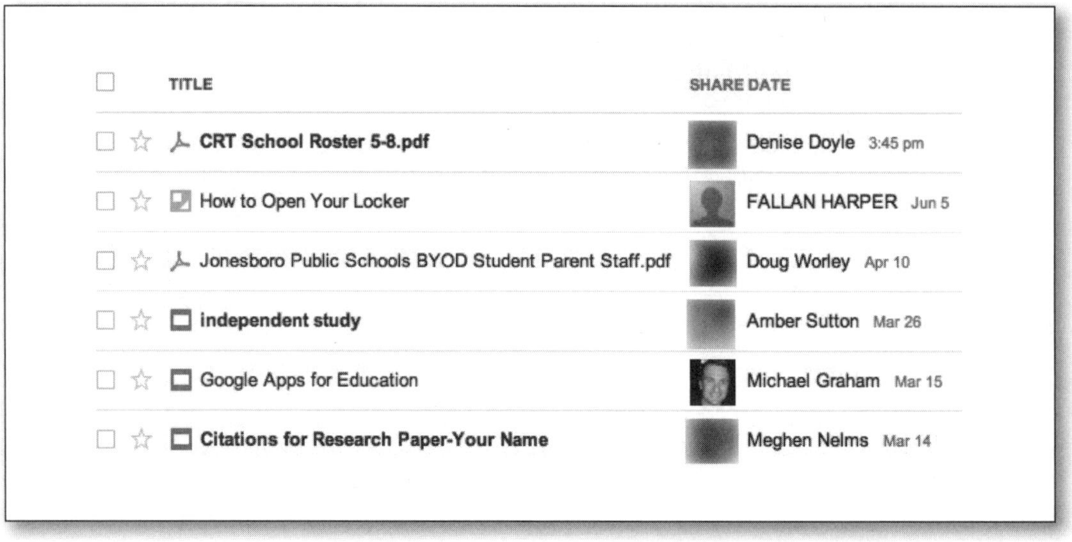

- **Trash** shows the files that the user has deleted. Google never deletes files unless the user empties the trash. It is like the old school recycling bin found in Microsoft Operating Systems.
- Click on the **Other, type, more** option to reveal more specific ways to display documents in the drive.
- Click any of the words in Figure 10.6 to display specific files in the documents list. Click on **Your School District (**Harrisburg School District) under visibility as in the box in Figure 10.6 to find files that are public in the domain. This refers to files that users across the entire domain have made available for public viewing. For example, the superintendent may place district forms such as sick leave, bus request, or purchase order forms to share with the entire district. They could be found by searching with this action.

Figure 10.6	Other, Type, More View of Documents List

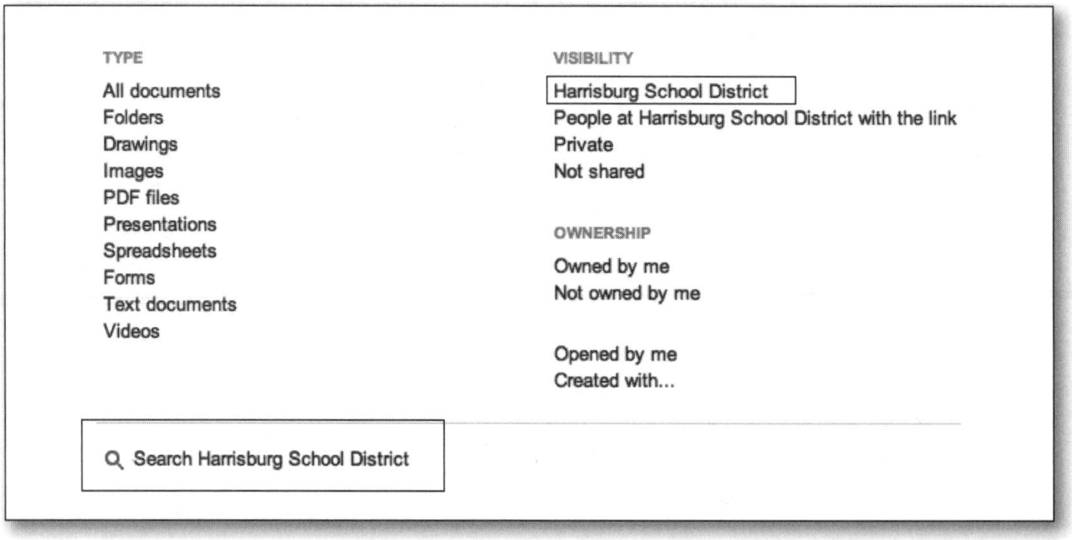

More specifically, in Figure 10.6, think about how this search will help the teacher and student find what they are looking for. Options like this further organize the digital lives of users. Users no longer have to worry when or where they saved a particular file because they are always accessible with a simple search or a more advanced search using the commands in Figure 10.6. Clicking on any of them will display all files that are of that particular type.

Icons of Drive

Google Drive houses files and folders and offers ways to organize the huge amount of digital content that is encountered from day to day. Drive has many organizational options to choose from that can benefit teacher and student. Thinking past the Common Core State Standards, students in college and career will be exposed to a large amount of digital information that they create, consume, and share. Look at the following steps and lists to learn more about how to retrieve and organize files in Google Drive. Figure 10.7 shows a list of icons that can be used to organize and search for files.

| Figure 10.7 | Organization Icons |

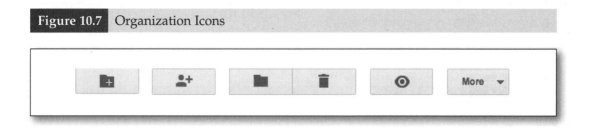

To **organize, remove, preview,** or perform **more** actions to a file or files place a checkmark next to the file or files that the user wants to modify. When checked the icons ₊ ▪ ▪ ⊙ More ▾ appear like in Figures 10.7 and 10.8.

| Figure 10.8 | Managing Files |

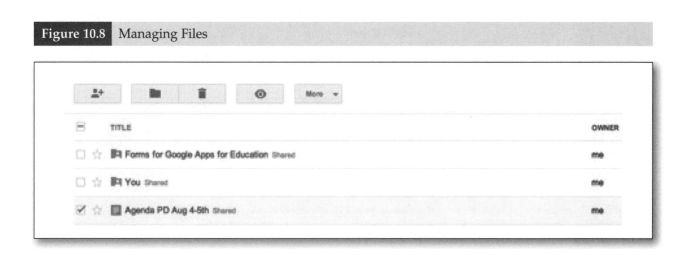

Figure 10.9	Preview File

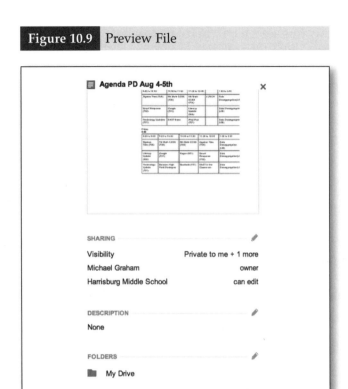

- Click the **Add New Folder** icon to create folders.
- Click the **Share** icon to share the checked file or files with others using the share settings.
- Click the **Organize folder** icon to manage files and folders.
- Click the **Remove** icon to move the checked file or files to the trash.
- Click the **Preview** icon to reveal a detailed overview about the file including (see Figure 10.9):
  - Image of the file
  - Who it is shared with
  - Description
  - What folder it is in
- Click the **More** icon to manage additional options to the checked file shown in Figure 10.10.

Figure 10.10	More Options

More ▾

- Open
- ♣+ Share...   ▶
- ☆ Add star
-     Don't show in Activity list
- 📁 Organize...
-     Rename...
-     Mark as unviewed
-     Download...
-     Submit to template gallery
- 🗑 Remove

In Figure 10.10 **Open, Share, Add star, Organize, Rename, Mark as unviewed**, and **Remove** have been previously discussed; follow the rest of the bullets below for explanation.

- **Don't show in Activity list** will hide the file from the activity view. Activity view shows the user the last few files that were accessed by the owner of the file or a person who it is shared with.
- Select **Download** to save the file to the hard drive of the computer.
- **Submit to template gallery** is a feature that will allow Google Docs to enter the template gallery for others in the domain to use. For example, if the whole school is using the same graphic organizer for writing, then the teacher should submit the file to the template gallery so all users in the domain can access it. Use templates to search for commonly used files such as invoices, time sheets, purchase orders, and resumes.

Sorting Files in Documents List

Sorting files in the documents list is an easy way to access files quickly. Use the icons in Figure 10.11 to organize the documents in a variety of ways.

- Click the drop-down menu on the Sort icon to reveal more options shown in Figure 10.12.

Clicking any one of these options will display the files in the documents list with the particular format. For example, selecting the **Quota used** option will arrange the files from the largest to the smallest with respect to file size. Expect videos and pictures to appear first on the list because they are most likely the largest files.

- Click the **list view** icon ≡ to view the files in a list.
- Click the **grid view** icon ⠿ to see the files in a grid. This shows parts of the actual file cuing the user visually of what the file looks like. This is opposed to the list view that only reveals the file name.
- Click the **settings** gear ⚙ to drop-down more view options shown in Figure 10.13.
- **Display Density** is for aesthetics only. These options change the distance between file names displayed in the documents list.
- **Settings** displays the current storage usage of your Google Drive.
- **Upload settings** will set how the user wants to upload files into Google Drive (Figure 10.14). These options are important to consider because if the user is

Figure 10.11 Viewing Files

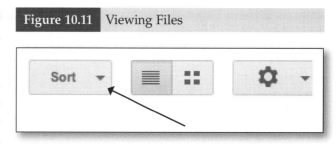

Figure 10.12 Sort Drop-Down Menu

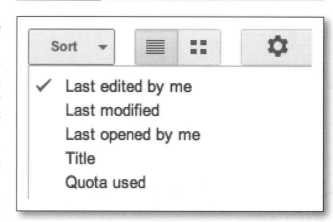

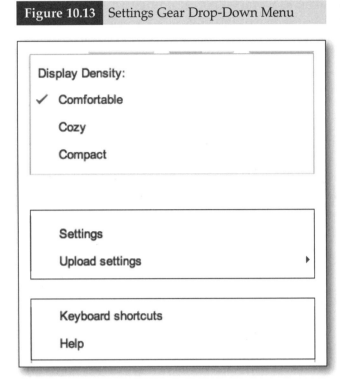

Figure 10.13   Settings Gear Drop-Down Menu

Display Density:

✓ Comfortable

Cozy

Compact

Settings

Upload settings ▸

Keyboard shortcuts

Help

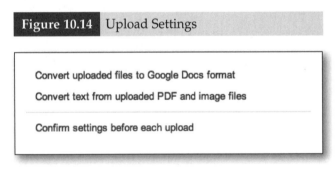

Figure 10.14   Upload Settings

Convert uploaded files to Google Docs format

Convert text from uploaded PDF and image files

Confirm settings before each upload

uploading a file from another format such as Microsoft Word, the user cannot edit it with the Google Documents program. The file must be converted to a Google Docs format before editing can occur using the online collaborative tools. Alternatively, do not convert the file and leave it as a .doc format to simply store the information and download it to a device where Microsoft Word is available to edit the document.

- **Keyboard shortcuts** are quick commands that are ideal for experienced users. Some examples include **Command+C** for copy and **Command+V** for paste. Click keyboard shortcuts for a list.
- Click **Help** to be taken to Google's help files online.

SEARCH

Google's search power does not stop with www.google.com. It is permeated into everything it does. This includes Google Drive. Use the search bar at the top of the page in Drive to search for:

- File names
- Text in files
- File types
- Text in images or PDF—Google reads text in PDF and image files and reports that in their search results from drive.

DOWNLOAD GOOGLE DRIVE

Mac and PC users may download the Google Drive folder to their computer. This installs a folder on the computer similar to other folders like the My Documents folder on a PC. When a file is saved into the folder called Google Drive, the file is synced into the user's My Drive folder in the cloud. This allows the file to be accessed from anywhere with an Internet connection and syncs any changes automatically to Google Drive. The user can drag and drop files into the drive for instant access across all of the users' devices. Files that are too big to e-mail can easily be saved in the My Drive folder for sharing. Share them within drive instead of using attachments. Sharing creates a unique URL that allows users to download the file to their computer or start editing right away if it is a Google Doc. To share a non-Google Doc files with the Google Drive app, follow these steps:

1. Install the Google Drive folder onto your computer by clicking on the **Download Google Drive** link at the bottom of Figure 10.2.

2. Save any file type into the folder called Google Drive on your computer.

   a. This will automatically upload the file to the My Drive folder in the cloud. For example, when working on a Microsoft Word document, you could save the file into the Google Drive folder on your computer and later download the file again to a different device. When editing from another device save the file to Google Drive again and the most recent version of the file will be saved in the cloud. This reduces multiple versions of files that were saved on many different devices.

3. Click on the **My Drive** folder in Google Drive to see the documents list.

4. Find the file in which to share.

5. Place a check mark into the box next to the file name.

6. Select the ⬚ More ⬚ icon. When selected, the drop-down menu will appear as in Figure 10.10.

7. Click **Share** to reveal sharing options as discussed in previous chapters.

SUMMARY

Google Drive is the storage solution for Google Apps for Education that provides 5 gigabytes of storage for users to store any file type. Students and teachers can share, manage, and upload files and folders easily to their online hard drive giving them flexibility to work anywhere. With Google Drive students can create folders and organize their digital content creating student progress portfolios that can track their academic record. For example, students entering college may be required to submit a writing sample from their high school work. With Google Drive, students can access all of their work from any grade level and not worry about where they saved it. Similarly, teachers can create their professional learning folders where they can store information found online and share it with coworkers through share settings.

Wherever the users go, so do their files. Google Drive is the final piece of the puzzle for storage for Google Docs, giving the user mobility. College and career will increasingly rely on mobility of its students and employees to get work done on the go. Although this is the last of the official Google Apps for Education, the next chapter will explore an array of supportive tools produced by Google to make Google Apps for Education even better.

RESOURCE LINK

Access videos, video tutorials, and other Web content by accessing this link:

- http://goo.gl/r2Oj3

11

Even More

KEY FEATURES

❖ Search secrets

❖ A Google a Day trivia search game

❖ http://goo.gl URL Shortener

❖ Quick-response (QR) codes

❖ Chrome

❖ Panaramio

❖ Google Maps

❖ Google Scholar

Throughout the previous chapters, we have been learning about the suite of Google tools called Google Apps for Education. In that suite of applications, students and teachers have access to Gmail, Google Docs, Google Calendar, Google Sites, and Google Video. These five apps are not the end of the story when learning and working with Google, they are just the ones nicely packaged and controlled by the school's domain administrator. Other apps exist that are not part of the Google Apps for Education service, and they can be accessed with ease and have high educational value linking to the Common Core State Standards. This chapter explores other free Google products that can supplement the Google Apps for Education package to help students and teachers thrive in a technologically based learning environment.

SEARCH

Search is Google's most popular product. It is so popular that it is now part of the English language. USAToday.com reported in June 2006 that the word *Google* was added to the *Merriam-Webster's Collegiate Dictionary* as a verb (http://goo.gl/db1fz). To *Google* means to do a Web search for something. Google frowns on this use of the word because it may take away from its brand if people start to use it generically as *any* Web search and not specifically a *Google* Web search. Xerox faced this problem.

Search is Google's first priority. Google's familiar search bar is in every Google App for Education, where it can help users find what they have created in Google Docs, e-mailed in Gmail, or can help users search for appointment details in Google Calendar. Most people's first experience with Google is using the search engine www.google.com. Google has a clean look with no advertisements on its front page. The crisp, clean backdrop clears the mind and reminds the user to think simply when searching. Simple search terms are often the best. For example, when a user wants to find websites that contain information about how to cite using American Psychological Association (APA) style, type the search term *APA citation example* in the search box and press **Enter** to reveal websites that Google has ranked based on its search algorithm. The simple approach using the fewest words possible will reveal the most relevant results. The most relevant websites are found near the top of the search results. This directs the user to a webpage that may contain the information the user seeks.

Search is difficult to teach. It requires trial and error and attention to precision. The user should learn from the first few searches and tailor subsequent searches to acquire information that is useful. Students who do not find what they are looking for in the first few results that Google provides tend to give up and report their findings with incomplete or inaccurate information. Google provides online courses for anyone to learn how to search better. Sign up for Google's Power Searching Course at this link: http://goo.gl/Gopye. It is student friendly and it is a required part of our middle school technology classes. Use the following tips to help students avoid misinformation in searches.

Use quotes. Placing quotes around a specific word or phrase will signal Google to only provide search results that contain the exact spelling and order of the words in quotes. For example, when searching for *education technology*, the search results will give the user content that has the words *education* and *technology*. By placing quotes around the two words "*education technology*," Google will provide search results that have the words *education technology* exactly as it appears in the quotes. This will narrow down search results and save the user time.

Search a specific site. Search a specific website by typing the word **site** followed by a colon. For example, *site:www.nytimes.com education technology* would return results that only come from www.nytimes.com that have to do with education technology.

Use the minus sign. Use the minus (-) or the dash sign to eliminate terms from the search results. For example, a student wants to know about King Tut but the teacher explicitly does not want the information to come from www.wikipedia.org. To exclude search results that originate from www.wikipedia.org, place a minus sign in front of the website like in the following example: *King Tut -site:www.wikipedia.org.*

Use the calculator. Every Google search bar is a calculator. Place common or complex math in the search bar, and Google will give you the answer. For example, students are able to type into the Google bar *2*8+(sqrt 64)^3* and Google will calculate the expression and display the result. It even recognizes functions such as y=2x+4 or y=x^2. Google will graph the function as the first search result (see Figure 11.1). For an example of higher level math, watch the YouTube videos at these links in the list to see amazing three-dimensional graphs and explanations of their functions. It is a must-see for any math teacher!

- http://goo.gl/GikKu
- http://goo.gl/yFqdW
- http://goo.gl/OvTgo

Figure 11.1 Calculator in Search Bar

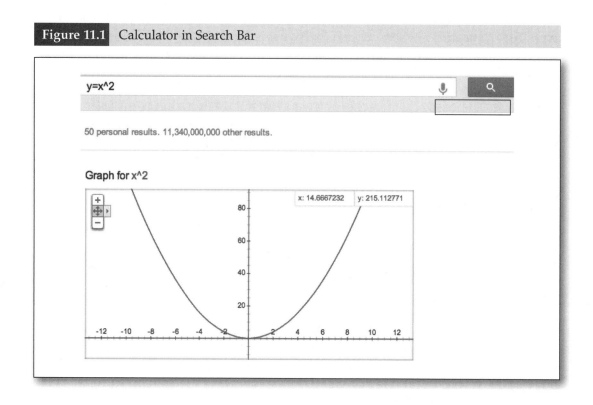

The box in Figure 11.1 below the search query, $y=x^2$, notes that there are more search results than just the graph. Google ranks the graph of the function above the other search results because it thinks that the graph is the most useful for the query. In case the user was looking for more information about the function, he or she can scroll down below the graph and Google will provide webpages associated with that search.

Search public data. Users may search the public data provided by the United States, World Bank, United Nations Economic Forum, and others. The data are searchable through the site http://www.google.com/publicdata/directory. Search through several databases and take advantage of the charts generated by Google for stunning visualizations. For example, popular data are displayed in the form of graphs and charts that are interactive. Students can interact with the information by changing variables based on different views. Motion charts are a great example of this. In these charts, the data are shown on the graph with a play button in the bottom left-hand corner. Clicking play shows the data move in response to time. One of the best examples of this is the public data of births per woman versus life expectancy of the nation in which they live. Clicking play will show how the data have changed over time. Find this example at http://goo.gl/AX8k1. An example of a simpler use of public data is U.S. population. Search from the Google bar: *population of United States,* and it will yield a graph of the nation's population over time. In addition to this information, the user can select specific states to compare (see Figure 11.2).

Figure 11.2 State-by-State Comparison of Population

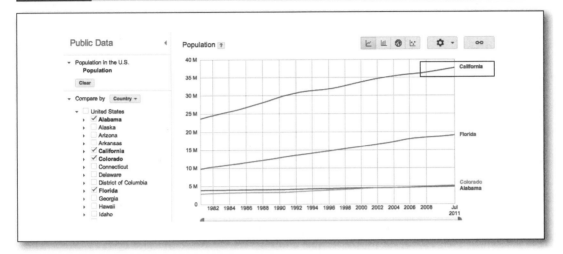

Convert units. Users can convert any comparable units of measure, including but not limited to length, volume, weight, and time. For example, students can easily convert fathoms into feet by searching for *12 fathoms to feet*. This query will yield the answer as shown in Figure 11.3. The graphic in the box in Figure 11.3 next to the answer lets the user know that the answer came from the Google Calculator rather than regular search results. For instance, you would cite Google itself with the information, not a website Google brought you to.

Figure 11.3 Fathoms to Feet Conversion

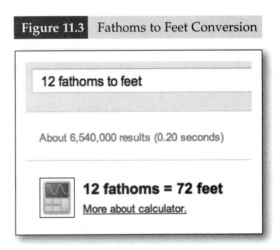

Knowledge Graph

Google has developed the Knowledge Graph to make it easier to find important information about a topic being searched. Simple searches like names of places, people, or things yield the Knowledge Graph located on the right side of the regular search results. The Knowledge Graph contains facts, pictures, maps, and informational highlights about the query. Look at Figure 11.4 for an example of a search for *Memphis, TN*.

The Knowledge Graph will be different depending on the search term. Memphis, TN is a place, so located in its Knowledge Graph is the population, area, and current weather conditions, among other items. If searching for a person, then the graph will contain different information such as birthplace, age, contributions to society, etc. Students and teachers can use the Knowledge Graph as a starting point for research. It is fantastic for elementary searchers because of the quick facts that it provides the users without having to wade through webpages for information.

Searching Specified

Google provides many ways to get information. The most common way is to type a query in the search bar, and Google will provide the user with webpages that

Figure 11.4   Knowledge Graph

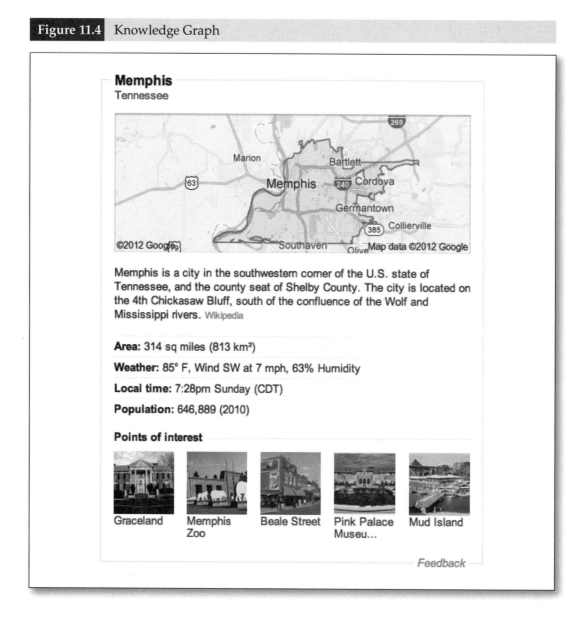

Memphis
Tennessee

Memphis is a city in the southwestern corner of the U.S. state of Tennessee, and the county seat of Shelby County. The city is located on the 4th Chickasaw Bluff, south of the confluence of the Wolf and Mississippi rivers. Wikipedia

Area: 314 sq miles (813 km²)

Weather: 85° F, Wind SW at 7 mph, 63% Humidity

Local time: 7:28pm Sunday (CDT)

Population: 646,889 (2010)

Points of interest

Graceland   Memphis Zoo   Beale Street   Pink Palace Museu...   Mud Island

Feedback

contain the information. Sometimes, the information given is too broad. Google will perform specialized searches that can narrow down the results to the user's specific needs. For example, students in science class may be researching current science news for a project. But, every time the student searches for the *Large Hadron Collider,* news results are buried deep in the search results that may contain off-topic content. The student would then perform the search and click on **News** search shown in Figure 11.5 to access only news articles about the topic. This list is located on the left side of the search results. Specifically search the Internet using the filters in Figure 11.5 to maximize searching efficiency.

- **Web** searches everything on the Web and does not exclude any of the other specific searches on the list in Figure 11.5.
- **Images** will search any image file from the Web, even search for a particular color in the images.

- **Maps** searches Google Maps and provides driving directions if the search query follows this example: *Portland, OR to Little Rock, AR*
- **Videos** searches videos related to the query from across the Web.
- **News** searches news related websites and provides results accordingly.
- **Shopping** searches various Web and brick-and-mortar stores, including amazon.com and Wal-Mart, to provide pricing and ordering of products.
- **Books** searches the books.google.com database providing samples or in some cases full copies of books.
- **Places** searches will result in information concerning the location in the search. For example, to find the best barbecue in Memphis, search in Google places and it will reveal restaurant reviews along with a map. Click on the map to be given directions from your current location.
- **Blogs** searches only information found in blogs. Many influential experts and organizations write blogs on a variety of topics. For example, the blog from *Education Week* (http://blogs.edweek.org/) has great information for teachers about professional practice. Use this search to add to your professional learning network.
- **Flight** information can be searched using this filter. Flight search includes:
  - Departure/Arrival times
  - Prices
  - Map of flight

Figure 11.5 Special Search

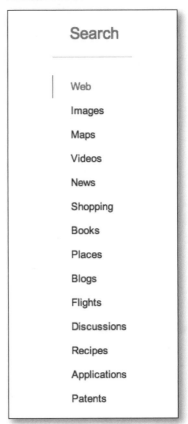

- **Discussions** search shows discussion forum conversations only. This is particularly useful when wanting to know how to do a particular task, but you cannot find the right search terms to express it or cannot find results from a traditional website. Discussion forums often are treasure troves of complicated information where people have voiced concerns or questions. Read the questions to find out if people are having the same trouble as you are.
- **Recipes** searches the Web for recipes. This search option lets the user filter specific ingredients to include calorie content and cook time.
- **Applications** searches for apps for mobile devices from various app stores. Search for education games or other content using this feature.
- **Patents** searches the United States Patent Office.

A GOOGLE A DAY

Being good at search takes experience and knowledge of how the search engine operates. Goggling something without giving it thought may lead to results that do not yield the best information; experience is necessary. Google's algorithm that ranks pages and Web content based on the search query is constantly evolving, and staying up-to-date can be challenging. To gain experience, teachers and students can play the game *A Google a Day*. This trivia game asks players to use their search skills to find the answers to questions posed by Google. The game is a great way for teachers to implement a little fun in the classroom while teaching the students a lot about search skills. The Common Core State Standards do not specifically address using computerized search algorithms like Google's to find digital information. Although search is not a skill demanded by the Common Core State Standards, it will be an imperative skill for the college- and career-ready student. Practicing search skills and becoming competent in finding information will be one of the most important skills for life after high school. Have students try it at www.agoogleaday.com. This will make excellent bell work or a class starter to get students warmed up for learning. See Figure 11.6 for a screenshot of the game.

Follow these steps to play:

1. Enter www.agoogleaday.com into a Web browser's address bar.

2. Click on the **regular game** link as shown in Figure 11.7 to reveal the page in Figure 11.6.

   a. Signing in with Google Plus (Google's social networking service) will challenge the user's Google Plus friends and post scores to their profile page.

3. Read the question in the box as shown in Figure 11.6.

4. Use the Google search bar above the question to search for the answer.

   a. Answers may take longer than one query; be diligent and remind students of Standard for Mathematical Practice 1: *Make sense of problems and persevere in solving them.*

5. Click the box | Enter your answer | to answer the question.

6. Press | Submit | to check the answer. If correct, points will be awarded based on speed.

Figure 11.6 A Google a Day

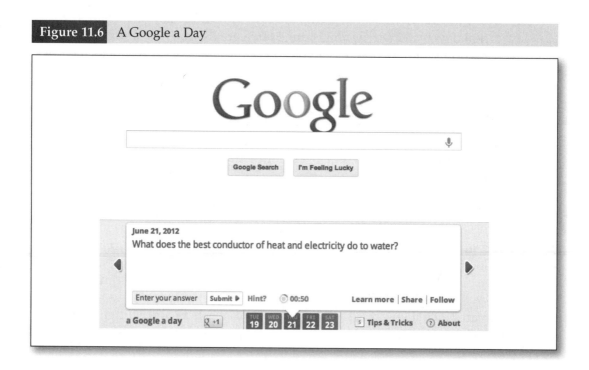

Figure 11.7 Regular Game

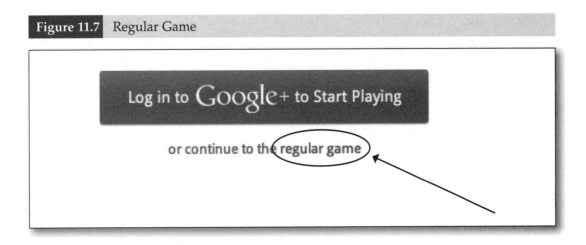

GOOGLE URL SHORTENER

Long, complicated URLs are cumbersome to students and teachers. Long URLs can make it very difficult for students or teachers to type the original URL into the address bar to be directed to a website. Google provides a service that shortens the URL and gives it a new manageable link. For example, the URL for a document a teacher wants to share with students is https://docs.google.com/document/d/1TNd9xj4hVWiiz7VHTfmSX7JZVnYd_tOJJ-oYcBRrDRs/edit. Imagine typing this entire URL in the address bar; it is difficult to get it right because every character in the URL must exactly match for the Web browser to find the page. The teacher can use the Google URL Shortener to shorten the URL. For example, the URL above now turns into http://goo.gl/mZP6T. This new URL will direct the user to the exact same document or webpage as the long URL but without the confusion. Follow these steps to create a shortened URL:

1. Enter http://goo.gl into a Web browser's address bar.

2. Copy the long link to the computer's clipboard (right-click, then copy).

3. Paste the long link into the box shown in Figure 11.8 (right-click, then paste).

4. Click the **Shorten URL** icon.

Follow these steps to shorten a long URL; a new shortened link is now created. The user is limited only by her imagination of how to use the shortened link. If the

Figure 11.8 Regular Game

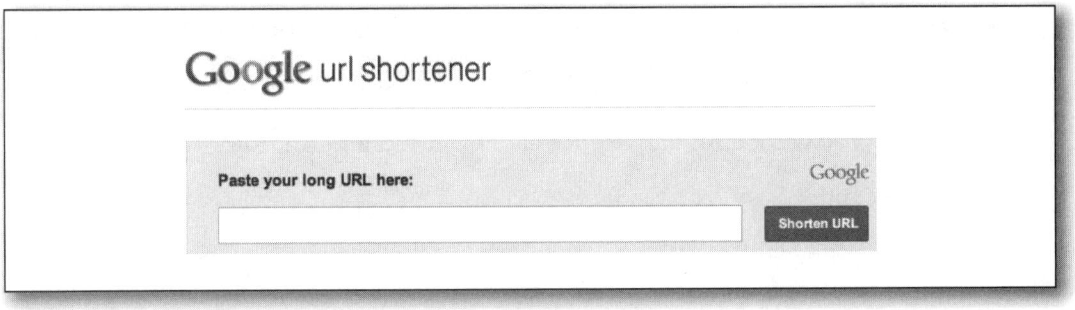

Google url shortener

Paste your long URL here: Google

[   ] **Shorten URL**

shortened link is a Google Doc or a file from the user's Google Drive, then the user can share the file by providing the shortened URL. Share the URL through Twitter, Facebook, e-mail, or print it out on a flier or parent newsletter. If it is a document that is used by the class regularly, have the students memorize the shortened link or have them write it down in their notebooks.

QR Codes and goo.gl

In addition to shortening URLs, http://goo.gl automatically creates QR codes. QR codes are like traditional barcodes found on library books or at the supermarket, but they can hold many times the information a regular barcode can hold. The most frequent use of QR codes in education is to make accessing URLs easy on mobile devices. With the QR code, the user does not have to type long URL into his mobile device's address bar. Instead, he can snap the QR code with his QR code reader application and have instant access to the link that is encoded into the image. Figure 11.9 depicts an example of what a QR code looks like.

| Figure 11.9 | QR Code Watermelon |

TECHNOLOGY-INFUSED TEACHING TIP

Use your phone's QR code reader application to snap the QR code in Figure 11.9 or go to this link if you do not have a QR Reader (http://goo.gl/YbSN6). This code is attached to a link of a Google Document. The Google Doc is an informational sheet made by a student to inform readers about items in our school garden. The codes were printed and laminated, then placed on stakes next to the plants. The codes serve as extra information to the people who visit our garden and for our classes that go to the garden to research the produce grown there.

TECHNOLOGY-INFUSED TEACHING TIP

Visit the links below for a list of free QR Readers for iOS and Android.

- Android: http://goo.gl/yCA3D
- iOS: http://goo.gl/xccVu

To create a QR code from http://goo.gl, follow these steps.

1. Follow the steps to shorten a link located near Figure 11.8.
2. Click on the **Details** link located below the Shorten URL box as shown in Figure 11.10.

Figure 11.10 Click Details to Access QR Code

3. Copy or save the QR code image located in the upper right-hand corner of the **Details** screen as shown in Figure 11.11.
   a. This allows the user to print on paper, post to social media, or print on a t-shirt the QR code that was created. This may be read by any tablet or smartphone to directly take the user to the link encoded in the image.

Figure 11.11 Google URL Shortener QR Code

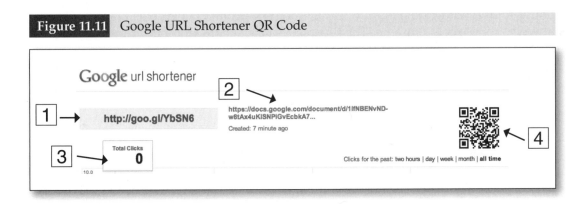

In Figure 11.11, valuable statistics and information about the link are recorded. Follow the list here to understand what this image displays:

1. The shortened link is displayed in blue.
2. The long URL is displayed in green to the right of the shortened link.
3. The total number of clicks or snaps of the QR code is located below the shortened link.
4. The QR code is prominently displayed in the right-hand corner of the page.
   a. This image can be copied, saved, and transmitted anywhere.

TECHNOLOGY-INFUSED TEACHING TIP

You may have seen QR codes in magazines, advertisements, or on product packaging in a store. Take the time to practice with your device's QR code reader to gain experience. One activity teachers can do with QR codes is to create a scavenger hunt. Students are given a mobile device such as an iPad or Android tablet to read the codes. The codes are linked to Google Documents that contain questions or clues to find the next code leading the user to another clue. See the Resource Link section for more amazing uses for QR codes in the classroom.

GOOGLE CHROME

Mashable, an online tech magazine, reported in May 2012 that Google Chrome is the number-one portal to the Web in the world, outranking all other browsers, including Microsoft Internet Explorer, Mozilla Firefox, and Apple Safari in number of users (http://mashable.com/2012/05/21/chrome-is-tops). It is a Web browser developed by Google that offers users a complete Google experience when interacting with Google's apps and features. Other browsers like Microsoft's Internet Explorer, Apple's Safari, and Mozilla's Firefox are designed to access the Web differently than Google. It stands to reason that using Google Chrome will work better with Google Apps and its other tools. The other browsers do work with Google Apps, but they may not have all the features that are available in Google Chrome. For example, users can only upload individual files in non-Chrome browsers, but they can upload entire folders into Google Drive using Google Chrome. Download Google Chrome at www.google.com/chrome. The browser is fast, secure, and built for Google Apps.

Chrome OS

In addition to Chrome browser, Google has developed Chrome OS. Chrome OS is Google's Chrome Operating System for computers. Google has developed a lightweight, fast, and inexpensive computer made by Samsung and ACER that runs Google Chrome OS totally going away from Microsoft Windows and Apple OSX. The notebook version is called Chromebook and the desktop version is called Chromebox. The advantage of Chromebooks and Chrome OS is that when students turn on the computer, the log-in screen is their Google Apps account. There is no reason to install or buy third-party office software for these machines because the first thing that comes up is Google Drive and access to Google Apps for Education. Students may store their work in the cloud and access it from any computer with Internet access. Domain administrators working with Chrome OS can deploy apps to the user's account that are downloaded from the Chrome Web Store. In the Chrome Web Store, users can download apps to their specific username and can have access to them anywhere where they sign into Chrome.

Chrome Web Store

The Google Chrome Web Store is the application store for Google Chrome. Here users can download specific applications that make the Google Chrome experience better. Many educational apps are available free for download that will help students learn and teachers be more productive. Visit https://chrome.google.com/webstore/ to search the database of apps.

To search and download apps from the Chrome Web Store, follow these steps:

1. Download the Google Chrome Web browser at www.google.com/chrome.

2. Install the program on your computer.

3. Click the Google Chrome icon to access the browser from your desktop or programs list.

4. Click on the chrome web store link located in the bottom right-hand corner of Chrome to access the store.

5. Search for apps by using the search bar located in the upper left-hand corner of the webpage as shown in Figure 11.12.

PANORAMIO

Panoramio is a photo-sharing platform owned by Google. Users can explore the world in photos uploaded by users. Photos are tagged by keywords and location then placed on a Google Map. Teachers and students can find wonderful photos of places that they are studying. Remember that the owners of the photos set the copyrights to the images. Be sure to follow all copyright rules.

Figure 11.12 Searching the Chrome Web Store

Panoramio and Common Core State Standards

The Common Core State Standards want students to be college and career ready by the time they leave high school. Google Apps for Education provides experience with the tools they need to enter the workforce or college. Tools like Panoramio are different and more specialized and are ideal to offer students experiences with enrichment. When students have time to discover places and photos, they will have a better understanding of the culture or features that makes a location unique. A picture is worth a thousand words, and there are thousands of photos from different points of view concerning the same topic in this app. For example, when studying the White House in social studies class, teachers can direct students to use Panoramio to search for photos that were taken by people near the White House. There are hundreds of images uploaded of that location all with their own unique perspective. Students can study the photos and discover for themselves the political, cultural, or artistic points of view of the photographers. To take it one step further, students who have taken photos of the White House can upload their own version and describe their feelings and political motivations in the caption. This action will aid others in their understanding of the topic. When students get to contribute to the existing knowledge of the topic, it is my experience that the quality of work improves.

To start exploring the world through photos, follow these steps:

1. Go to http://www.panoramio.com/ in a Web browser.

2. Search for specific places by typing in the name of the location in the search box shown in Figure 11.13.

Figure 11.13	Search Photos by Location

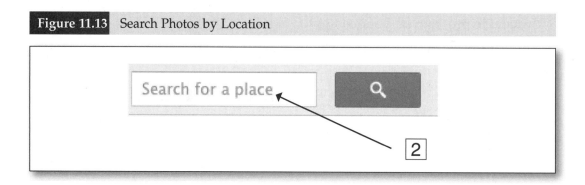

3. Click on the drop-down menu **Explore** to reveal options shown in Figure 11.14.

Figure 11.14	Explore

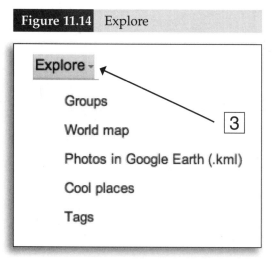

- Click on **Groups** to explore photos that describe a user's general interest.
  - Examples of Groups include:
    - ☐ Sunrise and sunset
    - ☐ Rivers, lakes, and streams
    - ☐ Mountains
    - ☐ Best beaches
    - ☐ Historic places
- Click on **World Map** to reveal a world map with thumbnail photos connected to a specific location on the map. For example, zoom in on the Pacific Northwest to reveal pictures of the world specific to that location.
- Click on **Photos in Google Earth** to open Panoramio Photos in the Google Earth Application (if it is downloaded on the user's computer).
- Click on **Cool places** to open another window that displays photos overlaying a map of a random location that is noted for its beauty, political importance, or other cool features. Click on the **See next** ⇨ button on that page to go on to the next "cool place."
- Click on **Tags** to open the window pictured in Figure 11.15. Tags are keywords users can "tag" photos with to make it easy to search. In Figure 11.15, words that are larger are proportional to the number of times that word was used to tag a photo. For example, the tag *Nature* found in Figure 11.15 is used most to describe photos. Click in the search box to enter a keyword for a tag that may interest the user.

Figure 11.15 Search Photos by Location

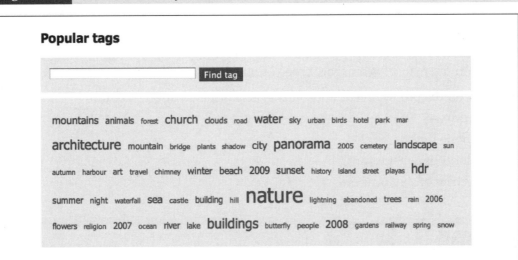

TECHNOLOGY-INFUSED TEACHING TIP

Teachers of literature and reading often are left with the task of describing places involved in the reading based on the author's words alone or with the aid of illustrations. Use Panoramio as a tool to get students to understand the places and people of a region they are reading about. For example, when reading the works of Mark Twain, students can search for cities and towns that the characters visit in Panoramio. Imagine the light bulb going off in the mind of the inner-city 14-year-old boy when he looks at a photo from the bank of the Mississippi just as Huck Finn would have seen it more than a century earlier.

MAPS

Google Maps is a first-class map program that uses Google's search power to help users find anything in any place. Google Maps allows users to search for directions to and from places by car, walking, or public transportation. The search results for directions overlays routes onto the map and provides driving mileage and time of travel, including the current traffic conditions. Google Maps allows the user to view satellite images of locations and zoom in for detail. Users can also use the hybrid view to overlay roads and streets on satellite images. To search directions or locations on Google Maps, follow these steps:

1. Go to http://maps.google.com.

2. Enter a search term into the search bar. Use the following search examples to get started using Google Maps.

   a. ZIP code

   b. City, state

    c. Physical address

    d. Landmarks example: *Grand Canyon*

    e. Places example: *Cuban restaurants, Orlando, FL*

3. Click search to reveal pins that are dropped onto the map, pinpointing the location on the map of your search (see Figure 11.16).

4. Click on the pin to reveal information about the location, including:

    a. Address

    b. Phone number

    c. Menu (if a restaurant)

    d. Picture of the location

Figure 11.16	Dropped Pins and Information

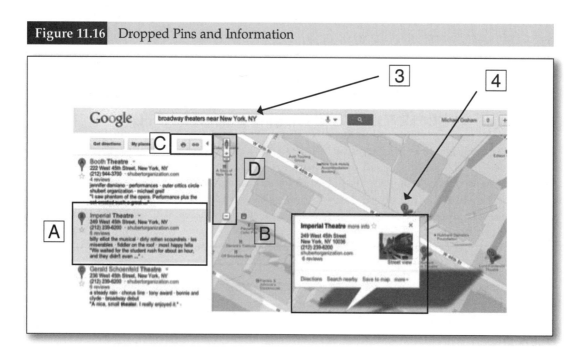

- The pins are labeled by alphabet and correspond with more detailed information on the left side of the page.
- The box labeled **A** represents snippets of information about the pins dropped on the map.
- The box labeled **B** appears when the user clicks on a pin.
- The box labeled **C** contains print and the link to the map so it can be shared with friends.

To share the map:

1. Click on the link icon [GO] to open the box in Figure 11.17.

2. Copy the link in the box.

3. Paste the link in an e-mail, instant message, Facebook, or Twitter post.

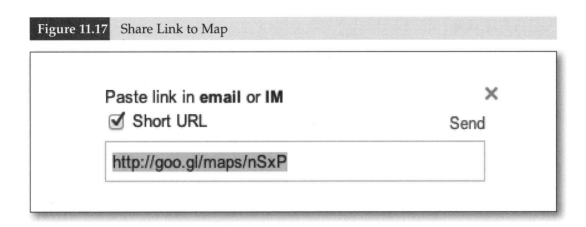

Figure 11.17 Share Link to Map

> Paste link in **email** or **IM**   ✕
>
> ☑ Short URL   Send
>
> http://goo.gl/maps/nSxP

- The box labeled **D** contains the zoom plus and minus buttons as well as Pegman. See more about Pegman in the next section.

Street View and Pegman

Street View is a feature in Google Maps that lets the user see street-level imagery of a location in Google Maps. Google has a fleet of cars that have driven many of the roads in the world, and they have taken a 360-degree picture every few feet. The image captures buildings, passersby, and interesting landmarks. The purpose of this for the regular Google user is to be able to see what the location looks like from the street before they travel there. This gives them a way to know exactly what they are looking for when they arrive. In education, Street View could be used in a variety of contexts. Students can research places where Street View is enabled to see what the places look like as if they were standing there. For example, a search for Rome, Italy, places a pin next to the *Colosseum*. Activate Street View to see the *Colosseum* from the street. Sometimes Google has gone off the street with Street View. This means that they have taken their cameras inside buildings like the White House, the Roman *Colosseum*, and in a boat on the Amazon River. For a full list of Street View places, go to the Street View Gallery located at http://goo.gl/9MzCK. To use Pegman to activate Street View from any map, follow these steps:

1. Follow the steps to search for locations on Google Maps described earlier.

2. Click and drag Pegman (box D in Figure 11.16) onto the map where the user wants to see street-level imagery (if the street turns blue, Pegman has taken a photo from that location).

3. Use the arrows that are overlaid on the image to navigate the street.

   a. Using the arrows allows the student to virtually walk the streets of the location to explore the area.

4. Exit Street View by clicking on the ✕ in the upper right-hand corner of the map.

SCHOLAR

Google Scholar is an easy way to search for scholarly literature. Searching through Google Scholar will yield search results only from journals, scholarly books, articles, university libraries, and other trusted sources. Google ranks its search results in the same manner as publishers do. Google carefully measures the work's contribution to the field as well as the number of citations in other works. Google Scholar is a great place to start a research project. For example, senior research papers will require that the information be from trusted sources that are scholarly in nature. The students get a chance to read some of the abstracts and articles to gain a starting point of information. Often, students believe that information is true or trustworthy because it was published on the Internet. It will be valuable for students to know the difference between a plain Google search and a Google Scholar search as they become college and career ready. Reading evidence-based text and writing about its impact is an important skill. To access Google Scholar, follow these steps:

1. Go to http://scholar.google.com.

2. Type a search query into the search bar shown in Figure 11.18.

Figure 11.18 Search Photos by Location

3. Review the results.

4. Narrow the results by selecting the parameters located in Figure 11.19 (opposite).

   The box labeled **A** indicates Articles/ Legal Documents: Click on one or the other to filter search results accordingly. In the box labeled **B**, click on a time interval. In box **C**, check to include or exclude patents or citations.

SUMMARY

Throughout this book, we have been learning how Google Apps for Education can be a great resource in implementing the Common Core State Standards. It is the goal of the standards to get every student college or career ready to face the challenges of life after high school. It is apparent that the Common Core State Standards want educators to infuse more technology into the learning environment. Standards like Anchor Standard 6 for Writing want students to "produce and publish writing using the Internet." Google Apps for Education makes that a reality with the use of Google Docs. It seems like the team of Google employees that built Google Apps for Education must have read the Common Core State Standards and then wrote software to improve the learning experiences of students.

Although the Google Apps for Education package includes many apps that are perfect for school and learning, it does not contain all of the products Google offers. Search,

A Google a Day, Google URL Shortener, QR code generator, Chrome, Chrome OS, Chrome Web Store, Panoramio, Google Maps, and Google Scholar support the Google Apps for Education package and give even more learning tools to students. Educators who are well versed in these tools can make an impact on the proper use of the Internet for learning. Students who have access to learn and work with tools like the ones found at Google will be well-prepped for success in college or a career. Look for lesson plans linked to specific Common Core State Standards in the next part of the book. The Lesson Plan Correlation Chart (found in the Resource section following this chapter) will direct you to the appropriate lesson for your grade level. These lessons will refer to the use of Google Apps for Education and the supporting tools learned about in this chapter.

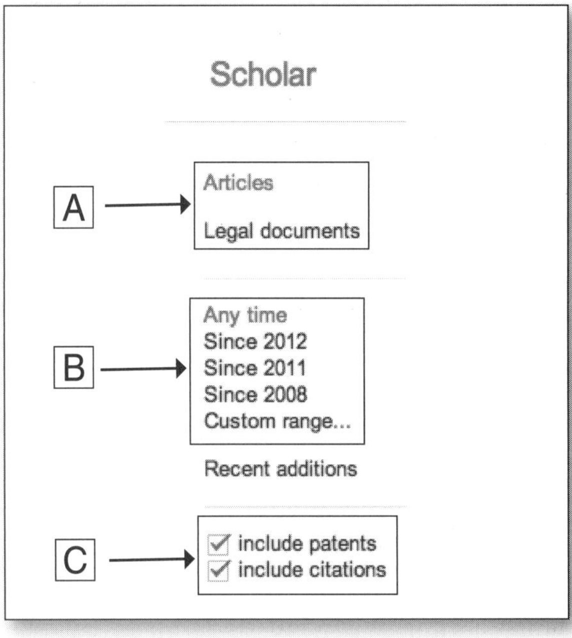

I hope you have enjoyed this resource. But, remember, the learning is not over. Come to the companion website www.21learning.net to get even more lesson plans, content, and insight on how to use Google Apps for Education. Take an active role and become a contributor to the website by using Lesson Cloud. Use Lesson Cloud to upload lesson plans you have developed using Google Apps or other Google products. The Lesson Cloud link and instructions are located on the website.

Figure 11.19 Scholar Search Parameters

RESOURCE LINK

Lesson Plans

Grade Level	Lesson Plan Title	Digital copy found at the link. Lesson plans with numbers are in order in the resource section.	
Elementary School	Book Buddies by Lucie deLaBruere, Jackie Richardson, and Joy Walsh	http://goo.gl/BwGXm	Online Only
Middle School	Historical Novel *My Brother Sam Is Dead* by Carol LaRow	http://goo.gl/SGkkn	Online Only
High School	Datapalooza	http://goo.gl/hHZl2	#14

For additional resources, including lesson plans, videos, and video tutorials, access this link:

■ http://goo.gl/4eyjL

Resources

R.1: Lesson Plan Correlation Chart

Title	Lesson #	Location on the Web	Grade Level	Common Core State Standard(s)	Gmail	Documents	Presentations	Spreadsheets	Forms	Drawings	Calendar	Even More
E-mail the Author (Gmail)	1	http://goo.gl/EOhG7	Elementary	3.RL.5, 3.RL.5	X							Google Search
Call the Expert (Gmail)	2	http://goo.gl/D9WnT	Middle	SL Anchors 1-6	X	X					X	Google Search
E-mail the Journalist (Gmail)	3	http://goo.gl/VRTp7	High School	11-12.RST.1	X	X						Google Search
Reader's Workshop Online Activities (Documents) Joseph Hartman		http://goo.gl/Qz0Pi	Elementary	4.W.6, 5.W.6, 6.W.6, 5.RF.4, 6.RF.4		X						
Jefferson, Adams, and History (Documents)	4	http://goo.gl/rHn33	Middle	6.RL.1, 6.L.1a-e, 6.L.6, 6.W.6		X	X		X	X		
Political Campaign (Documents)	5	http://goo.gl/rHBmn	High School	8.SL.2, 11-12. RH.1-2,6, 11-12. WHST.2,4-6								
Biomes (Presentations) Ronna Van Veghel		http://goo.gl/ILJ3V	Elementary	K-2.W.7, K-3. SL.4		X	X					Google Image Search
Peter Pan (Presentations)	6	http://goo.gl/I9XmX	Middle	7.W.6, 7.W.9a, 7.RL.6		X	X			X		YouTube

(Continued)

(Continued)

Activity	#	URL	Level	Standards						Google Tools
Introduction to the Salem Witch Trials (Presentations) Heather Eggers	7	http://goo.gl/wmf7h	High School	11-12.RI.7, 11-12.W.6, 11-12.W.7, 11-12.SL.1-6	X	X		X		Google Search, http://goo.gl
Introduction to Scientific Method (Spreadsheets) Mary Fran Lynch		http://goo.gl/WtCm6	Elementary	1.MD.4, 2.MD.10, 3.MD.4,			X	X	X	Google Search
iTravel Vacation (Spreadsheets)	8	http://goo.gl/KZuI5	Middle	6.RP.3a-d, 6.W.4-6	X	X		X		Google Maps, Street View, Google Search
Collaborative Lab Experience (Spreadsheets) Cheryl Davis		http://goo.gl/LzaTz	High School	9-10.WHST.6, 9-10.WHST.7, 9-10.WHST.9, 9-10.RST.1	X		X	X		Google Search, http://goo.gl
About Us (Forms)	9	http://goo.gl/zIFu0	Elementary	1.MD.4, 2.MD.10, 3.MD.4			X	X	X	Google Search
Slow Down! (Forms)	10	http://goo.gl/XnXki	Middle	6-8.SL.4-6, 6.SP.2-3	X	X		X	X	Google Search
Attitude Survey (Forms)		http://goo.l/2Zfx3	High School	S-IC.1-6	X	X		X	X	Google Search
Exploring Shapes (Drawings)	11	http://goo.gl/rgg4U	Elementary	1.G.1, 2.G.1, 3.G.1				X		Google Image Search

Project	#	URL	Grade Level	Standards							Google Tools
Tangram Square (Drawings)	12	http://goo.gl/ehls8	Middle	5-6.W.4-6, 5-6.SL.4-6,		X					
Graphic Design in Science (Drawings)	13	http://goo.gl/4mgU9	High School	11-12. WHST.6-10, 11-12.SL Anchor 4-6		X		X			Google Search, YouTube
Telling Time and Google Calendar (Calendar) Caitlin Kelly		http://goo.gl/1Ya5x	Elementary	1.MD.3, 2.MD.7, 3.MD.1	X						Google Search
History of Life on Earth (Calendar) Jason Borgen		http://goo.gl/gWF0k	Middle	6-8.RST.1-4, 6-8.RST.6	X				X		Google Search
Great Moments in Art (Calendar)		http://goo.gl/oSc2J	High School	9-10.W.6-10,	X						Google Search, Google Scholar
Book Buddies (Even More) Lucie deLaBruere, Jackie Richardson, and Joy Walsh		http://goo.gl/BwGXm	Elementary	K-3.RL.4-6		X				X	Google Search
Historical Novel My Brother Sam Is Dead (Even More) Carol LaRow		http://goo.gl/SGkkn	Middle	6-8.RL.9						X	Google Blogger, Google Earth, Google Scholar
Datapalooza (Even More)	14	http://goo.gl/hHZl2	High School	F-IF.4, F-IF.7, SL Anchor 2-3, SMP 4				X		X	Google Data Explorer

Title: E-mail the Author

Elementary

Reading

Overview

This lesson will explore technology skills of composing an e-mail and practicing with a keyboard. Students will read an assigned piece of writing and formulate questions that they will ask directly to the author through e-mail. Students should know in advance that they will be required to ask the author questions they have about the characters or plot. The students will make notes as they read.

Objective

The students will read an assigned text, for example, poem, article, or book. While reading, the students will formulate questions that they would like to ask the author of the work. The students will then compose an e-mail using their school Gmail account and ask the questions directly to the author.

Materials

- Computers with Internet access

Teachers need to access the Internet to search for authors' e-mails. Many newspaper and magazine articles have the e-mail address at the end. It is a good idea to only assign text that the teacher can find e-mails. If no e-mails are found, contact the publisher.

Instructions

The teacher will . . .

1. Assign students an article, poem, or book to read.
2. Explain to the students that they must come up with at least five questions and/or comments for their author about their reading.
    a. They must include the terms that apply to their genre. For example:

  i. Chapter

  ii. Scene

  iii. Stanza

  iv. Plot

  v. Characters

3. Assign students to introduce themselves and tell why they are writing this e-mail.

  a. Students need at least one page of text.

  b. Third grade must be able to write using keyboard skills (see Anchor Standard 6 for Writing Third Grade).

4. Instruct the students to make notes as they read and to formulate any questions they have for the author. Students reading the same article could collaborate on their questions using a Google Document shared with each student. Students can use the shared document to help each other with their questions.

5. Assess the questions before the student e-mails their author and offer feedback as to what makes a good question. After all edits are made, the teacher will tell the students to e-mail their questions to the author's e-mail.

COMMON CORE STANDARDS 3.RL.5, 3.RL.5

Refer to parts of stories, dramas, and poems when writing or speaking about a text, using terms such as chapter, scene, and stanza; describe how each successive part builds on earlier sections.

Distinguish their own point of view from that of the narrator or those of the characters.

Assessment

  Students are informally assessed on the comprehension of their text. They must at least have a working knowledge of the text to ask appropriate questions. Help the student make revisions before the e-mail is sent. Consider grading the student's ability to make revisions in response to collaboration with the teacher, not necessarily the first draft.

LESSON PLAN 2

Title: Call the Expert

Middle School

Overview

Speaking and listening are two of the most important learning modalities used by humans. Learning is an active process, and oftentimes a conversation can replace hours of reading about a topic. In this lesson, students will use the Gmail Call Phone or Video Chat feature to call an expert in the student's topic of study. This lesson plan can be used for any discipline. Adapt this to your class for a fun and exciting use of Gmail.

Objective

The students will call a person that works, studies, or has special knowledge of a topic they are studying in class. Students will use the Call Phone or Video Chat features in Gmail to speak and listen with an expert.

Instructions

Teachers need to plan ahead and make a list of potential people to contact. Each discipline will have different people to contact. For example, when students are studying renewable energy in middle school science class, the teacher would collect a list of people to contact from the local power plant or biodiesel company. A Web search will be a sufficient starting point for teachers to get information.

The teacher will . . .

1. Introduce the topic they are studying.

2. Contact professionals ahead of time asking permission to be contacted.

3. Gather contact information, including e-mail, so students can make the initial contact and set up an appointment.

4. Assign students to create a Google Doc of the questions and rationale of questions to be asked with sufficient research and share that with the teacher for review.

5. Schedule time for students to use their Gmail accounts to call or video chat.

6. Assign students to document through notes on a shared document what the discussion taught them about their topic.

COMMON CORE STATE STANDARDS

Speaking and Listening Anchor Standards

Comprehension and Collaboration

1. Prepare for and participate effectively in a range of conversations and collaborations with diverse partners, building on others' ideas and expressing their own clearly and persuasively.

2. Integrate and evaluate information presented in diverse media and formats, including visually, quantitatively, and orally.

3. Evaluate a speaker's point of view, reasoning, and use of evidence and rhetoric.

Presentation of Knowledge and Ideas

4. Present information, findings, and supporting evidence such that listeners can follow the line of reasoning and the organization, development, and style are appropriate to task, purpose, and audience.

5. Make strategic use of digital media and visual displays of data to express information and enhance understanding of presentations.

6. Adapt speech to a variety of contexts and communicative tasks, demonstrating command of formal English when indicated or appropriate.

Assessment

Students will be assessed on their speaking and listening skills and their content-specific standards. Students may also be assessed on their questions.

LESSON PLAN 3

Title: E-mail the Journalist

High School

Overview

This lesson will focus on using e-mail for formal communication. Using electronic communication is one of the hallmarks of a college- and career-ready student. Critical analysis of informational text and asking questions, challenging the author's facts or conclusions with evidence will be a valuable skill.

Objective

The students will read an article of their choice from any newspaper, magazine, or digital publication relating to science and technology. The students will look for evidence in the text about the various claims the author makes and research them extensively. The students will analyze the piece, looking for any inconsistencies or gaps in reasoning. The students will then compose an e-mail to the author of the piece asking questions and offering supporting evidence with citations to refute or agree with the author's claims.

Instructions

The teacher will . . .

1. Provide research time for the students to find an article to critique.

2. Provide discussion time for each student to talk about his or her article.

3. Instruct the students to study the claims or assertions made in the article and to fact check them.

   a. If the student believes that the author has gaps or inconsistencies in the writing, the student must provide and cite evidence in the reply.

   b. If no problems are found with the article, instruct the students to supply more corroboration and cite specific studies or other examples where the claims are made.

COMMON CORE STANDARDS (11–12.RST.1)

Cite specific textual evidence to support analysis of science and technical texts, attending to important distinctions the author makes and to any gaps or inconsistencies in the account.

Assessment

Students are to present the e-mail to the teacher for review before sending it. The teacher will grade and give students time to make corrections.

LESSON PLAN 4

Title: Jefferson, Adams, and History

Middle School

Overview

In this lesson the sixth-grade students will be exposed to informational text to gain understanding of what they are reading while citing specific evidence from it to support their claims. Students will make a personalized vocabulary help sheet where the students may enter words into a Google Form for later review. This is kept in their

COMMON CORE STATE STANDARDS

Anchor Standard #1 for Reading

Read closely to determine what the text says explicitly and to make logical inferences from it; cite specific textual evidence when writing or speaking to support conclusions drawn from the text.

Sixth-Grade Standard (6.RL.1)

Cite textual evidence to support analysis of what the text says explicitly as well as inferences drawn from the text.

Anchor Standard #2 for Language

Demonstrate command of the conventions of Standard English capitalization, punctuation, and spelling when writing.

Sixth-Grade Standard (6.L.1a-b)

Demonstrate command of the conventions of Standard English capitalization, punctuation, and spelling when writing.

- Use punctuation (commas, parentheses, dashes) to set off nonrestrictive/parenthetical elements.
- Spell correctly.

Anchor Standard #6 for Language (6.L.6)

Acquire and use accurately grade-appropriate general academic and domain-specific words and phrases; gather vocabulary knowledge when considering a word or phrase important to comprehension or expression.

Anchor Standard #6 for Writing

Use technology, including the Internet, to produce and publish writing and to interact and collaborate with others.

Sixth-Grade Standard (6.W.6)

Use technology, including the Internet, to produce and publish writing as well as to interact and collaborate with others; demonstrate sufficient command of keyboarding skills to type a minimum of **three pages** in a single sitting.

Google Drive for the duration of the lesson to help them prepare to produce and publish a minimum of three pages of writing. In this lesson, teachers will share a copy of the *Letter on Thomas Jefferson* by John Adams from 1776 into their Google Drive.

Objective

The students will read closely a piece of informational text. The students will also cite evidence from the text and use that to form a writing response using Google Documents to produce and publish writing while collaborating with peers and the teacher.

The teacher will . . .

1. Share the text *Letter on Thomas Jefferson* with the entire class with the view only restriction in Google Docs.
   a. This is best done by copying the text from the letter from Appendix A of the Common Core State Standards for English Language Arts or finding it on a licensing website. The letter is in the public domain so copyright is not a problem.

2. Instruct the students to create a Google Form that will log unknown vocabulary words that they encounter in the text. The form should be in another tab on their Web browser for easy access while reading the text in the shared, view only document.
   a. The teacher should practice with the students Google Form creation prior to this activity. The point of the form is to collect unknown or confusing vocabulary words that appear in the text. When the students create this form, Google will automatically generate a Google Spreadsheet that is saved in their Google Drive with the words that they enter. This is valuable differentiation. Instruct the students at a later time in the unit to go back and define the words. The teacher can have access also to this information to individualize vocabulary lessons. For an example of the vocabulary collection form, access this link in a Web browser: http://goo.gl/ExZrC.

3. Instruct the students to read the entire text silently to gain familiarity.

4. Read the text to the students, emphasizing main points with their speaking while stopping to explain and discuss main points and what the text is conveying, supplying evidence.
   a. One question might be: Why did Adams repeat the word "science" twice in Jefferson's reputation that he brought to the Congress?
      i. Was it to emphasize his commitment to evidence-based decision making?
      ii. Did Adams make a mistake in his writing?
      iii. Was Adams making a joke?
      iv. What document were they talking about Jefferson writing and why was it important for an eloquent writer to take on this challenge?
   b. This process will take three days or more. Probe deep and elicit responses from students that make them think of the context of the letter. Questions to ask are:
      i. What events can you think of that surround the year 1776?
      ii. Why were these men meeting and what is the argument that Adams is trying to make for Jefferson?

5. Insist that students' responses to these questions be cited with evidence from the text or other research that the students are allowed to review.

The students will . . .

1. Read the text closely, making notes when necessary in a Google Doc.

2. Listen to the teacher as he or she reads the text with inflection and making note of the main points. (Speaking and listening Common Core State Standards apply here.)

3. Make note and type vocabulary words that they do not understand or words that seem confusing in the Google Form that they have created.

4. Define the words in the list using a variety of print and digital resources in the spreadsheet. These words will be used as a differentiation tool during another class time devoted to vocabulary.

   a. In essence, the students need to spend some time with the words looking them up in a Google Search or paper dictionary. This gives them the opportunity to slowly take in the deeper meaning of the words and have access to the words used in a slightly different context. This will connect meaning back to the *Letter on Thomas Jefferson.* Remember, the Common Core State Standards want the teacher to have the courage to slow down and spend time focusing on a deep understanding.

5. Respond to writing prompt on a Google Document. The document should be shared with a peer or peer group and the teacher. These small groups of no more than three students should read each other's writing and discuss strengths and weaknesses. The students must develop a trusting rapport with the group and be open to constructive criticism. When students get a chance to explain their reasoning, they are much more likely to be engaged in the assignment. (This activity ties into the Standard for Mathematical Practice #3: Construct viable arguments and critique the reasoning of others.)

6. Finalize the writing and complete a response of at least three pages in a single setting.

Assessment

Students will be assessed by the completion of their vocabulary Google Form. This is meant to be an activity for personal growth and a way to differentiate the lesson. In addition to the vocabulary list, the student will write a rough draft of the response to the writing prompt taking into account the suggestions of the teacher and peers. Collaboration of ideas is key. Later, the student will complete a final draft of the response to the prompt in a single setting with a minimum of three pages. The draft must be produced and published on the Internet using Google Documents.

Possible writing prompts to respond:

- What is the main purpose of this letter?
- What evidence did Adams cite in order to convince his readers that Jefferson was the right man for the job?

Title: Political Campaign

High School

Objective

The students will become knowledgeable of the political process of the United States. Students will participate in a group effort to create a campaign for President of the United States. The students will research the platform for the various political parties and design and run a four-week campaign for President. The students will debate and hold a primary and a general election within their classes.

Overview

High school students are approaching voting age. It is important for them to realize how the political system in the United States operates. Students need to be exposed to the structure of campaigns and what the political parties believe will be the right direction for the country. This lesson will explore these points in a group project that will take on the feel of a campaign for President of the United States.

Instructions

1. Students will break up into groups of four assigned by the teacher.
2. Each group will consist of a
   a. Candidate
   b. Campaign manager
   c. Media manager
   d. Party chair
3. Each position in the group will be responsible for their share of the campaign.
   a. Students must research the roles and report to the teacher a plan of action for all members of the group, including a summary of their responsibilities, citing sources.
4. The teacher will assign the groups to a political party based on a random selection.
   a. Democratic
   b. Republican
      i. Choose one group to portray the Tea Party. (Be creative about this group. The teacher may have a secret meeting instructing the Tea Party to try to

push the debate in the Republican camp to the right. Judge the success of their secret mission by how far to the right the Republicans can be pushed.)

    c. Some students may be knowledgeable of the political parties and may identify with a particular group already. Encourage them to participate as their assigned party and to not be discouraged, but to take the opportunity to learn about their perceived opposition.

5. The students will research the platforms of each party and create their own agenda for the campaign. The students will narrow down the issues that are most important to the group as they feel will help them win the election. The goal is for the candidate to win the class election.

6. After students design a platform of the issues that are the most important (a mini convention), the students will create campaign materials using Google Documents and distribute them to the student body using various Google tools.

    a. Leave this up to the imagination of the students but encourage them to be as creative as possible. For example, a campaign document may have many elements:

        i. Google Drawings—graphic design

        ii. Images

        iii. Campaign slogans

        iv. Videos embedded

        v. Links to videos

        vi. Campaign website using Google Sites

    b. Videos made by the participants communicating their plan

    c. Campaign advertisements made by students

7. Students are instructed to make posters, signs, and create Google Docs that can be e-mailed—anything that will attract viewers of their campaign materials.

8. Campaign materials are judged by the rubric found here: http://goo.gl/gVwF9.

9. After the campaign has been run for four weeks, leaders from the party are required to debate the issues in their classes. The teacher will serve as moderator.

10. Each candidate will debate once.

    a. The candidates must be supported by their staff.

    b. Each role will help the candidate prepare for the debate.

11. After the debates, students in their class period will nominate two classmates from both parties and hold a primary election using Google Forms.

    a. The teacher will create a primary ballot and use Gmail to mail it only to their political party members in the class (unless the state has an open primary). Students will vote.

12. Hold a debate for the general election and short campaign.

    a. The teacher will create a general election ballot using Google Forms and mail it to the entire class period. Students will vote.

COMMON CORE STATE STANDARDS

Eighth-Grade Speaking and Listening (8.SL.2)

Analyze the purpose of information presented in diverse media and formats (e.g., visually, quantitatively, orally) and evaluate the motives (e.g., social, commercial, political) behind its presentation.

11th–12th-Grade Reading (11–12.RH.1–2,6)

1. Cite specific textual evidence to support analysis of primary and secondary sources, connecting insights gained from specific details to an understanding of the text as a whole.
2. Determine the central ideas or information of a primary or secondary source; provide an accurate summary that makes clear the relationships among the key details and ideas.
6. Evaluate authors' differing points of view on the same historical event or issue by assessing the authors' claims, reasoning, and evidence.

11th–12th-Grade Writing (11–12.WHST.2,4–6)

2. Write informative/explanatory texts, including the narration of historical events, scientific procedures/ experiments, or technical processes.
4. Produce clear and coherent writing in which the development, organization, and style are appropriate to task, purpose, and audience.
5. Develop and strengthen writing as needed by planning, revising, editing, rewriting, or trying a new approach, focusing on addressing what is most significant for a specific purpose and audience.
6. Use technology, including the Internet, to produce, publish, and update individual or shared writing products in response to ongoing feedback, including new arguments or information.
7. Conduct short as well as more sustained research projects to answer a question (including a self-generated question) or solve a problem; narrow or broaden the inquiry when appropriate; synthesize multiple sources on the subject, demonstrating understanding of the subject under investigation.

Assessment

Students must share all writing projects with the teacher for grading. Teachers are encouraged to create their own rubrics for debate and debate prep from other members of the group. All documents submitted as campaign materials should be evaluated for accuracy, spelling and grammar, and creativity.

LESSON PLAN 6

Contributed by Betsy Davis

Title: Contrasting Peter Pan

Middle School

Objective

The students will participate in an electronic writing event done entirely in Google Documents. Students will watch a performance of *Peter Pan* the Broadway musical and then read the book *Peter Pan* to produce a compare-and-contrast essay. Students will take notes with Google Presentations and use them while writing in Google Docs. Student will produce and publish their writing directly on an electronic device and understand the format for a compare-and-contrast essay.

COMMON CORE STATE STANDARDS

Seventh-Grade Standard (7.W.6)

Use technology, including the Internet, to produce and publish writing and link to and cite sources as well as to interact and collaborate with others, including linking to and citing sources.

Seventh-Grade Standard (7.W.9a)

Draw evidence from literary or informational texts to support analysis, reflection, and research.

 a. Apply grade 7 Reading standards to literature (e.g., "Compare and contrast a fictional portrayal of a time, place, or character and a historical account of the same period as a means of understanding how authors of fiction use or alter history").

Seventh-Grade Standard (7.RL.6)

Analyze how an author develops and contrasts the points of view of different characters or narrators in a text.

Instructions

The teacher will . . .

1. Share the graphic organizer Four Square with the students through Google Docs (http://goo.gl/8Hdrq).

2. Instruct the students to watch the musical *Peter Pan* and make notes on the Four Square.

    a. Make a copy of the Four Square.

3. Instruct the students to read *Peter Pan* and makes notes on a different Four Square.

    a. Make a copy of the Four Square.

4. Instruct the students to write a compare-and-contrast essay in Google Docs and share the document with the teacher for commenting and grading.

5. The teacher will help the students edit their drafts of their writing by making comments on the students' writing live in the document. Teachers could spend 3–5 minutes with each student's document while they are typing live in class.

Assessment

The student will share the document with the teacher for grading and e-mail the results through Gmail.

Contributed by Heather Eggers

Title: Introduction to the Salem Witch Trials

High School

Objective

To prepare for the studying of *The Crucible,* the students will work in groups with a computer device to research a topic from the period of the Salem Witch Trials. All notes will be made in a Google Document to produce and publish writing while collaborating with peers and the teacher. Students will then create a Google Presentation using their notes, incorporating pictures along with the information that they will present to the class. In addition to the teacher's evaluation, all students will use a prepared Google Form to provide peer evaluations.

COMMON CORE STATE STANDARDS

Anchor Standard #7 for Reading

Integrate and evaluate content presented in diverse formats and media, including visually and quantitatively, as well as in words.

11th–12th Grade Standard (RI.11–12.7)

Integrate and evaluate multiple sources of information presented in different media or formats (e.g., visually, quantitatively) as well as in words to address a question or solve a problem.

Anchor Standard #6 for Writing

Use technology, including the Internet, to produce and publish writing and to interact and collaborate with others.

11th–12th Grade Standard (W.11–12.6)

Use technology, including the Internet, to produce, publish, and update individual or shared writing products in response to ongoing feedback, including new arguments or information.

Anchor Standard #7 for Writing

Conduct short as well as more sustained research projects based on focused questions, demonstrating understanding of the subject under investigation.

11th–12th Grade Standard (W.11–12.7)

Conduct short as well as more sustained research projects to answer a question (including a self-generated question) or solve a problem; narrow or broaden the inquiry when appropriate; synthesize multiple sources on the subject, demonstrating understanding of the subject under investigation.

Anchor Standards # 1–6 for Speaking and Listening

1. Prepare for and participate effectively in a range of conversations and collaborations with diverse partners, building on others' ideas and expressing their own clearly and persuasively.

2. Integrate and evaluate information presented in diverse media and formats, including visually, quantitatively, and orally.

3. Evaluate a speaker's point of view, reasoning, and use of evidence and rhetoric.

4. Present information, findings, and supporting evidence such that listeners can follow the line of reasoning and the organization, development, and style are appropriate to talk, purpose, and audience.

5. Make strategic use of digital media and visual displays of data to express information and enhance understanding of presentations.

6. Adapt speech to a variety of contexts and communicative tasks, demonstrating command of formal English when indicated or appropriate.

11th–12th Grade Standards (SL.11–12.1–6):

1. Initiate and participate effectively in a range of collaborative discussions with diverse partners, building on others' ideas and expressing their own clearly and persuasively.

2. Integrate and evaluate information presented in diverse media and formats, including visually, quantitatively, and orally to make informed decisions and solve problems.

3. Evaluate a speaker's point of view, reasoning, and use of evidence and rhetoric, assessing the stance, premises, links among ideas, word choice, points of emphasis, and tone used.

4. Present information, findings, and supporting evidence, conveying a clear and distinct perspective, such that listeners can follow the line of reasoning and the organization, development, and style are appropriate to purpose, audience, and a range of formal and informal tasks.

5. Make strategic use of digital media (e.g., textual, graphical, audio, visual, and interactive elements) in presentations to enhance understanding of findings, reasoning, and evidence and to add interest.

6. Adapt speech to a variety of contexts and communicative tasks, demonstrating command of formal English when indicated or appropriate.

Overview

In the 11th grade students will be exposed to research pertaining to the Salem Witch Trials of 1692 in preparation for reading *The Crucible*. Students will set up a Google Document that they will share with their group members and the teacher to create a collaborative document with researched information. Students will then create a Google Presentation, where they will incorporate visual graphics and their researched information to present their topic to the other students. During the presentation, other students will evaluate the presentation using a Google Form to provide feedback.

Instructions

The teacher will . . .

1. Assist students with creating a Google Document and sharing that with their group members and the teacher.

2. Provide assistance in finding research pertaining to topics from *The Crucible* and the Salem Witch Trials.

3. Help students determine credibility of sources, as well as evaluate what information should be presented.

4. Create a Google Form for students to use for peer evaluations.

The students will . . .

1. Research topic pertaining to the Salem Witch Trials individually and in groups.

2. Take notes on the research gathered in a shared Google Document where each student will provide input and information.

3. Create a shared Google Presentation using the information gathered, providing key details and important facts about their topic.

4. Present information to the class detailing their research topics paying close attention to the oral presentation guidelines.

5. Evaluate student presentations using Google Forms providing feedback to the group.

Assessment

Presentations will be assessed by peer evaluation as well as teacher evaluation. See the Google Form: http://goo.gl/YldPi.

LESSON PLAN 8

Title: iTravel Vacation

Middle School

Objective

The students will use Google Maps and Street View to take a virtual travel adventure. The students will research their destination, plan activities, and use the student information sheet to know the parameters of their budget. Students will calculate their expenses based on their activities and not go over budget. Students will learn how to use unit rates to make sense of linear relationships and report their findings. The students will also write about their adventure making a brochure detailing the trip.

COMMON CORE STATE STANDARDS

Math Sixth Grade (6.RP.3a–d)

1. Use ratio and rate reasoning to solve real-world and mathematical problems, e.g., by reasoning about tables of equivalent ratios, tape diagrams, double number line diagrams, or equations.
2. Solve unit rate problems including those involving unit pricing and constant speed. For example, if it took 7 hours to mow 4 lawns, then at that rate, how many lawns could be mowed in 35 hours? At what rate were lawns being mowed?

English Language Arts Anchor Standard 4–6 Production and Distribution of Writing

a. Produce clear and coherent writing in which the development, organization, and style are appropriate to task, purpose, and audience.
b. Develop and strengthen writing as needed by planning, revising, editing, rewriting, or trying a new approach.
c. Use technology, including the Internet, to produce and publish writing and to interact and collaborate with others.

Writing Standard (6.W.4–6)

4. Produce clear and coherent writing in which the development, organization, and style are appropriate to task, purpose, and audience.
5. With some guidance and support from peers and adults, develop and strengthen writing as needed by planning, revising, editing, rewriting, or trying a new approach. (Editing for conventions should demonstrate command of Language standards 1–3 up to and including Grade 6 on page 52.)
6. Use technology, including the Internet, to produce and publish writing as well as to interact and collaborate with others; demonstrate sufficient command of keyboarding skills to type a minimum of three pages in a single sitting.

Overview

> ### *STUDENTS:*
>
> Plan a trip anywhere in the world that you can get there by driving a vehicle. You have $3,000 to spend and you need to take into account the number of people you want to go with you, food, gas, and hotel. Assume that the gas costs $3.50 a gallon. Food will cost you $50 per day per person. Please be creative as possible and make sure to have fun on your trip, but you must not go over budget. When you get to your location or along the journey use Google Street View to see interesting things the place has to offer. Take note of what you learn as you tour the location.

Students discuss their grouping based on how many are going on the trip with them.

Additional Information that will help you plan the trip:

—A SUV can hold up to 7 people with luggage and average 15 miles to the gallon.

—A car gets 30 miles to the gallon and can hold 4 people with luggage.

Use Google Maps to plan your trip, including finding miles driven and routes.

1. Use Expedia.com or hotels.com to find your cost of lodging per night.

2. Use Google Search to find fun activities and their estimated prices.

   Use official websites such as the city's chamber of commerce website or other websites that are official. **(Ask the teacher for help determining this.)**

Activities include:

Professional Sports Teams

Museums

Theme Parks

Beaches

Water Parks

Tours (e.g., Grand Canyon tour)

- Once you get to your location use Google Street View to sightsee.
- Create a brochure using a Google Document; the brochure must include at least the four things below.

1. The top sites to see

2. Description of city, including population and other notable aspects

3. Detail the expenditures of the trip, including a review of the hotel

4. Descriptive narrative describing the adventure

The teacher will . . .

1. Share student documents with each class period.
2. Instruct the students to log in to their Google Apps for Education Account.
   a. Find the document titled iTravel Adventure.
   b. Find the document titled Expenditure Report.
   c. Find the document titled Brochure.
3. Instruct students to read the documents and fill them out appropriately, then share the project with the teacher for grading.
4. Prior understanding of Google Maps, Google Docs, and Street View is suggested.

Driving Questions

1. What are the steps involved in planning a vacation?
2. What mathematics do I need to understand to properly plan my trip?

Expenditure Report

The students will create their own expenditure report with guidance from the teacher. The goal is to have the students explore different tools that will help them organize their information in a legible report. Have students create the report with any Google Doc they choose.

Brochure

The students will create a brochure that will serve as the writing portion of their document. Students need to use the collaborative tools of Google Apps to create their own templates and other ways to achieve the goals of the lesson. Cookie-cutter brochures will not score as high as creative ways to display the required information. Have students create the brochure with any Google Doc they choose.

Assessment

Students will share their work through Google Documents with the teacher for grading with the rubric given previously.

Student Documents

http://goo.gl/X4x2S

Demo Slam Street View

Use the link below to give your students an idea about what Street View can do. Notice that the users can focus in on the sides of the road and be able to even off-road in particular places.

http://goo.gl/FrFwL—Demo Slam

http://goo.gl/maps/0usrI—White House Washington, D.C. (Drag PegMan on top of the White House)

LESSON PLAN 9

Title: About Us

Mathematics

Elementary

Overview

This lesson will expose students to data collection and analysis in a fun way using Google Forms and Spreadsheets. Students will answer questions about themselves using a premade Google Form. The information will be automatically sent to a Google Spreadsheet, where the teacher will ask questions about the data and the students will draw conclusions and read graphs.

Objective

The students will practice technology skills while collecting data. The student will learn to analyze and interpret data as well as read graphs and make conclusions and predictions based on the data.

Materials

- Computers for students with Internet Access
- Premade Google Form

Instructions

The teacher will . . .

- Create a Google Form with questions that students would want to know about each other. Questions could come from students if the teacher asked in advance.
- Use goo.gl URL Shortener to shorten the link of the form.
   □ Sample form: http://goo.gl/PDVVB
- Share the link to the form in an e-mail to the student, or
   □ For students who are unable to sign in to their Google Account, write the shortened link on the board for students to type into their Web browser.
   □ Have the form on the screen when the students enter the computer lab.

- Instruct the students to answer the questions on the form.
- Discuss students' answers to the questions using the Summary of Responses.
  □ Summary of Responses shows graphs to students, not just the raw spreadsheet data.
  □ Discuss what types of graphs, asking questions that force students to think about the data and draw conclusions.
- Questions could be
  □ How many more students have pets than do not have pets?
  □ How many students have pets and at least one brother or sister?
- Vocabulary
  □ Percentage
  □ Bar graph
  □ Sample

COMMON CORE STATE STANDARDS

1.MD.4

Represent and interpret data.
Organize, represent, and interpret data with up to three categories; ask and answer questions about the total number of data points, how many in each category, and how many more or less are in one category than in another.

2.MD.10

Draw a picture graph and a bar graph (with single-unit scale) to represent a data set with up to four categories. Solve simple put-together, take-apart, and compare problems using information presented in a bar graph.

3.MD.4

Draw a scaled picture graph and a scaled bar graph to represent a data set with several categories. Solve one- and two-step "how many more" and "how many less" problems using information presented in scaled bar graphs. *For example, draw a bar graph in which each square in the bar graph might represent 5 pets.*

Enrichment

Students will be given time to analyze the raw data found in the spreadsheet to construct their own graphs. Focus on bar and double bar graphs using spreadsheets.

Title: Slow Down!

Middle School

Overview

Students will participate in a guided inquiry lesson to explore problems in their school community. Students are often just given problems to solve, but in this lesson, students get a chance to identify their own problems, research ways to solve them, and present that information back to the class using technology in meaningful ways. In this lesson, students will use Google Forms and Google Spreadsheets to collect data about their hypothesis (problem), research using Google Search; and present their data in the form of graphs and charts using Google Presentations. This is guided inquiry because students are given only a limited set of tools to identify, solve, and research their problem.

Objective

The students will use speed detection devices (radar guns) to test the speeds of vehicles on or around campus. Students will be directed to form a hypothesis and test it using Google Forms to collect data into a Google Spreadsheet for analysis. Students will research their findings and provide solutions to increase student safety on campus.

Instructions

1. Open this lesson with a discussion about safety on campus. Let the students make the conclusion that cars are a danger and certain regulations should be in place to prevent serious accidents. Use the questions below to start the conversation.
   a. What are some of the easiest ways to be injured on campus?
   b. What are some dangers of inattentive drivers?
   c. What are some of the ways people are distracted while driving?
   d. Are teens allowed to drive on campus?
2. Assign students to a group of 2–3.
3. Ask them to come up with a hypothesis that they would like to study.
   a. For example: People are more likely to speed on or near campus when using a cellphone while driving.
   b. Any hypothesis that can be tested with the use of the radar gun will suffice.

4. Assign students to formulate their study minimizing error.

   a. For example: Students should figure out that if the driver of the car sees them pointing a radar gun at their vehicle, then they are likely to slow down, causing error in the data.

5. Introduce the students to Google Forms and Google Spreadsheets for data collection.

   a. Students will create their own Google Form that will serve as their data collection piece to their study. The data collected in the form will automatically be sent to an accompanying Google Spreadsheet for analysis.

   b. Two ways to collect data: If the students are allowed to use their smartphones then students may access the Google Form they created on their phone, allowing them to directly enter data from the field into their spreadsheet. As the cars go by and they collect speed and other categorical data they may simply access the form and fill in the appropriate boxes and submit to the spreadsheet for each data entry. Later the students may access their data in their Google Drive.

   c. Sample form located here: http://goo.gl/cPdpD.

   d. Video tutorial for shortening links and accessing it on a Web browser found here: http://goo.gl/FIUG5.

   e. If students are not allowed to use their cell phones, then have the students take down the information on paper and then transfer it to their Google Form for entry into the spreadsheet.

6. Let the groups of students go and collect their data.

7. Arrange for students to research using Google Search ways to help them solve their problem.

8. Assign the students to create graphs and charts inserted into a Google Presentation for students to present their findings and research along with their solution to the problem they are studying.

COMMON CORE STATE STANDARDS

Speaking and Listening Grade 6–8 (6–8.SL.4–6)

Present claims and findings, emphasizing salient points in a focused, coherent manner with pertinent descriptions, facts, details, and examples; use appropriate eye contact, adequate volume, and clear pronunciation.

5. Include multimedia components and visual displays in presentations to clarify claims and findings and emphasize salient points.
6. Adapt speech to a variety of contexts and tasks, demonstrating command of formal English when indicated or appropriate.

Mathematics Sixth Grade (6.SP.2–3)

2. Understand that a set of data collected to answer a statistical question has a distribution, which can be described by its center, spread, and overall shape.

3. Summarize numerical data sets in relation to their context, such as by:

   a. Reporting the number of observations.

   b. Describing the nature of the attribute under investigation, including how it was measured and its units of measurement.

   c. Giving quantitative measures of center (median and/or mean) and variability (interquartile range and/or mean absolute deviation), as well as describing any overall pattern and any striking deviations from the overall pattern with reference to the context in which the data were gathered.

   d. Relating the choice of measures of center and variability to the shape of the data distribution and the context in which the data were gathered.

Assessment

Students will be assessed on the quality of their presentations as described in the standards as well as their quality of research and the design of their study.

Presentation rubric: http://goo.gl/IqN1

LESSON PLAN 11

Title: Exploring Shapes

Elementary

Overview

Google Drawings uses terms used in mathematics like *rotate 90 degrees, flip horizontal, flip vertical.* When students understand these terms, they are more likely to create and manipulate shapes using graphic design programs while learning geometry. While playing with the shapes, students will be introduced to vocabulary of the shapes, learn how to build and draw shapes, and manipulate them in a graphic design program. This activity will be a good introduction to learning shapes and vocabulary.

Objective

The students will learn to distinguish between the defining attributes of shapes by creating, manipulating, and using commands such as rotate 90 degrees, flip horizontal, flip vertical.

Instructions

The teacher will . . .

1. Share the Google Drawing (http://goo.gl/wlEkk) with the students asking them to make a copy of the document.
   a. **Making a copy** of the drawing allows each student to edit his or her own version without editing the shared document.

2. Instruct the students to manipulate, create, rotate, and flip various shapes.

3. Encourage students to explore the many different kinds of shapes that Google Drawings allows students to make.

4. Ask students to construct a drawing with the shapes.

Enrichment: Students may change the size of the shapes recognizing that size of the shape does not affect the name of the shape. Explore polygons and irregular polygons.

The student will . . .

1. Make and manipulate various polygons.

2. Double-click in the center of the shape to name it.

3. Share the drawing with the teacher for grading.

COMMON CORE STATE STANDARDS

Elementary Mathematics (1.G.1)

Distinguish between defining attributes (e.g., triangles are closed and three-sided) versus nondefining attributes (e.g., color, orientation, overall size); build and draw shapes to possess defining attributes.

Elementary Mathematics (2.G.1)

Recognize and draw shapes having specified attributes, such as a given number of angles or a given number of equal faces. Identify triangles, quadrilaterals, pentagons, hexagons, and cubes.

Elementary Mathematics (3.G.1)

Understand that shapes in different categories (e.g., rhombuses, rectangles, and others) may share attributes (e.g., having four sides), and that the shared attributes can define a larger category (e.g., quadrilaterals). Recognize rhombuses, rectangles, and squares as examples of quadrilaterals, and draw examples of quadrilaterals that do not belong to any of these subcategories.

Assessment

The teacher grades the shared drawing and grades the name of the shapes.

Title: Tangram Square

Middle School

Overview

In this lesson, students will be exposed to a digital set of tangram puzzle pieces. These pieces are digitally made using Google Drawings. The students will learn about the properties of each shape and how they can interact with them in the digital environment. In addition, literacy aspects are introduced by the video explaining the origin myth of tangrams.

Objective

The students will learn about the tangram puzzle, explore shapes, and construct their own tangram creations using Google Drawings. Students will learn key vocabulary such as flip 90 degrees, flip horizontal, flip vertical, and the names of the shapes.

Instructions

1. Watch the video http://youtu.be/X5mc-dkYLfI exploring the history of tangrams with your students.

2. Access http://goo.gl/GqJuP and make a copy of this drawing to share with the class.

3. Share the Google Drawing tangram with the class and instruct the students to make a copy and give it a name.

4. Give the students time to explore the tangram puzzle.

5. Ask students to:

   a. Complete the tangram square.

   b. Work with a partner to flip, slide, and turn the digital pieces to mix them up and share that puzzle with another student to make the square.

   c. Create characters with their tangram pieces and tell a story using Google Presentations.

      i. Use Google Drawings to copy and paste the premade shapes onto a Google Presentation slide or save a Google Drawing as a slide in Google Presentations.

6. Present the story to the class.

COMMON CORE STATE STANDARDS

Writing Standards (5–6.W.4–6)

4. Produce clear and coherent writing in which the development, organization, and style are appropriate to task, purpose, and audience.
5. With some guidance and support from peers and adults, develop and strengthen writing as needed by planning, revising, editing, rewriting, or trying a new approach. (Editing for conventions should demonstrate command of Language standards 1–3 up to and including Grade 6 on page 52.)
6. Use technology, including the Internet, to produce and publish writing as well as to interact and collaborate with others; demonstrate sufficient command of keyboarding skills to type a minimum of three pages in a single sitting.

Speaking and Listening (5–6.SL.4–6)

4. Present claims and findings, emphasizing salient points in a focused, coherent manner with pertinent descriptions, facts, details, and examples; use appropriate eye contact, adequate volume, and clear pronunciation.
5. Include multimedia components and visual displays in presentations to clarify claims and findings and emphasize salient points.
6. Adapt speech to a variety of contexts and tasks, demonstrating command of formal English when indicated or appropriate.

Mathematics Fifth Grade (5.G.3–4)

3. Understand that attributes belonging to a category of two-dimensional figures also belong to all subcategories of that category. For example, all rectangles have four right angles and squares are rectangles, so all squares have four right angles.
4. Classify two-dimensional figures in a hierarchy based on properties.

Additional Resources

http://goo.gl/PY7Ds—Lesson Plan With Tangrams

LESSON PLAN 13

Title: Graphic Design in Science

High School

Overview

Scientists rely on artists to portray a particular scientific process to make it clear for the public. Science would be less understood without the ability of complex graphic designs to represent the unseen process of science. For example, think of a computer graphics artist building a three-dimensional model of DNA and how transcription works in the nucleus. Without knowledgeable graphic design artists that are also scientists, science would be even less understood by the public and students. Read this article for more information: http://goo.gl/jvHez.

Objective

The students will use Google Drawings to create a graphic design of a topic in science. They will research the topic and design flow charts, animations, and infographics that describe a process in science. The students will create many of these drawings and place them in a Google Presentation to share with the class.

Instructions

1. Instruct students to research a topic that they are studying in science.
    a. For example, the water cycle could be researched and studied, and then students could use Google Drawings to put together an artistic representation of the cycle explaining it to the class.

2. With their research, students should explore the drawings program knowing its limitations; have students watch this demo slam from Google to see what is possible: http://youtu.be/bt9F7tKcZcU.

3. After the students know how to use the program, instruct them to create their slides for their project.

4. Give students ample time to be creative and to research.

COMMON CORE STATE STANDARDS

Writing 11th–12th Grades (11–12.WHST.6–10)

6. Use technology, including the Internet, to produce, publish, and update individual or shared writing products in response to ongoing feedback, including new arguments or information.
7. Conduct short as well as more sustained research projects to answer a question (including a self-generated question) or solve a problem; narrow or broaden the inquiry when appropriate; synthesize multiple sources on the subject, demonstrating understanding of the subject under investigation.
8. Gather relevant information from multiple authoritative print and digital sources, using advanced searches effectively; assess the strengths and limitations of each source in terms of the specific task, purpose, and audience; integrate information into the text selectively to maintain the flow of ideas, avoiding plagiarism and overreliance on any one source and following a standard format for citation.
9. Draw evidence from informational texts to support analysis, reflection, and research.
10. Write routinely over extended time frames (time for reflection and revision) and shorter time frames (a single sitting or a day or two) for a range of discipline-specific tasks, purposes, and audiences.

Reading 11th–12th Grade (11–12.RST.1–2)

1. Cite specific textual evidence to support analysis of science and technical texts, attending to important distinctions the author makes and to any gaps or inconsistencies in the account.
2. Determine the central ideas or conclusions of a text; summarize complex concepts, processes, or information presented in a text by paraphrasing them in simpler but still accurate terms.

Speaking and Listening 11th–12th Grade (Anchor 4–6)

Presentation of Knowledge and Ideas

4. Present information, findings, and supporting evidence such that listeners can follow the line of reasoning and the organization, development, and style are appropriate to task, purpose, and audience.
5. Make strategic use of digital media and visual displays of data to express information and enhance understanding of presentations.
6. Adapt speech to a variety of contexts and communicative tasks, demonstrating command of formal English when indicated or appropriate.

Assessment

Assess scientific knowledge
Presentation Rubric: http://goo.gl/JyYIW

LESSON PLAN 14

Title: Datapalooza

High School

Overview

The Common Core State Standards describe an entire high school set of standards called Modeling. Modeling stresses the importance in collecting, understanding, and manipulating data when used in decision making and predicting. The Common Core State Standards define modeling as "the process of choosing and using appropriate mathematics and statistics to analyze empirical situations, to understand them better, and to improve decisions." Data are everywhere, and with the Internet, interesting and useful data can be accessed with ease. One just has to know where to look. In this lesson, students will explore sources of data that Google indexes with the use of Google Data Explorer. This service by Google shows charts, graphs, and other interactive data displays that can make understanding a topic easier.

Objective

Students will use the interactive Google Data Explorer to analyze a complex data system. The students will explore the fertility of countries versus various other independent variables to understand how certain variables affect change. Students will study how the Google Data Explorer works and they will understand how access to this information may help them with data for other projects they encounter in their schooling.

Instructions

1. Direct the students to the webpage http://goo.gl/4DLU0.

2. Instruct the students to explore the graph as it is currently (not changing variables).

   a. Hover mouse over particular parts of the graph to reveal country names.

   b. Click the play button to set the graph in motion.

      i. Notice how the fertility rates change over time, and ask the students what world events during particular times would change the rate of births per woman.

   c. Click on different ways to display this information and discuss what chart type or graph most appropriately displays information.

3. Instruct students to change variables on the graph to compare other data with fertility rate.

   a. The students should be seeing changes in birthrate in response to other factors such as poverty, education, and region.

4. Assign students to make observations from the data and make written statements in a Google Doc as to why a certain event is true. Students must make at least five statements with evidence from the chart and from the Web to back up their claims from the data. All sources must be cited.

5. Instruct students to present the statements and supporting evidence to the class.

COMMON CORE STATE STANDARDS

Functions (F-IF.4)

For a function that models a relationship between two quantities, interpret key features of graphs and tables in terms of the quantities, and sketch graphs showing key features given a verbal description of the relationship. Key features include: intercepts; intervals where the function is increasing, decreasing, positive, or negative; relative maximums and minimums; symmetries; end behavior; and periodicity.

Functions (F-IF.7)

Graph functions expressed symbolically and show key features of the graph, by hand in simple cases and using technology for more complicated cases.

Standard for Mathematical Practice #4 Model With Mathematics

Speaking and Listening Anchor #2–3

2. Integrate and evaluate information presented in diverse media and formats, including visually, quantitatively, and orally.
3. Evaluate a speaker's point of view, reasoning, and use of evidence and rhetoric.

Assessment

Students share statements with the teacher to be evaluated for accuracy. Students will be assessed on their speaking and listening standards as they present their findings.

Glossary

Address Bar: This is the location in a Web browser where a user will type in a specific Web address to go directly to the website in question.

Anchor Standards: Anchor Standards are used in the Common Core State Standards for English Language Arts. They are meant to represent the overreaching goal of the standards. Each anchor is broken down by grade level, with increasing complexity and difficulty as the grades increase.

Case Sensitive: Each character in a Web address must be typed into the address bar exactly as shown. For example, goo.gl/9KUnm is not the same as goo.gl/9kUNM; the uppercase or lowercase letters will affect the meaning of the URL.

Common Core State Standards: The Common Core State Standards are an initiative created by the Chief Council of State School Officers and the National Governors Association to improve the quality of K–12 education. Forty-five states and many territories adopted the standards to narrow the focus on important student learning expectations. In addition, the almost nationwide implementation means that students are held to the same high standards no matter what ZIP code they live in.

Device Neutral: Device neutral refers to the ability for a software program to be accessed by any device. Google Apps are device neutral because the user can access them from PC, Mac, iPad, iPhone, or Android.

Documents List: This is where the documents appear in Google Drive.

Domain Administrator: The domain administrator is the controller of the Google Apps for Education domain.

Domain: A domain represents a system of Internet activity. Inside the domain, the domain administrator may block access or grant access to the outside world of Internet activity. In the purposes of Google Apps for Education, the domain is the school's bubble in which to operate its own set of preferences regulating Google Apps. Each school system using Google Apps has its own domain, where they may set restrictions on how users may use the apps.

Gigabyte: 1,024 megabytes.

Google Docs: Suite of free office software that is device neutral. Each Google Doc creates a unique URL or link to be shared with the classroom or the world.

Hosted Solution: Google Apps is a hosted solution for e-mail and document storage for schools. With Google Apps, schools no longer have to maintain expensive servers to store information. Google provides this service with storage limits for free.

Megabyte: 1,000 bytes—one byte of information is approximately one character of text at 12-point font.

Search Bar: This is the location in a Web browser where a user will type a query to be answered by the search engine, providing webpages for the user to read. This will not take the user directly to a webpage.

Share: Sharing a document in Google Apps allows the recipient of the shared document to edit, view only, or comment only, depending on the share settings.

URL: Uniform Resource Locator is the way Web browsers find webpages. The URL is a link that directs the browser to a specific page. Google Apps for Education creates a unique URL for each Google Doc.

Index

CORWIN
A SAGE Company

The Corwin logo—a raven striding across an open book—represents the union of courage and learning. Corwin is committed to improving education for all learners by publishing books and other professional development resources for those serving the field of PreK–12 education. By providing practical, hands-on materials, Corwin continues to carry out the promise of its motto: **"Helping Educators Do Their Work Better."**